REPTILES AND AMPHIBIANS

REPTILES AND AMPHIBIANS

EDITED BY JOHN P. RAFFERTY, ASSOCIATE EDITOR, EARTH AND LIFE SCIENCES

Britannica
Educational Publishing

IN ASSOCIATION WITH

ROSEN
EDUCATIONAL SERVICES

Published in 2011 by Britannica Educational Publishing
(a trademark of Encyclopædia Britannica, Inc.)
in association with Rosen Educational Services, LLC
29 East 21st Street, New York, NY 10010.

First Edition

Britannica Educational Publishing
Michael I. Levy: Executive Editor
J.E. Luebering: Senior Manager
Marilyn L. Barton: Senior Coordinator, Production Control
Steven Bosco: Director, Editorial Technologies
Lisa S. Braucher: Senior Producer and Data Editor
Yvette Charboneau: Senior Copy Editor
Kathy Nakamura: Manager, Media Acquisition
John P. Rafferty: Associate Editor, Earth and Life Sciences

Rosen Educational Services
Jeanne Nagle: Senior Editor
Nelson Sá: Art Director
Cindy Reiman: Photography Manager
Matthew Cauli: Designer, Cover Design
Introduction by David Nagle

Library of Congress Cataloging-in-Publication Data

Reptiles and amphibians / edited by John P. Rafferty.
    p. cm.—(Britannica guide to predators and prey)
"In association with Britannica Educational Publishing, Rosen Educational Services."
Includes bibliographical references and index.
ISBN 978-1-61530-344-1 (library binding)
1. Reptiles. 2. Amphibians. I. Rafferty, John P.
QL641.R464 2011
597.9—dc22
                                                              2010028543

Manufactured in the United States of America

On the cover and silhouetted pp. 1, 18, 48, 69, 100, 136, 160, 181, 189, 209, 230:
A rattlesnake bares its fangs, which are capable of injecting deadly venom into its prey.
© *www.istockphoto.com/Cory Thoemke*

On page xii: Snakes (suborder Serpentes). *Encyclopædia Britannica, Inc.*

On page xx: A giant tortoise of the Galapagos Islands. *Rodrigo Buendia/AFP/Getty Images.*

On pages 1, 18, 48, 69, 100, 136, 160, 181, 189, 209, 230, 253, 255, 264: Banner. *Siede Preis/Photodisc/Getty Images*

CONTENTS

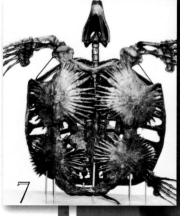

7

41

44

56

82

fang

ae)

fang

ged snake
ae)

90

fang

107

119

137

152

169

189

205

210

220

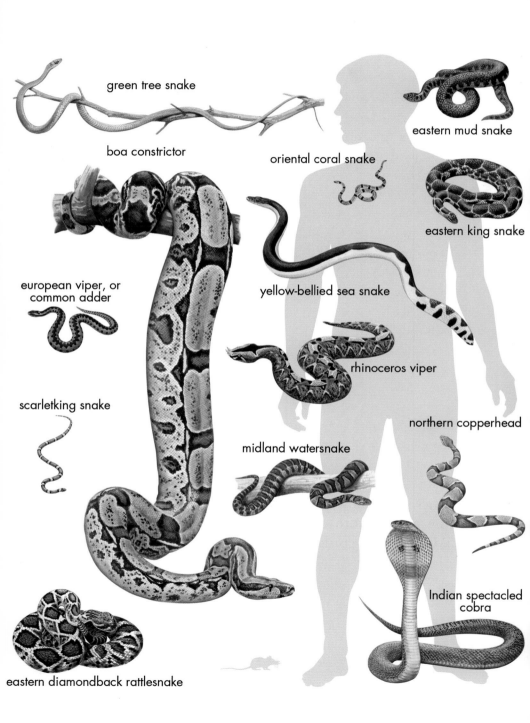

green tree snake

eastern mud snake

boa constrictor

oriental coral snake

eastern king snake

european viper, or common adder

yellow-bellied sea snake

rhinoceros viper

scarletking snake

northern copperhead

midland watersnake

Indian spectacled cobra

eastern diamondback rattlesnake

Perhaps it is due to the fact that, according to some scientists, humans and reptiles shared a common ancestor over 300 million years ago, or, conversely, that reptiles appear to be completely dissimilar to human beings. No matter the core reason, these ubiquitous creatures—there are more than 8,700 reptilian species on Earth—have aroused strong feelings of fascination in humans for thousands of years. Who could help but be intrigued by dinosaurs, "thunder lizards" crashing through primeval jungles or cruising through primordial seas?

Alas, dinosaurs are but one example of a group of reptiles that are now extinct. Other extinct lines include the mosasaurs, plesiasaurs, and ichthyosaurs. The reptiles that now exist, and are examined thoroughly—in broad strokes and by particular species—in this book, are snakes, lizards, turtles, and tuataras. The world's amphibians, noted and even named for their ability to lead a "double life" on land and water, are carefully explored in much the same fashion in this volume.

What makes a reptile a reptile? In general, all reptiles are air-breathing vertebrates. They have scales and reproduce through internal fertilization. Embryonic development involves a fluid-filled sac called the amnion. Singly, these features could be applied to other vertebrate groups, including mammals. However, taken together, only their close relatives the birds share these characteristics. Birds, however, are warm-blooded, or endothermic; the temperature of the body is maintained internally. All modern reptiles are cold-blooded, or ectothermic; the temperature of the body is largely dependent on the external environment. (Some extinct groups of reptiles, such as the ichthyosaurs and certain dinosaur lineages, are thought to have been warm-blooded.)

Nevertheless, from the smallest (skinks and geckos) to the largest (pythons and crocodiles), all reptiles depend upon heat from their surroundings for functional life processes, including locomotion. This helps account for the fact that the vast majority of reptiles are located in warmer climates, between 30° N and 30° S latitude. The highest diversity and number of reptiles have habitats in tropical and subtropical areas. Survival in changing environments can prove difficult for ectothermic creatures, so reptiles have adopted a number of behaviours that best help them cope. They tend to seek out habitats where there is minimal competition for land or mates. Many put on displays of ferocity rather than actually fight for territory or breeding partners.

More than half of all reptile species are classified in the order Squamata, a group that includes lizards and snakes. The defining characteristics of lizards—the possession of legs, movable eyelids, and external auditory openings—are flexible in that many different types of lizards may not have one or more of these attributes. While most reptiles lay leathery fertilized eggs or bear live young, certain types of lizards can, under limited conditions, reproduce by parthenogenesis—that is, produce offspring from eggs that have not been fertilized.

Snakes are essentially legless lizards that have evolved to become more specialized, yet simplified, in the process. The possession of a skull characterized by several movable parts, the lack of external ear sites, and pronounced fangs are some of the traits that set these fascinating creatures apart from their lizard cousins. Taking into account certain characteristics of most snakes—shedding of skin, ever-open eyes, dangerous jaws and fangs—it is easy to see why many people are disturbed by these creatures. Truth be told, only a few species of snakes are poisonous, and very few of these are aggressive towards humans.

As for behaviour, snakes gather rarely, with only the need to breed breaking up their solitary existence. Like lizards, they must deal with the challenges of ectothermic regulation, as well as the search for food. These basic survival activities keep snakes on the go. Despite lacking legs, snakes use a variety of techniques, including S-shaped loops, the so-called "caterpillar" and "concertina" motions, and side-winding in order to move from one place to another. Each of these places stress upon and wears down the most external layer of scales. The process of molting, in which a snake actually sheds its skin, aids in the repair of all but the most egregious wear and tear. It also allows for the growth of the snake's body. After molting, the snake's coloration and patterning remain, albeit in slightly altered form. The bright colours of some species get brighter, but camouflaging elements still allow for background blending.

Turtles are reptiles with a body encased in a bony shell. Each turtle is born with a shell that it keeps throughout its life. Tremendous diversity exists among the roughly three hundred different species of turtles. In general, they are aquatic in nature, but not the tortoise, which is a specific kind of turtle that lives exclusively on land. The name "tortoise" has been attached to a few land-dwelling turtles, but entomologically speaking, these are not truly tortoises. In addition to living on land, true tortoises also have a unique anatomy. Their hind limbs and feet are cylindrical, and their digits have only two or fewer phalanges, or bones connected by joints to form "fingers" and "toes." By contrast, the average turtle has three phalanges in each of its digits except the thumb. Another differentiating feature is that a tortoise shell is domed in a more pronounced fashion than that of most turtles.

For years people had used the term "terrapin" as a generic description of all turtles. Currently, the preferred scientific usage of the word applies only to a specific species of turtle, the North American diamondback terrapin.

These creatures are found in saltwater habitats, including the salt marshes and coastal waters of New England and the Gulf of Mexico.

One way in which all turtles are similar is their method of reproduction. Essentially, they lay their eggs on land and thereafter show no parental care to the clutch of eggs or emerging offspring whatsoever. The eggs and young turtles frequently fall victim to predation by all manner of wildlife. To ensure survival, then, huge numbers of young are usually produced. Environmental temperatures often influence whether the offspring develop as male or female, with clutches of eggs yielding approximately equal numbers of males and females. Surviving newborns gravitate toward the sea or skulk into the surrounding underbrush. Those that make it to these locations safely have a shot at living relatively long lives, particularly compared to other members of the animal kingdom. Turtle life spans fall between 20 and 30 years on average, but some, such as certain species of sea turtles, can reach or exceed 70 years of age. (Stories of turtles reaching ages of two hundred plus years appear to be, as Mark Twain noted in regard to false reports of his death, "greatly exaggerated.")

Turtles have been around for the past 220 million years or so, but their origin has been the subject of disagreement among zoologists for years. One school of thought holds that turtles arose as a distinct offshoot of an ancient, seminal reptile group called the Parareptilia. Others believe that turtles were an early divergence from the same lineage that evolved into the dinosaurs, pterosaurs, crocodiles, birds and lizards. Additional evidence and research are needed to determine exactly whence came these reptiles.

The largest and heaviest reptiles existing on earth today are crocodiles, with certain species reaching in excess of 6 metres (20 feet) in length and over a ton in weight. Their backs covered with thick, bony plates and tough scales covering their bodies, crocodiles eerily resemble the dinosaurs of old. It is much more difficult to see them as the nearest living relatives of birds. Today's crocodiles make up the sole-surviving suborder of the order Crocodylia, which includes alligators, caimans, and gavials, as well as the "true" crocs.

Crocodylia are differentiated primarily by skull shape. The snout, teeth, and certain bony protuberances are all characteristics that distinguish species. True crocodiles have a large fourth tooth that sits outside the mouth when closed—perhaps due to the narrow V-shape of the croc jaw line—while alligators possess a severe "overbite" with their huge U-shaped jaw.

The tuataras are a relatively unknown members of the reptile class, existing solely on the islands that make up New Zealand. Distantly related to snakes and lizards, these nocturnal creatures, in a wonderful example of exploitation, usually share the burrows of the fairy prion, a burrow-nesting seabird. Insects attracted to the bird excrement present in the burrows draw smaller lizards, and these animals are readily consumed by the resident tuatara. Tuataras also are not above eating the eggs and chicks of their host bird. Underground, interconnected tunnel systems can be shared by numerous tuataras. Although tuataras are generally solitary, mating season allows for a bit more social interaction. Eggs deposited in the ground require a year or so to incubate. At just over half a metre (2 feet) in length, tuataras are one of the few reptiles that remain active at lower temperatures.

Amphibios is a Greek word that means "living a double life," which aptly describes an amphibian's existence. The double life of these creatures is exhibited by their ability to exist in both aquatic and terrestrial habitats.

Approximately 6,500 species live today, descended from ancestral amphibians that first appeared over 340 million years ago. Amphibians were the first wave of vertebrates to switch from a wholly aquatic environment to one that included land.

There are three orders of amphibians: Anura (frogs and toads), Caudata (newts and salamanders) and Gymnophiona (caecilians). All of these groups share traits such as moist skin through which respiration occurs, a double-channeled hearing system, two-part teeth, and true colour vision. Members of each of the three orders differ markedly in appearance. While frogs and toads are tailless and have long back legs, caecilians are wormlike. The bodies of newts and salamanders appear as though they might be a fusion of these two designs, with plain features, smaller appendages, and something of a tail. Amphibians exist almost everywhere on earth with the exceptions of Antarctica, isolated islands, and extremely arid lands.

While they often are the object of revulsion by many due to the belief that they are capable of transmitting warts to the hands of handlers, toads are actually benign in this aspect. They differ from frogs due mostly to their rough, relatively drier skins. Anurans (frogs and toads) make up approximately 5,400 of the 6,500 amphibian types. Wonderful consumers of insects, these leaping animals (along with other amphibians) may serve as bellwethers of ecosystem health. The rapid decline in their numbers during the 1980s was thought to be the result of increased adverse environmental conditions, a belief since modified by the discovery of a parasitic fungus called *Batrachochytrium dendrobatidis* (or Bd) that attacks amphibian life.

Most amphibians lay eggs in moist or wet environments, with the developing embryo advancing through one or more larval stages on its way to reaching adulthood. From these eggs arise hugely diverse iterations of these moist-skinned animals, including giant frogs, poisonous frogs, blind and limbless burrowing caecilians, bright red or completely camouflaged salamanders, salamanders with external gills, and lungless frogs.

As this book explores in-depth the different reptiles and amphibians that the world holds, readers should come to a greater appreciation of the incredible diversity of species, their wide and varied areas of geographic distribution, their roles in the ecosystems they inhabit, and their purity of form and function.

CHAPTER 1

REPTILES

A reptile is any member of the class Reptilia, the group of air-breathing vertebrates that have internal fertilization, amniotic development, and epidermal scales covering part or all of their body. The major groups of living reptiles—the turtles (order Testudines), tuataras (order Sphenodontida), lizards and snakes (order Squamata), and crocodiles (order Crocodylia)—account for over 8,700 species. Birds (class Aves) share a common ancestor with crocodiles in subclass Archosauria and are technically one lineage of reptiles, but they are treated separately.

Common king snake (Lampropeltis getula). Jack Dermid

The extinct reptiles included an even more diverse group of animals that ranged from the marine plesiosaurs, pliosaurs, and ichthyosaurs to the giant plant-eating and meat-eating dinosaurs of terrestrial environments. Taxonomically, Reptilia and Synapsida (a group of mammal-like reptiles and their extinct relatives) were sister groups that diverged from a common ancestor during the Middle Pennsylvanian Epoch (approximately 312 million to 307 million years ago).

For millions of years representatives of these two groups were superficially similar. Slowly, lifestyles diverged, and from the synapsid line came hairy mammals that possessed an endothermic (warm-blooded) physiology and mammary glands for feeding their young. All birds and some groups of extinct reptiles, such as selected groups of dinosaurs, also evolved an endothermic physiology. The majority of modern reptiles possess an ectothermic (cold-blooded) physiology. Today, only the leatherback sea turtle (*Dermochelys coriacea*) has a near-endothermic physiology. So far no reptile, living or extinct, has developed specialized skin glands for feeding its young.

GENERAL FEATURES OF REPTILES

Most reptiles have a continuous external covering of epidermal scales. Reptile scales contain a unique type of keratin called beta keratin. The scales and interscalar skin also contain alpha keratin, which is a trait shared with other vertebrates. Keratin is the main component of reptilian scales. Scales may be very small, as in the microscopic tubercular scales of dwarf geckos (*Sphaerodactylus*)or relatively large, as in the body scales of many groups of lizards and snakes. The largest scales are the scutes covering the shell of a turtle or the plates of a crocodile.

Other features also define the class Reptilia. The occipital condyle (a protuberance where the skull attaches to the first vertebra) is single. The cervical vertebrae in reptiles have midventral keels, and the intercentrum of the second cervical vertebra fuses to the axis in adults. Taxa with well-developed limbs have two or more sacral vertebrae. The lower jaw of reptiles is made up of several bones but lacks an anterior coronoid bone. In the ear a single auditory bone, the stapes, transmits sound vibrations from the eardrum (tympanum) to the inner ear. Sexual reproduction is internal, and sperm may be deposited by copulation or through the apposition of cloacae. Asexual reproduction by parthenogenesis also occurs in some groups. Development may be internal, with embryos retained in the female's oviducts, and embryos of some species may be attached to the mother by a placenta. Development in most species is external, with embryos enclosed in shelled eggs. In all cases each embryo is encased in an amnion, a membranous fluid-filled sac.

IMPORTANCE

In the agriculture industry as a whole, reptiles do not have a great commercial value compared with fowl and hoofed mammals. Nonetheless, they have a significant economic value for food and ecological services (such as insect control) at the local level, and they are valued nationally and internationally for food, medicinal products, leather goods, and the pet trade.

Reptiles have their greatest economic impact in some temperate and many tropical areas, although this impact is often overlooked because their contribution is entirely local. A monetary value is often not assigned to any vertebrate that provides pest control. Nonetheless, many lizards control insect pests in homes and gardens; snakes are major predators of rodents, and the importance of rodent control has been demonstrated repeatedly when populations of rodent-eating snakes are decimated by snake harvesting for the leather trade. The absence of such snakes allows rodent populations to explode.

Turtles, crocodiles, snakes, and lizards are regularly harvested as food for local consumption in many tropical areas. When this harvesting becomes commercial, the demands on local reptile populations commonly exceed the ability of species to replace themselves by normal reproductive means. Harvesting is often concentrated on the larger individuals of most species, and these individuals are often the adult females and males in the population; their removal greatly reduces the breeding stock and leads to a preciptious population decline.

Regulated harvesting of large snakes and lizards is under way in parts of Indonesia. In addition, several groups of reptiles (tegu lizards in Argentina, freshwater turtles in China, and green iguanas [*Iguana iguana*] in Central America) are raised as livestock. Often the process of regulated harvesting begins with the removal of a few eggs, juveniles, or adults from wild populations. Stocks of reptiles are raised on farms and ranches. Farms and ranches then sell some individuals to commercial interests, while others are retained as breeding stock.

Reptiles have contributed significantly to a variety of biomedical and basic biological research programs. Snake venom studies contributed greatly to the care of heart-attack patients in the 1960s and 1970s and are widely studied in the development of pain-management drugs. Field studies of lizards and other reptiles and the manipulation of populations of various lizard species, such as the anoles (*Anolis*) have provided scientists opportunities to test hypotheses on different aspects of evolution. Reptile research remains an important area of evolutionary biology. Similarly, lizards and other reptiles have provided experimental models for examining physiological mechanisms, especially those associated with body heat.

SIZE RANGE

Most reptiles are measured from snout to vent, that is, the tip of the nose to the cloaca. However, measurements of total length are common for larger species, and shell length is used to gauge the size of turtles. The body size of living reptiles varies widely. *Sphaerodactylus parthenopion* and *S. ariasae*, which are the smallest dwarf geckos and also the smallest reptiles, have a snout-to-vent length of 16-18 mm (0.6-0.7 inch). In contrast, giant turtles, such as the leatherback sea turtles (*Dermochelys coriacea*), possess shell lengths of nearly 2 metres (about 7 feet). In terms of total length, the largest living reptiles are the reticulated pythons (*Python reticulatus*) and saltwater crocodiles (*Crocodylus porosus*), which may grow to more than 7 metres (23 feet) as adults. Some ancient reptile groups had members that were the largest animals ever to live on the land—some sauropod dinosaur fossils measure 20–30 metres (66–98 feet) in total length. The largest marine reptiles, the pliosaurs, grew to 15 metres (50 feet) long.

The reptile groups also show a diversity of morphologies. Some groups, such as most lizards and all crocodiles, possess strongly developed limbs, whereas other groups, such as the worm lizards and snakes, are limbless. Reptilian body flexibility ranges from the highly flexible forms found in snakes to the inflexible armoured bodies of turtles. In addition, the tails of most turtles tend to be short, especially when compared with the long heavy tails of crocodiles.

Giants in any animal group always attract attention and are often exaggerated. Anacondas (*Eunectes*), gigantic

Eastern diamondback rattlesnake (Crotalus adamanteus). Jack Dermid

snakes from South America, are undoubtedly the largest living snakes. The largest species, the green anaconda (*E. murinus*), likely only rarely exceeds 9 metres (30 feet) in length. Nonetheless, persistent but unsubstantiated reports have been made of anacondas that are 12 metres (40 feet) long. The reticulated python (*P. reticulatus*) of Southeast Asia and the East Indies has been recorded at 10.1 metres (33.3 feet).

At about 5.5 metres (18 feet), the king cobra (*Ophiophagus hannah*) of Asia and the East Indies is the longest venomous snake. The heaviest venomous snake is probably the eastern diamondback rattlesnake (*Crotalus adamanteus*); its length does not exceed 2.4 metres (7.9 feet), but it may weigh as much as 15.5 kg (34 pounds). The largest of the common nonvenomous snakes is probably the keeled rat snake (*Ptyas carinatus*), at about 3.7 metres (12 feet).

Five species of crocodiles may grow larger than 6 metres (20 feet). Nile crocodiles (*Crocodylus niloticus*) and estuarine (or saltwater) crocodiles (*C. porosus*) regularly exceed this length. The American crocodile (*C. acutus*), the Orinoco crocodile (*C. intermedius*), and the gavial (*Gavialis gangeticus*) may also grow larger than 6 metres; however, this is less common. The gavial normally attains a length of about 4–5 metres (12–15 feet).

The giant among living turtles is the marine leatherback sea turtle (*D. coriacea*), which reaches a total length of about 2.7 metres (9 feet) and a weight of about 680 kg (1,500 pounds). The largest of the land turtles is a

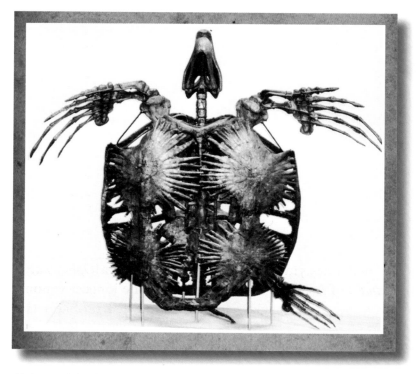

Skeleton of the Cretaceous marine turtle Archelon, *length 3.25 metres (10.7 feet)*. Courtesy of the Peabody Museum of Natural History, Yale University

Galapagos tortoise (*Geochelone nigra*), weighing about 255 kg (560 pounds).

The largest modern lizard, the Komodo dragon (*Varanus komodoensis*) of the East Indies, is a monitor lizard that attains a total length of 3 metres (10 feet). In addition, two or three other species of monitors reach 1.8 metres (5.9 feet). The water monitor (*V. salvator*) may grow to a greater total length than the Komodo dragon, but it does not exceed the latter in weight. The green iguana (*I. iguana*), which grows to a length of about 2 metres (7 feet) comes close to that size, but no other lizard does.

Within each reptile group, with the possible exception of snakes, no living member is as large as its largest extinct representative. At about 2.7 metres (9 feet) in total length, the leatherback sea turtle is smaller than *Archelon*, a genus of extinct marine turtles from the Late Cretaceous (100 million to 65.5 million years ago) that was about 3.6 metres (11.8 feet) long. No modern crocodile approaches the estimated 15-metre (49-foot) length of *Phobosuchus*, and the Komodo dragon does not compare with *Tylosaurs*, a mosasaur that exceeded 6 metres (20 feet) in length. Some quadrapedal browsing dinosaurs grew to lengths of 30 metres (100 feet) and weights of 91,000 kg (200,000 pounds) or more.

The smallest reptiles are found among the geckos (family Gekkonidae), skinks (family Scincidae), and microteiids (family Gymnopthalmidae); some of these lizards grow no longer than 4 cm (about 2 inches). Certain blind snakes (family Typhlopidae) are less than 10 cm (4 inches) in total length when fully grown. Several species of turtles weigh less than 450 grams (1 pound) and reach a maximum shell length of 12.5 cm (5 inches). The smallest crocodiles are the dwarf crocodiles (*Osteolaemus tetraspis*), which grow to about 2 metres (7 feet), and the dwarf caimans (*Paleosuchus*), which typically grow to 1.7 metres (6 feet) or less.

DISTRIBUTION AND ECOLOGY

Reptiles are mainly animals of Earth's temperate and tropical regions, and the greatest number of reptilian species live between 30° N and 30° S latitude. Nevertheless, at least two species, the European viper (*Vipera berus*) and the common, or viviparous, lizard (*Lacerta vivipara*, also called *Zootoca vivipara*), have populations that edge over the Arctic Circle (66° 33'39" N latitude). Other species of snakes, lizards, and turtles also live at high latitudes and altitudes and have evolved lifestyles that allow them to survive and reproduce with little more than three months of activity each year.

Reptile activity is strongly dependent on the temperature of the surrounding environment. Reptiles are ectothermic—that is, they require an external heat source to elevate their body temperature. They are also considered cold-blooded animals, although this label can be misleading, as the blood of many desert reptiles is often relatively warm. The body temperatures of many species approximate the surrounding air or the temperature of the substrate, hence a reptile can feel cold to the human touch. Many species, particularly lizards, have preferred body temperatures above 28 °C (82 °F) and only pursue their daily activities when they have elevated their body temperatures to those levels. These species maintain elevated body temperatures at a relatively constant level by shuttling in and out of sunlight.

Reptiles occur in most habitats, from the open sea to the middle elevations in mountainous habitats. The yellow-bellied sea snake (*Pelamis platurus*) spends all its life in marine environments. It feeds and gives birth far from any coastline and is helpless if washed ashore, whereas other sea snakes live in coastal waters of estuaries and coral reefs. Sea turtles are also predominately coastal animals, although most species have a pelagic, or open-ocean, phase that lasts from the hatchling stage to the young juvenile stage. Many snakes, crocodiles, and a few lizards are aquatic and live in freshwater habitats ranging from large rivers and lakes to small mountain streams. On land, turtles, snakes, and lizards also occur widely in forests, in grasslands, and even in true deserts. In many arid lands lizards and snakes are the major small-animal carnivores.

NORTH TEMPERATE ZONE

Reptiles of the North Temperate Zone include many ecological types. Aquatic groups are represented in both hemispheres by the water snakes, many testudinoid turtles, and the two species of *Alligator*. Terrestrial groups include tortoises, ground-dwelling snakes, and many genera of lizards. Arboreal snakes are few, and arboreal lizards are almost nonexistent. There are few specialized burrowing lizards in this region, but burrowing snakes are common.

The viviparous lizard (*L. vivipara, or Z. vivipara*) and the European viper (*V. berus*) are the most northerly distributed reptiles. A portion of each reptile's geographic range occurs just north of the Arctic Circle, at least in Scandinavia. Other reptiles—the slowworm (*Anguis fragilis*), the sand lizard (*L. agilis*), the grass snake (*Natrix natrix*), and the smooth snake (*Coronella austriaca*)—also appear at high latitudes and reach to 60° N in Europe. Of these six northern species, all but the grass snake are viviparous (live-bearing). Across Siberia only *L. vivipara* and *V. berus* live north of 60° N.

In North America no reptile is found at 60° N latitude or higher. Two species of garter snakes (*Thamnophis*) live as far north as 55° N in western Canada; however, it is only south of 40° N that numerous species of reptiles occur. In the eastern United States and eastern Asia, several colubrid snake species, northern skinks (*Plestiodon*), glass lizards (*Ophisaurus*), and softshell turtles (Trionychidae) are common.

Across North America and Eurasia, the northern limit of turtles is about 55° N. Even though these regions are characterized by many species of turtles, most families and genera are unique to one region or another. This phenomenon also occurs in other groups of reptiles. Many lizards of temperate Eurasia belong to the families Agamidae and Lacertidae, which do not occur in the Americas, whereas many lizards of North America are in the families Iguanidae and Teiidae, which do not live in Eurasia. Nonetheless, of the two living species of *Alligator*, one (*A. mississippiensis*) lives in the southeastern United States, and the other (*A. sinensis*) lives in China.

The reptiles of the eastern United States are almost as distinct from those of the western United States and northern Mexico as they are from those of eastern Asia. The eastern region (that is, the eastern United States) has many genera and species of emydid turtles. In contrast, the western region (that is, the western United States and northern Mexico), which is defined by a diagonal line running southeast to northwest through Texas, then northward along the Continental Divide, has only four or five species of emydids. Few genera and species of iguanid lizards inhabit the eastern region, whereas the western region has many. Although the eastern region has more species of water snakes, the western region contains more garter snakes. Whereas more species of snakes appear in the eastern United States than in the western areas, the converse is true of lizard species.

CENTRAL AND SOUTH AMERICA

Nearer to the Equator, reptiles become more numerous and diverse. This is true of crocodiles; Mexico is home to three species, but nine countries in South America are home to four or more crocodilian species. Turtles, lizards, and snakes are also particularly diverse in this region.

Some groups of North American turtles are represented in the New World tropics. For example, the mud turtles (*Kinosternon*) and sliders (*Trachemys*) appear in both regions, but the majority of species are members of genera and even families (such as the side-necked turtles of families Podocnemididae and Chelidae) that are unknown in North America. In addition, Central America has three endemic genera of turtles (*Dermatemys*, *Claudius*, and *Staurotypus*).

Many of the genera of iguanid lizards occurring in the western United States have species in Mexico. One genus of spiny lizards (*Sceloporus*) is most diverse in Mexico. South of Mexico the North American iguanids disappear and are replaced by tropical groups such as the black iguanas (*Ctenosaura*), the helmeted iguanids (*Corythophanes*), the casque-headed iguanids (*Laemanctus*), and the basilisks (*Basiliscus*). Iguanid lizards of the anole genus (*Anolis*) are represented in northern South America and the West Indies by more than 200 species. Other iguanid genera—the long-legged *Polychrus*—make an appearance.

The lizard family Teiidae, though represented in the United States by the racerunners and whiptails of the genus *Cnemidophorus*, is primarily tropical, and its area of greatest biological diversity begins in Central America with the large, conspicuous, and active ameivas (*Ameiva*). The Gymnophthalmidae (or microteiids), close relatives of the teiids, are a diverse group of small-bodied lizards that live largely in and under leaf litter in the West Indies, Central America, and South America north of central Argentina.

Among snakes, fer-de-lances (*Bothrops*), coral snakes (*Micrurus*), rear-fanged snakes (such as the cat-eyed snakes [*Leptodeira*]), and certain nonvenomous genera (such as the tropical green snakes [*Leptophis*]) do not occur north of Central America. Farther south these groups become more diverse. Vine snakes (*Oxybelis* and *Imantodes*), false coral snakes (*Erythrolamprus*), coral snakes (*Micrurus*), slender ground snakes (*Drymobius*), and the burrowing spindle snakes (*Atractus*) are some of the most biologically diverse groups in this region.

Several groups of reptiles that form important, if not dominant, elements of the fauna of the Eastern Hemisphere are largely or completely absent from the American tropics. Such groups include the lizard families Agamidae, Chamaeleonidae, Lacertidae, and Scincidae and many genera, subfamilies, and families of snakes.

South of the tropics, in the temperate regions of South America, the diversity of reptiles diminishes rapidly. Crocodiles and turtles do not occur south of northern Argentina; however, the range of one viviparous pit viper reaches to almost 50° S, and the ranges of two iguanid lizards, Magellan's tree iguana (*Liolaemus magellanicus*) and the Cascabel rattlesnake (*Crotalus durissus*), extend to almost to 55° S.

ASIA

The temperate zone of Eurasia is noted for its many lizards of the families Agamidae and Lacertidae, and, to lesser degrees, Gekkonidae and Scincidae. Most of the lizards are terrestrial, and extremely specialized burrowers include desert-dwelling skinks (*Ophiomorphus* and *Scincus*). Most of the snakes characteristic of this vast area are also terrestrial, and the leaf-nosed snakes (*Lytorhynchus*) and the sand boas (*Eryx*) are the distinctive burrowing snakes of the region. Arboreal snakes are represented almost exclusively by the rat snakes (*Elaphe*).

A few types of reptiles characteristic of the Asian tropics extend into the temperate zone—such as several rear-fanged snakes (*Boiga trigonata* and *Psammodynastes*), some cobras of the genus *Naja*, several species of softshell turtles (Trionychidae), and some species of skinks and geckos. Except for the Chinese alligator (*Alligator sinensis*) and the Indian gavial (*Gavialis gangeticus*), crocodiles are absent from temperate Eurasia.

In the Asian tropics, the reptilian fauna is extremely rich in species and encompasses several diverse types. Aquatic reptile groups are represented by snakes of various genera (such as *Natrix*, *Enhydris*, and *Acrochordus*), several groups of lizards (*Tropidophorus* among the skinks and *Hydrosaurus* among the agamids), many batagurids and soft-shelled turtles, and five species of crocodiles. Asia's numerous terrestrial reptiles include the small kukri snakes (*Oligodon*), the big Asian rat snakes (*Ptyas*), cobras (family Elapidae), monitor lizards (*Varanus*), many species and genera of skinks, some geckos, and several land turtles (*Cuora*, *Indotestudo*, and *Geochelone*). Specialized burrowing snakes (such as those of family Uropeltidae and the colubrid genus *Calamaria*) and lizards (such as the family Dibamidae and the skink genus *Brachymeles*) contain many.

Many distinctive life forms of reptiles in tropical Asia are arboreal. They include pythons and Asian pit vipers (*Trimeresurus*), vine snakes (*Ahaetulla*), slug-eating snakes (*Pareas*), flying snakes (*Chrysopelea*), and tree racers (*Gonyosoma*). Some lizards, such as the monitors, climb only with the aid of claws. A few others—such as the deaf agamids, *Cophotis*—climb with the help of prehensile, or grasping, tails. Other Asian reptiles, such as several species of geckos, climb with the help of clinging pads under the digits. The most striking arboreal reptiles of this area are the flying lizards (*Draco*), which possess spreadable rib wings, and the parachuting gecko (*Ptychozoon*), which has fully webbed digits, a fringed tail, and wide flaps of skin along its sides.

AUSTRALIA

As a result of close geological relationships and faunal similarities, the general characteristics of reptiles in the Australian faunal region also apply in New Guinea. Australia is the only continent in the world in which venomous snake species outnumber nonvenomous ones. The family Colubridae, which encompasses the majority of the nonvenomous or slightly venomous snakes of the world, is poorly represented in Australia, with fewer than a dozen species. The reptilian fauna also includes several pythons and minute blind snakes (family Typhlopidae); a great variety of geckos, skinks, and agamid lizards; side-necked turtles (family Chelidae); and three species of crocodiles. The Australian region is home to a diverse group of cobras (family Elapidae) but no vipers.

AFRICA

The reptilian fauna of Africa has two main components. The first, the fauna of North Africa, is akin to that of central and southwestern Asia and southern Europe and thus is mainly a Eurasian fauna. The racers (*Coluber*), the burrowing sand skink (*Scincus*), and the batagurid turtle (*Mauremys caspica*) are elements of this fauna in North Africa.

North African reptiles, though representing many families, are principally terrestrial and burrowing. Many lacertid and agamid lizards scamper over rocks and sand by day; they are replaced at night by small geckos and are preyed upon by the racers and sand snakes. In addition to cobras, the venomous snakes of North Africa include the common vipers, the saw-scaled viper (*Echis carinatus*), and the horned vipers (*Cerastes*). The last two are true desert animals and also occur in Southwest Asia.

Some reptilian genera from sub-Saharan Africa also occur in North Africa and in southwestern Asia. Examples include the sand snakes (*Psammophis*), cobras, and chameleons (family Chamaeleonidae).

The second and much larger component of the African herpetofauna is the sub-Saharan assemblage that ranges from the Sahara southward to the Cape of Good Hope. In common with tropical Asia, this vast area is home to cobras and many skinks and geckos. Its fauna differs from that of Asia by the absence of pit vipers (subfamily Crotalinae), the absence of batagurid turtles, and the presence of a few agamid lizards. These groups are replaced in tropical Africa by the many true vipers (subfamily Viperinae), the side-necked turtles (family Pelomedusidae), the wall lizards (family Lacertidae), and the spiny-tailed lizards (family Cordylidae). Numerous species of chameleons and tortoises and three species of crocodiles occur in sub-Saharan Africa.

The large island of Madagascar, off the eastern coast of Africa, has a peculiar fauna with its affinities mainly to African reptile groups. Because of its long isolation, Madagascar possesses distinct genera and subfamilies of chameleons and other reptiles.

HOW CROCODILES DIFFER FROM OTHER REPTILES

As a group, the largest and heaviest reptiles are the crocodiles, which also includes alligators, gavials, and caimans. Crocodiles are often set apart from other reptiles by the presence of scutes (scales reinforced with bone) and bony plates covering their dorsal parts, which serve functions similar to the scales found in snakes and lizards. Internally, one of the most significant differences between crocodiles and all other reptiles is that crocodiles possess a four-chambered heart that separates deoxygenated blood from oxygenated blood. All crocodile species prey on other animals, a role shared with many other reptiles. All female crocodiles produce hard-shelled eggs which are deposited in nests. In addition, crocodiles and birds share a close evolutionary affinity.

With only 23 extant species, crocodiles are not a diverse group. These amphibious animals are treated in more detail elsewhere in this series. In ensuing chapters, this book takes a more detailed look at several of the smaller, yet more diverse, groups of reptiles around the world.

CHAPTER 2
LIZARDS

Lizards (suborder Sauria) account for nearly 4,450 species of reptiles belonging in the order Squamata, which also includes snakes (suborder Serpentes). Lizards are scaly-skinned reptiles that are usually distinguished from snakes by the possession of legs, movable eyelids, and external ear openings. However, some traditional (that is, non-snake) lizards lack one or more of these features. For example, limb degeneration and loss has occurred in glass lizards (*Ophisaurus*) and other lizard groups. Movable eyelids have been lost in some geckos, skinks, and night lizards. External ear openings have disappeared in some species in the genera *Holbrookia* and *Cophosaurus*. Most of the living species of lizards inhabit warm regions, but some are found near the Arctic Circle in Eurasia and others to the southern tip of South America.

Snakes arose from lizards and are thus considered to be a highly specialized group of limbless lizards. In addition to those traits they have in common with non-snake lizards, snakes are often separated from other lizards in popular literature because they share a set of unique traits that are relatively easy to observe.

GENERAL FEATURES OF LIZARDS

Lizards are by far the most diverse group of modern reptiles in body shape and size. They range from 2 cm (0.8 inch) snout to vent in geckos (family Gekkonidae) to 3 metres (10 feet) in total length in monitor lizards (family Varanidae). The weight of adult lizards ranges from less than 0.5 gram (0.02 ounce) to more than 150 kg (330 pounds).

Day gecko (genus Phelsuma*).* © Digital Vision/Getty Images

The popular conception of a lizard as a scampering reptile about 30 cm (12 inches) in total length with a slender tail may be applied accurately only to a small number of species. Representatives of several families are limbless and resemble snakes, whereas others have long hind legs that permit bipedal locomotion. Male lizards may be outfitted with a wide array of ornamentation—such as extensible throat fans and frills, throat spines, horns or casques on the head, and tail crests.

Lizards occupy diverse habitats that range from underground warrens and burrows to the surface and elevated vegetation. Some move slowly and rely on cryptic coloration for protection, whereas others can run swiftly across desert sands. Lizards of the family Mosasauridae, an extinct group, were strictly marine. Some mosasaurs were giants and grew to lengths of 10 metres (33 feet). One living lizard, the marine iguana (*Amblyrhynchus cristatus*) of the Galapagos Islands, feeds on algae in the sea; however, it spends much of its time basking on lava rocks on the islands. No other extant lizard species is marine, but several are partially aquatic and feed on freshwater organisms.

The role lizards play in human ecology is poorly known. Some lizards are sources of food and clothing or agents of pest control, whereas others are pests. Some larger lizards (such as the iguanas [*Iguana* and *Ctenosaura*] of Mexico, Central America, and South America) are eaten and are an important food source. Others are used for leather goods. Monitor lizards and tegus (family Teiidae) are harvested for their skins, and these skins have a major effect on local economies of rural areas in Third World countries. Although lizards are often portrayed as insectivores, many also consume small vertebrates and at least some plant material; strict herbivory has evolved independently in several groups of lizards. Nevertheless, lizards eat large numbers of insects and other invertebrates, particularly in the tropics and in deserts. These insect-control services affect humans in many subtle ways; however, such effects have not been well studied. Large predatory lizards (such as monitors and tegus) can be pests—often preying on farm animals or stealing chicken eggs—that affect the livelihoods of ranchers and farmers.

Some relatively small lizard species, such as geckos, have not only colonized many islands by rafting with humans on boats but have also invaded cities and towns throughout the world. For example, throughout Brazil, one of the best-known lizards, the Mediterranean gecko (*Hemidactylus mabouia*), is so common in houses and buildings that most Brazilians know more about it, based on their own observations, than they know about any of the endemic species. As is the case with many introduced lizards, the Mediterranean gecko appears to do very well living with people in disturbed areas but does not seem to invade undisturbed habitats.

For the most part, lizards are not disease vectors and pose little danger to humans who take proper precautions when handling them. Lizards are often infected with various parasites, including a type of malaria, but these parasites tend to be species specific. *Salmonella* bacteria may be transmitted from a lizard to a human, particularly if the lizard is placed in a person's mouth. Tuberculosis (*Mycobacterium tuberculosis*) and some viral and fungal infections may also pass from lizard to human. Persons handling lizards are advised to practice good personal hygiene.

Only two species, the Gila monster (*Heloderma suspectum*) of the southwestern United States and northwestern Mexico and the Mexican beaded lizard (*H. horridum*) of western Mexico, are venomous. Both species bite humans only when provoked, and fatalities are very rare. Among the most harmless of lizards are geckos, which are falsely believed to be highly venomous by many indigenous cultures throughout the world. Reasons for this suspicion are unclear; however, the geckos' nocturnal activity, elliptical pupils, and ability to walk up smooth vertical surfaces could make them seem supernatural to some cultures.

Lizards are also valued as subjects for biological research. Their varied modes of reproduction and their ability to regulate body temperatures are two of many areas studied by comparative physiologists. The great abundance and observability of numerous species make them ideal subjects for ecologists and ethologists. The ability of some species to regenerate broken tails has led to their use as research subjects by behavioral ecologists and developmental biologists. Since they are relatively clean and easy to keep, lizards are also quite popular as house pets.

NATURAL HISTORY OF LIZARDS

Reproductive and parental-care strategies vary among lizard species. Although most lizards are egg layers, some give birth to live young. Some species, such as *Lacerta* and *Aspidoscelis*, are parthenogenetic and do not even require egg fertilization to produce offspring. Behaviours, especially as they relate to feeding, territorial defense, and courtship, also vary between species. Despite these differences, all lizards must consider the effects of the temperature of their surroundings on their daily activities, and many species have innovative strategies to keep their bodies within a preferred temperature range.

LIFE CYCLE AND LIFE HISTORY

Most lizards reproduce by laying eggs. In some small species, the number of eggs is rather uniform for each laying or clutch. For example, all anoles (*Anolis*) lay but a single egg at a time, many geckos lay one or two eggs (depending upon the species), and some skinks have clutches of two eggs. A more general rule is that clutch size varies with the size, age, and condition of the mother. A clutch of four to eight eggs may be considered typical, but large lizards such as the iguanas may lay 50 or more eggs at one time. Lizard eggs are usually leathery-shelled and porous; they can expand by the absorption of moisture as the embryos grow. An exception occurs in the majority of egg-laying geckos, whose eggs have shells that harden soon after they are deposited and then show no further change in size or shape.

EMBRYONIC DEVELOPMENT AND SEX DETERMINATION

Viviparity, or the birthing of live young, occurs in some lizard species. For skinks, this is true for about one-third of the species, many of which live in tropical climates. In most other families that have live-bearing representatives, the species that are frequently exposed to cold conditions—either at high altitude or at extreme latitude—tend to be live-bearers. For example, all New Zealand geckos give birth to live young, yet all other geckos lay eggs. A great diversity of mechanisms exists that results in the production of live young. In some lizards the only difference between egg laying (oviparity) and live bearing (viviparity) is that shells never form around the "eggs." The female retains them inside the oviduct until development is complete, and each egg already contains all of the energy necessary for development in its large yolk. In these cases, no additional nutrients pass from the mother to the offspring.

In other lizards, eggs released from the ovary contain most, but not all, of the energy necessary for development in the yolk. Several kinds of placentae can develop, depending on the species of lizard. The result is that some nutrients pass from the mother to the offspring during development. In just a few species, such as *Mabuya heathi*, tiny eggs with almost no yolk are released from the ovary and deposited in the oviduct. An advanced and complex placenta develops, and more than 99 percent of the nutrients required for embryonic development pass from the mother to the offspring. In these species the gestation period is usually very long (8–12 months).

Sex in most lizards is genetically and rigidly determined; a hatchling normally has either male or female reproductive structures. In representatives of most iguanian lizard families (Iguania) and in some species of whiptails, tegus, geckos, and skinks, the males have dissimilar sex chromosomes, comparable to the sex-chromosome system of most mammals. Some female geckos and wall lizards and all monitor lizards have sex-chromosome differences that are similar to those found in snakes. In a few lizard species (some iguanids, geckos, and wall lizards), no sex chromosomes exist. They rely on temperature-dependent sex determination (TSD)—that is, temperatures occurring within the nest during egg development control the sex of the hatchlings.

PARTHENOGENESIS

Most lizard populations are evenly divided between females and males. Deviations from this pattern are found in parthenogenetic species, in which the young are produced from unfertilized eggs. Parthenogenesis in lizards was first discovered in all-female races of *Lacerta* in the Caucasus, but it is now known to occur in all-female species of whiptail lizards (*Aspidoscelis*) in the southwestern United States and parts of Mexico, several other Teiidae and Gymnophthalmidae (spectacled lizards or microteiids) in South America, and a few Gekkonidae. Parthenogenetic lizards appear to live in areas that are ecologically marginal for representatives of their genera. In *Aspidoscelis* and several other parthenogenetic species, convincing evidence exists that parthenogenetic forms arose through the hybridization of two bisexual species. The number of chromosomes in such species is usually double that in sexually reproducing species, but in a few cases, the number of chromosomes is triple. This results from the mating of a sexually reproducing species with one that is parthenogenetic. These offspring are called allotriploid because they represent a backcross that produces three sets of chromosomes.

PARENTAL CARE

Parental care among lizards tends to be minimal following egg deposition, but there are striking exceptions. Many species dig holes in which the eggs are placed, whereas others bury them under leaf litter or deposit them in crannies of trees or caves. In contrast, females of some species, notably the five-lined skink (*Eumeces fasciatus*) of the United States and many of its relatives, remain with their eggs throughout the incubation time (about six weeks); they leave the clutch infrequently to feed. These skinks turn their eggs regularly and, if the eggs are experimentally scattered, will return them to the nest cavity. As soon as the young disperse, family ties are severed. Glass lizards (*Ophisaurus*, family Anguidae) appear to do the same thing. In addition, a number of viviparous lizards remove and eat the placental membranes from young when they are born.

In Australia, juvenile sleepy lizards (*Tiliqua rugosa*) remain in their mother's home range for an extended period, and this behaviour suggests that they gain a survival advantage by doing so. Female sleepy lizards and those of the Baudin Island spiny-tailed skink (*Egernia stokesii aethiops*) recognize their own offspring on the basis of chemical signals. Consequently, parental care in lizards may be more widespread than previously thought. Nevertheless, since recognition systems are subtle, they are difficult to study.

Certain lizards, particularly some species of Gekkonidae, are known to be communal egg layers, with many females depositing their eggs at the same site. In addition, it appears that the same individual female may return to a particular site throughout her lifetime to deposit clutches of eggs. In *Tropidurus semitaeniatus* and *T. hispidus*, two species of South American ground lizards, females nest communally under slabs of rock situated on top of large boulders. In this specialized habitat, only a few appropriate nest sites are available, and thus they are limited resources. Males appear to take advantage of this situation, especially if nesting sites are located within their territories. It is likely that if a male defends a good nesting site, he should have access to more females than males who govern areas without high-quality nesting sites.

MATURATION

Juvenile lizards are essentially miniature adults; they do not go through any larval phase or any other stage where they are dependent upon adults. They often differ from the adult in body colour or pattern and in certain body proportions. For example, the heads of hatchling lizards of some species tend to be proportionally larger than the heads of adults. Certain ornamental structures, such as the throat fan of the male green anole (*Anolis*) or the horns of some true chameleons (family Chamaeleonidae), develop as the lizards become sexually mature. The tails of juveniles in many lizard species are coloured differently from those of adults. Juvenile tails are brilliant blue, orange, or red and easily discarded (autotomized) when escaping a predator. Tail colour usually changes when the lizards reach sexual maturity.

Some of the smaller lizards mature very quickly, and population turnover (that is, the replacement of one generation by another) is essentially an annual event. For example, in the small, side-blotched lizard (*Uta stansburiana*) of western North America, the young hatch in July and reach sexual maturity the following autumn. At this time, males undergo spermatogenesis and mating takes place. Female side-blotched lizards accumulate large quantities of fat, which appear to be utilized in the production of eggs the following spring. Adult mortality in this species is 90 percent or more per year and may be a result of predation, inclement weather, or other factors. Conversely, the population dynamics of a single species living under a variety of environmental conditions may be very different from one region to another. For example, in areas with long winters where lizards experience long periods of hibernation, they may have greater longevity and slower population turnover.

On the other hand, large lizards may take several years to reach sexual maturity, and little information exists on the dynamics of natural populations of most lizard species. In captivity, many species are long-lived. Gila monsters (*Heloderma*) have been kept in captivity for more than 25 years, and even some small geckos have been kept for as long as 20 years. There is a report of a 46-year-old captive male slowworm (*Anguis fragilis*) mating with a 20-year-old female.

ECOLOGY

At the individual level, lizards are very sensitive to changes in the temperature of their surroundings. They are less sensitive to water loss because of their method of excretion. At the level of the biological community, lizards prey on insects, small mammals, birds, and one another. Some groups of lizards, such as the anoles, partition food resources so effectively that several species can coexist with one another within a single habitat.

THERMOREGULATION

The most important environmental variable to a lizard is almost certainly temperature. Like fish and amphibians, lizards are ectothermic; they receive heat from their surroundings. Although the term *cold-blooded* is typically applied to such organisms, it is a misnomer. The blood of lizards is not cold unless the lizard is cold. Under conditions where normal activities occur, lizard blood is as warm as or warmer than that of mammals. Nevertheless, all temperatures are not equally acceptable to lizards. Most species seek out relatively specific body temperatures, called "preferred temperatures," that mostly range from 28 to 38 °C (82 to 100 °F).

Although metabolic energy is not utilized to control body temperature, considerable thermoregulation is

Black girdle-tailed lizard (Cordylus nigra). Heather Angel

accomplished through behavioral means, if the lizard has a choice. Typically, a diurnal lizard emerges early in the morning and suns itself, orienting the body to maximize exposure to the sun, until the preferred temperature is achieved. The ability to absorb heat from solar radiation may permit the lizard to warm itself well above air temperatures. For example, *Liolaemus multiformis*, a small lizard that lives high in the Andes, has the ability to raise its body temperature to 35 °C (95 °F) while air temperatures are at 10 °C (50 °F) or lower.

The preferred body temperature plays a critical physiological role in the life of a lizard. All physiological processes are temperature-dependent, and physiological function influences behaviour. In most instances, the lizard's "performance," (that is, the lizard's ability to execute various behaviours or function well metabolically) is optimal within a small range of temperatures. To maximize performance, the lizard should seek to maintain its body temperature within this temperature range when at all possible.

Traditionally, the immediate environment in which a lizard lives has been considered the primary determinant of the lizard's body temperature. However, since thermoregulation is complex, there are constraints. Lizards living in hot deserts might be expected to be active at higher body temperatures than those living in well-shaded tropical habitats. Nonetheless, a combination of factors including evolutionary history, the immediate thermal conditions, and the "costs" associated with behavioral thermoregulation determines temperatures at which a lizard will operate.

The effect of evolutionary history is obvious when comparing certain groups of lizards. All whiptail lizards and racerunners in the genera *Aspidoscelis* and *Cnemidophorus* are active at body temperatures between 37 and 40 °C (99 and 104 °F) whether they live in the hottest part of the Mojave Desert of southern California or along trails in the Amazon rainforest. In addition, all lizards in the family Xantusiidae, a group distributed from the Mojave Desert southward through the rainforests of Central America, are active at body temperatures between 25–28 °C (77–82 °F). Whiptails adjust their activity periods to take advantage of heat sources in environments where temperatures are relatively low, whereas the tiny desert night lizard (*Xantusia vigilis*) occupies a microhabitat that remains cool in an otherwise hot place. Although some desert lizards have slightly higher body temperatures than their close relatives in more moderate habitats, the immediate thermal conditions often determine when and where a lizard will be active rather than what its body temperature will be.

Several costs to thermoregulation exist, but only a few have been studied. Time spent basking to gain heat or escaping extremely high or extremely low temperatures cannot be used for feeding or reproduction. Basking in direct sunlight to gain heat places a lizard in an exposed location where predators can capture it. Lizards whose body temperatures are outside of the optimal range for their species may not perform as well in social interactions as those lizards at optimal body temperatures. Some of the lesser-known costs include reduced growth rates and longer time to sexual maturity, increased incubation times for eggs or embryos when optimal temperatures cannot be reached, and a reduced ability to escape falling temperatures, which may result in the freezing of body tissues.

WATER LOSS AND OTHER VARIABLES

Water is less of a problem to lizards than is temperature regulation. All reptiles excrete uric acid and thus do not need great amounts of liquid to rid themselves of nitrogenous wastes. All insectivorous lizards take in a large amount of water in the prey that they consume, and herbivorous lizards have salt glands for the active excretion of mineral salts. Because of their low metabolic rates relative to those of birds and mammals, lizards use less water. This may account for their success at colonizing oceanic islands and surviving in extreme deserts. Some lizards in extreme environments harvest water from the dew that collects on their skin in early morning, and thus deserts do not pose severe problems to them. In addition, lizards form a conspicuous portion of the fauna of oceanic islands, where the species diversity of amphibians and mammals is generally low. Even while riding on mats of floating vegetation in rivers and oceans, many lizards can survive for long periods without fresh water. This quality makes them ideal colonizers, and hard-shelled gecko eggs seem to be particularly equipped for such journeys.

Other variables that affect lizards are day length (photoperiod) and rainfall. Lizards living far from the Equator experience marked variation in photoperiod, with short winter days and long summer days. Certain species are adapted to respond to such cues. *Anolis carolinensis* of the southeastern United States ceases reproduction in the late summer and accumulates fat for winter hibernation. This change occurs while the days are still warm and appears to be triggered by decreasing day length. This environmental trigger is adaptive for the species, because eggs laid in September would essentially be wasted, as the young hatched in November would likely starve or freeze to death. Some tropical species respond to alternations between rainy and dry seasons, and egg-laying activities may cease during the driest months of the year when food resources are low. Under these conditions it is advantageous for the parent not to channel valuable energy into the production of eggs, and the eggs themselves might be less viable because of the threat of desiccation.

NICHE PARTITIONING

Lizards provide valuable models for the study of competition between species. On some Caribbean islands as many as 10 species of anoles (*Anolis*) may live in a single restricted area. For so many species to be accommodated, each must be specialized for a rather precise niche. The species come in a variety of sizes, feed on different sizes of prey, and have different preferences for structural and climatic niches. Some anoles live in tree crowns, whereas others live on trunks, and still others live in grass. Some species prefer the open sun, whereas others live in "filtered" sun environments, and still others live in deep shade. Thus, with 10 anole species in a single area, each has its own characteristic microhabitat.

Likewise, the deserts of Australia contain the greatest numbers of lizard species known, with 40 or more species occurring together in some areas. These lizard species separate themselves along three fundamental niche axes:

Green anole (Anolis carolinensis). Robert J. Erwin—The National Audubon Society Collection/Photo Researchers

time, food, and place. Some lizards are active only at night, others are active in the morning, and still others are active at midday. Some are generalists that eat almost anything that walks by them, whereas others specialize on termites or ants. Some species occur only within small shrubs, whereas others occur only in areas of open sand or on tree trunks. These differences between species, combined with a habitat containing high structural diversity (that is, many places to live), allow large numbers of species to coexist within a small area.

Lizard assemblages in the Amazon rainforest are arranged along niche axes similar to Australian desert lizards. However, species that are the most ecologically similar are also the most closely related. This pattern suggests that evolutionary history has played some part in determining where and how lizards live.

BEHAVIOUR

Predatory lizards are divided into those that sit and wait for prey to cross their paths and those that actively search. Alternatively, lizards may become food for other animals, and some lizards counter attacks from birds and mammals with tactics that combine their structural and behavioral uniquenesses. Many lizards engage in elaborate rituals and behaviours during the process of selecting mates. In some species, courtship is closely tied to the territories males defend.

FEEDING HABITS

Most lizards are active during daylight hours, when their acute binocular vision can be used to its greatest advantage, and vision is necessary for most nonburrowing species. The family Gekkonidae, however, is composed predominantly of species that are most active from dusk to dawn. In conjunction with night activity, geckos are highly vocal and communicate by sound, whereas most other lizards are essentially mute.

Lizards spend considerable time obtaining food, usually insects. Iguanian lizards—iguanas, anoles, agamas, chameleons, and others—tend to perch motionless at familiar sites and wait for prey. They detect their prey using visual cues, dash from their perches to where the prey item is, and capture it with their tongue in a process known as lingual prehension. Iguanian lizards are typically referred to as "sit-and-wait" predators. The true chameleons are the most extreme examples of this mode of foraging. They move slowly, scan the habitat with eyes that move independently of one another, and capture their prey by shooting out a sticky projectile tongue. (In some cases, their tongues can extend to twice their body length.) Chameleons effectively eliminate the need to pursue their prey, which is the most risky aspect of the sit-and-wait foraging mode.

In contrast, autarchoglossan lizards (the non-gecko scleroglossan lizards such as amphisbaenians, skinks, whiptails, and others) actively search for prey by probing and digging, using their well-developed chemosensory system in a process called vomerolfaction, as well as visual cues. These lizards do not use the tongue to capture prey; rather, they grab their prey in their jaws (jaw prehension). As a result, the tongue is free for use as an organ of chemoreception. Geckos also use jaw prehension, but they use olfaction for discriminating between chemical cues rather than vomerolfaction.

Some lizards are herbivorous. The largest of the iguanian lizards, such as the iguanas (*Iguana*, *Ctenosaura*, and *Cyclura*) and the spiny-tailed agamid (*Uromastyx*), eat plants. However, large body size is not necessary for herbivory (many small herbivorous species in the genus *Liolaemus* exist), and the very largest lizards, such as the Komodo dragon (*Varanus komodoensis*) and other monitor lizards, are carnivorous.

DEFENSIVE STRATEGIES

Many birds, mammals, invertebrates, and other reptiles prey on lizards. In response, lizards have a variety of defensive strategies to draw upon. For example, chuckwallas (*Sauromalus*) typically remain close to rock piles. When danger threatens, they move into small crevices and puff up their bodies to make their extrication difficult. A number of spiny-tailed lizards also move into crevices and leave only a sharp, formidable tail exposed. The African armadillo lizard (*Cordylus cataphractus*) holds its tail in its mouth with its forefeet and presents a totally spiny form to an attacker. Predators, such as snakes, that attempt to swallow an armadillo lizard will often fail because the lizard offers no start point from which swallowing can begin. The frilled lizard (*Chlamydosaurus kingii*) of Australia extends a throat frill that frames its neck and head to intimidate intruders on its territory. This frill is almost as wide as the lizard is long. In addition, the tails of many lizards break off (autotomize) easily. This broken-off section wriggles rapidly and often distracts the predator as the tailless lizard scurries for cover. Autotomized tails are often regenerated quickly.

JACOBSON'S ORGAN

The Jacobson's organ, also known as the vomeronasal organ, is part of the olfactory system of amphibians, reptiles, and mammals. However, it does not occur in all tetrapod groups. It is a patch of sensory cells within the main nasal chamber that detects heavy moistureborne odour particles. Airborne odours, in contrast, are detected by the olfactory sensory cells located in the main nasal chambers. Some groups of mammals also initiate a behaviour known as the flehmen response, in which the animal facilitates the exposure of the vomeronasal organ to a scent or pheromone by opening the mouth and curling the upper lip during inhalation.

This organ was named for its discoverer, Danish anatomist Ludvig Levin Jacobson, in 1811. It is a paired structure; in the embryo stages of all tetrapods, each half arises as an evagination of the floor of a nasal sac. In fully developed crocodilians, turtles, birds, cetaceans, and many advanced primates, this structure is absent or substantially underdeveloped. For most tetrapods that possess a Jacobson's organ, ducts connect the organ directly to the nasal cavity; however, in squamates (lizards and snakes) each organ opens on the roof of the buccal cavity (mouth). The tongue carries odour particles from the outside to the vomeronasal openings on the roof of the mouth, and the particles then move into the vomeronasal organ. After these particles reach the organ, some of the chemical compounds they contain bind to receptor molecules, and sensory messages are sent to the brain.

The Jacobson's organ is useful in the process of communicating chemical messages, such as readiness for sexual activity, between members of the same species. The organ also helps snakes hunt and track their prey. Much evidence suggests that this organ may also be involved in the detection of chemical signals related to aggression and territoriality.

COURTSHIP AND TERRITORIALITY

Social interactions among lizards are best understood for the species that respond to visual stimuli. Many lizards defend certain areas against intruders of the same or closely related species. Territorial defense does not always involve actual combat. Presumably to avoid physical harm, elaborate, ritualized displays have evolved in many species. These presentations often involve the erection of crests along the back and neck and the sudden increase in the apparent size of an individual through puffing and posturing. Many species display bright colours by extending a throat fan or exposing a coloured patch of skin and engage in stereotyped movements such as push-ups, head bobbing, and tail waving.

Large, colourful horns and other forms of conspicuous head and body ornamentation are often restricted to males, but females of many species defend their territories by employing stereotyped movements similar to those of males. A displaying male that stands out against his surroundings is vulnerable to predation; however, territoriality is evidently advantageous and has evolved through natural selection. Territories are usually associated with limited resources (such as nest sites, food, and refuges from predators), and a male that possesses a territory will likely attract females. Thus, he will have a higher probability of reproductive success than one living in a marginal area. The displays used by males in establishing territories may also function to "advertise" their presence to females; in species that breed seasonally, territoriality typically diminishes during the nonbreeding season. In iguanids, actual courtship displays differ from territorial displays in that males approach females with pulsating, jerky movements.

In addition to the visual cues used for bringing the sexes together, chemical stimuli play a role in some species of iguanian lizards. For example, desert iguanas (*Dipsosaurus dorsalis*) can discriminate between their own odours and those of other desert iguanas. In addition, numerous lizard species have femoral pores, which are small blind tubes along the inner surface of the thighs, whose function may be the secretion of chemical attractants and territorial markers.

The social systems of autarchoglossan lizards are fundamentally different. Rather than visual displays, chemical communication between individuals is used. Autarchoglossan males that rely heavily on vomerolfaction can distinguish species, sex, and sexual receptivity using chemical cues alone. Some lizards (such as those of families Teiidae, Varanidae, and Helodermatidae) have deeply forked tongues and may be able to use them to determine the direction of chemical signals in a manner similar to snakes. Geckos use auditory cues in social interactions, but they also have the ability to discriminate between chemical signals using olfaction.

Copulation follows a common pattern. The male grasps the female by the skin, often on the neck or side of the head, and places his forelegs and hind legs over her body. He then pushes his tail beneath hers and twists his body to bring the cloacae together. One hemipenis is then everted and inserted into the cloaca of the female. Depending upon the species, copulation may last from a few seconds to 15 minutes or more.

FORM AND FUNCTION

Rather than present a detailed anatomical report of a lizard, the following sections discuss certain structures that are either characteristic of lizards in general or specializations of certain groups.

SKULL AND JAWS

The skull is derived from the primitive diapsid condition, but the lower bar leading back to the quadrate bone is absent, however, giving greater flexibility to the jaw. In some burrowers (such as *Anniella* and the worm lizards) as well as some surface-living forms (such as the geckos), the upper and lower temporal bars have been lost. Small burrowing lizards have thick, tightly bound skulls with braincases that are well protected by bony walls. In most lizards, the front of the braincase is made up of thin cartilage and membrane, and the eyes are separated by a thin, vertical interorbital septum. In burrowing forms with degenerate eyes, the septum is reduced and adds to the compactness of the skull. Most lizard skulls, particularly in the Scleroglossa, are kinetic (that is, the upper jaw can move in relation to the rest of the cranium). Since the anterior part of the braincase is cartilaginous and elastic, the entire front end of the skull can move as a single segment on the back part, which is solidly ossified. This increases the gape of the jaws and probably assists in pulling struggling prey into the mouth.

DENTITION

Most lizards eat a variety of arthropods, with sharp, tricuspid teeth adapted for grabbing and holding. In most lizards, teeth are present along the jaw margin (on the maxilla, premaxilla, and dentary bones), although, in some forms, teeth may also be found on the palate. In the embryo, an egg tooth develops on the premaxilla bone and projects forward from the snout. Although it aids in piercing the shell, it is lost soon after hatching. This is a true tooth, unlike the horny epidermal point in turtles and crocodilians.

The teeth of some large predators are conical and slightly recurved. The Komodo dragon (*Varanus komodoensis*), for example, has serrated teeth that are curved like a scalpel blade; these teeth can cut through the leg muscle of a full-grown water buffalo (*Bubalus bubalis*) and cause it to bleed to death. In contrast, mollusk and crustacean feeders, such as the caiman lizard (*Dracaena*), have blunt, rounded teeth in the back of the jaw designed for crushing. Some herbivorous species (such as iguanas) have leaf-shaped tooth crowns with serrated cutting edges. The venomous lizards (*Heloderma*) have a longitudinal groove or fold on the inner side of each mandibular tooth; these grooves conduct the venom from the lizard to its victim.

The common mode of tooth implantation is pleurodonty, in which the teeth are fused to the inner side of the labial wall. In the other mode, acrodonty, teeth are fused to the tooth-bearing bone, often to the crest of the bone. Acrodont teeth are rarely replaced once a certain growth stage is reached. The dentition of the Agamidae is usually described as acrodont, but most species have several pleurodont teeth at the front of the upper and lower jaws.

LOCOMOTION AND LIMB ADAPTATIONS

Most lizards are quadrupedal and have a powerful limb musculature. They are capable of rapid acceleration and can rapidly change direction. The racerunners or whiptails (*Aspidoscelis*) can attain speeds of 29 km (18 miles) per hour, which, in terms of their own body length (less than 50 cm [20 inches] long), puts them in a class with fast terrestrial mammals. A tendency toward elongation of the body is found in some families, and a reduction of limb length or a complete loss of limbs often accompanies such elongation. Such lizards propel themselves entirely by lateral undulations emanating from highly complicated ventral abdominal muscles. Limbless lizards that move quickly on the surface or through sand (such as glass snakes [*Ophisaurus*]) tend to have elongate tails, whereas the burrowers have extremely reduced tails. Some burrowers (such as the amphisbaenians) dig by ramming the head into the substrate. This is followed by the rotation of the head around the head joint to compress the substrate. Others, like the California legless lizards (*Anniella*), literally "swim" through the sand.

Many modifications of the toes occur in lizards. Some desert geckos, the iguanid *Uma*, and the lacertid *Acanthodactylus* have fringes on the toes that provide increased surface area, preventing the lizard from sinking into loose desert sand. Arboreal geckos and anoles (*Anolis*) have lamellae (fine plates) on the undersides of the toes. Each lamella is made up of brushlike setae. The tips of each seta divide hundreds of times into tiny spatulae (spoon-shaped strands); the final strand is less than 0.25 micrometre (0.00001 inch) in diameter. (A tokay gecko [*Gekko gecko*], for example, has about half a million setae on each foot.) These fine hairlike processes greatly enhance the clinging ability of the lizards, allowing some

Spotted racerunner (Cnemidophorus sacki). John H. Gerard

to easily climb vertical panes of glass. Intermolecular forces between spatulae on the gecko's setae and the surface provide the adhesion.

The true chameleons (family Chamaeleonidae), a predominantly arboreal group, have a different type of highly specialized limb. The digits on each foot are divided into two groups by webs of skin. On each hind limb, three of the toes face away from the body, whereas two face toward the body; on each forelimb, the pattern is reversed. Each foot can thus be divided into an outer and an inner portion, which can be opposed as the branch is gripped. Chameleons and some other lizards have prehensile tails, which also aid in grasping branches.

Several terrestrial lizards are able to run bipedally. Basilisk lizards (*Basiliscus*) are actually able to run across water for short distances. During bipedal locomotion the tail is held out backward and upward and acts as a counterweight. The frilled lizard (*Chlamydosaurus kingii*) can also run bipedally.

Some lizards are able to parachute or glide through the air and make soft landings. The most highly adapted of these are the flying lizards (*Draco*), a group of agamids from Southeast Asia. The "wings" that enable this lizard to glide are extensible lateral folds of skin that are supported by elongate ribs.

SCALES AND COLOUR CHANGE

Except for openings of nostrils, mouth, eyes, and cloaca, most lizards are completely covered in scales. Scales may be smooth and overlapping, form a mosaic of flat plates, or have keels or tubercles. The arrangement varies among species and by body part. The outer parts of the scales are composed of dead horny tissue made up largely of the protein keratin. The dead layer is shed at intervals and is replaced by proliferating cells in the deep part of the epidermis. In some lizards, osteoderms, which are bony plates that develop in the dermis, underlie head and body scales. In addition, certain lizards have scale organs, with a stiff projecting seta emerging from the serrated edge of the scale. Presumably, these setae are responsive to touch.

Many lizards can change colour. The most notable groups in this regard are the chameleons and the anoles. Some species can change from bright green to deep, chocolate brown, and patterns such as lines and bars may appear and disappear along their bodies. Melanophores are the pigment cells that permit colour change, and the concentration of pigment granules within these cells determine the type of colour that is produced. In general, the animal appears lighter coloured when pigment is concentrated and dark when pigment is dispersed throughout the cells. The animal's colour state at any given time is controlled by a complex interaction of hormones, temperature, and the nervous system.

SCALES

Scales in zoology are small plates or shields that form part of the outer skin layers of certain animals. Scales provide protection from the environment and from predators. Fish scales are formed of bone from the deeper, or dermal, skin layer. The elasmobranchs (e.g., sharks) have placoid scales, which are bony, spiny projections with an enamel-like covering. Ganoid scales, which are found on such fishes as gars and the bowfin, are similar to placoid scales but are covered with a peculiar enamel-like substance called ganoin. It is thought that true teeth developed from placoid scales. The advanced fish have either cycloid scales (e.g., carp) or ctenoid scales (e.g., perch; sunfish). These are the typical overlapping fish scales. Cycloid scales are large, thin, and round or oval in shape, and exhibit growth rings. Ctenoid scales resemble cycloid scales but have comblike teeth on their overlapping edge.

Horny scutes, or corneoscutes, derived from the upper, or epidermal, skin layer, appear in reptiles and on the legs of birds. In crocodilians and some lizards, bony dermal scales (osteoderms) underlie the external scales. Bird feathers are developmentally modified epidermal scales. Modified epidermal tissue, mostly made up of keratin, forms the scaly surface found on some mammals (e.g., rats; pangolins); however, although mammalian hair is also largely keratin, it is not a modified scale.

The term scale is also applied to modified body coverings on certain insects, e.g., moths.

LIZARD EVOLUTION AND CLASSIFICATION

The common ancestor to all lizards was similar to the tuatara (*Sphenodon*), the only living representative of order Sphenodontida and sister group to the squamates. The tuatara is lizardlike in overall appearance; however, it differs from squamates in important ways. Male tuataras have no paired copulatory organ; they have saclike structures from which the paired hemipenes of squamates were likely derived. In addition, the tuatara does not have a movable quadrate bone in the jaw; this characteristic is present in all squamates.

Relationships between the major groups of squamates remain in flux. One hypothesis posits that early in the evolutionary history of lizards an important split occurred that not only influenced the disposition of taxonomic units but had cascading effects on the ecology of lizards and led to the diversification of snakes. This first split produced the iguanians (infraorder Iguania) and the scleroglossans (infraorder Scleroglossa), two large groups within order Squamata that were fundamentally different from each other. The ancestors of all lizards possessed an ability to capture and manipulate prey with the tongue (lingual prehension). Iguania retained the ability; however, this likely precluded the development of the tongue into an organ that transmitted chemical signals to a rudimentary vomeronasal system in this group.

Another hypothesis, based largely on unclear gene sequence data, posits that the group containing geckos

tuatara
(Sphenodon punctatus)

Tuatara (Sphenodon punctatus). Encyclopædia Britannica, Inc.

(and possibly the dibamids) diverged from all other squamates and that the iguanians are nested deeply within the stock of remaining lizards (that is, the autarchoglossans). If additional data support this hypothesis, then the presence of many of the ecological, morphological, and behavioral traits in iguanians suggests that the iguanians evolved independently within a group of squamates that had already diverged considerably from its squamate ancestors. At present, herpetologists operate under the assumption that the first hypothesis is better supported.

For the most part, Iguania is composed of foraging lizards that use cryptic coloration, morphology, and behaviour to escape detection by predators. Typically, they can be described as territorial, sit-and-wait predators that rely on visual cues to detect prey (usually by movement) and in social interactions. Within Iguania, one family, Iguanidae, retained the ancestral pleurodont dentition similar to the tuatara, in which teeth are essentially cemented to the inside of the jawbones. In contrast, the ancestor of two other families within Iguania, Agamidae and Chamaeleonidae, developed acrodont teeth, which are characterized by their attachment to the surfaces of jawbones. The most striking deviation from the typical Iguanian consumptive pattern is the evolution of herbivory in lizards, which occurred independently in several lineages. Herbivory evolved in the ancestor to the Leiolepinae (family Agamidae), the ancestor to the Iguaninae (family Iguanidae), and in some members of the Liolaeminae (family Iguanidae).

In some of these groups, the tongue is used less for prey capture and more for chemoreception. Scleroglossan ancestors retained pleurodont dentition, but use of the tongue in prey capture was replaced by grasping jaws (jaw prehension). Freed from its direct involvement in feeding, the scleroglossan tongue was allowed to develop into a carrier of chemical information. Although the actual sequence of events will never be known with certainty, the vomeronasal system grew in importance, and lizard evolution proceeded in an entirely new direction.

An early split within Scleroglossa produced the Gekkota (geckos) and the Autarchoglossa (snakes, skinks, and their relatives). Use of the vomerolfaction system did not develop within Gekkota to the extent that it did within Autarchoglossa; however, the tongue was increasingly used as a tool for cleaning the spectacle, a transparent scale covering the eye. A nasal chemosensory system became enhanced in the Gekkota, but many retained (or redeveloped) the sit-and-wait foraging mode of their ancestors.

Autarchoglossans took maximum advantage of the vomeronasal chemosensory system. It dominates social behaviour in extant groups. The vomeronasal system allows members of this group to discriminate species, sex, and sexual receptivity on the basis of chemical cues; it also allows lizards to discriminate among prey types. Autarchoglossans can select particularly energy-rich prey and avoid those containing noxious chemicals. They also can seek out prey that may not be visible on the surface, such as colonies of social insects and insect larvae in the soil and vegetation. Moreover, cryptic-coloured invertebrates that might never be detected visually by iguanian lizards are detectable chemically by autarchoglossans; by searching the habitat, autarchoglossans can locate prey not otherwise available. In contrast to the sit-and-wait foraging mode of the iguanians, autarchoglossans developed an active foraging mode where much time is spent searching for energy-rich prey items. An important trade-off must have existed in which the benefits of searching large areas for prey outweighed the benefits of maintaining defended territories.

The development of the vomeronasal system caused a major shift in social systems. Autarchoglossans developed a sort of sequential polygyny mating system in which a single male guards a number of females as they move about. This is quite different from the territorial systems in the Iguania in which males defend particular places where females reside. Maintaining all of this activity required autarchoglossans to make some major physiological adjustments. They have higher activity levels, appear more alert, use more energy while foraging, take in more energy, and often have higher body temperatures than iguanians.

An active, energy-intensive lifestyle, combined with keen chemosensory abilities, sets the stage for the evolution of limblessness and the use of subterranean habitats. Limblessness evolved independently in several groups of autarchoglossans, but it did not evolve within the Iguania. The extreme development of the tongue and vomeronasal system in superfamily Varanoidea (a group made up of monitor lizards, snakes, and their relatives) set the stage for the evolution of snakes.

CHAPTER 3
TYPES OF LIZARDS

Although scientists classify lizard groups by the physical features they have in common with one another, it is sometimes more useful to classify them in other ways. For many people, a number of lizard groups are known through educational programs put on by zoos and museums. Other groups, such as the frilled lizards, slowworms, and worm lizards, are less well known, but they possess distinctive physical characteristics.

FAMILIAR LIZARDS

Some groups of lizards are more easily recognized than others. Chameleons, iguanas, and geckos may be kept as pets and often appear in school collections and in the exhibits of zoos and museums. Other lizards, such as the monitors, are noted for their ferocity.

CHAMELEONS

Chameleons (family Chamaeleonidae) are described as a group of primarily arboreal (tree-dwelling) Old World lizards best known for their ability to change body colour. Other characteristics of chameleons include zygodactylous feet (with toes fused into opposed bundles of two and three), acrodont dentition (with the teeth attached to the edge of the jaw), eyes that move independently, and a long, slender projectile tongue. The name has also been applied to the false chameleon, or anole, a New World lizard of the genus *Anolis* (family Iguanidae).

Four genera of true chameleons have been described: *Bradypodion*, *Brookesia*, *Chamaeleo*, and *Rhampholeon*. Two additional genera (*Calumma* and *Furcifer*) are recognized by some researchers. More than 150 species are currently known, and additional ones remain to be named. About half of the species occur only in Madagascar, whereas others occur mostly in sub-Saharan Africa. Two species occur in Asia; one is native to southern India and Sri Lanka (*Chamaeleo zeylanicus*), and the other (the European chameleon, *C. chamaeleon*) is found from the Middle East to southern Spain. The most familiar chameleons belong to the genus *Chamaeleo*, and these have prehensile tails that wrap in a coil-like fashion around limbs to maintain balance. In contrast, most species of pigmy chameleons in the genera *Brookesia* (Madagascar) and *Rhampholeon* (Africa) have short stubby tails that are not prehensile, although pigmy chameleons in *Bradypodion* have longer tails that are.

Most chameleons are 17–25 cm (7–10 inches) long, and the longest grows to 60 cm (24 inches). The body is laterally compressed, the tail is sometimes curled, and the bulged eyes move independently of one another. Also, some chameleons possess helmet-shaped heads.

Some species have conspicuous head ornamentation that may include as many as three long horns projecting forward. Such features are either exclusive to or better developed in males, and at least some of these features are related to territorial defense. A defending male responds to an invader by expanding the body, puffing out the throat, and elevating or waving special head flaps. If this display fails to intimidate the intruder, the defender charges and snaps his jaws. The differences in appearance between the sexes result from a process known as sexual selection, in which individual males with extreme ornamentation have a higher breeding success. They pass on the genes that form the basis for these features at a faster rate than those individuals lacking ornamentation.

Each species is capable of undergoing a particular range of colour change. The mechanism involves the dispersal or concentration of pigment granules (melano-phore cells) in the cells that contain them. These cells are under the control of the autonomic nervous system. Colour change is determined by such environmental factors as light and temperature as well as by emotions — such as fright and those associated with victory or defeat in battle with another chameleon. Many chameleons can assume a green, yellow, cream, or dark brown coloration. Frequently, this occurs with lighter or darker spots on the background colour of the body. Some of the most striking colours appear in males during mating. Some achieve colour patterns that are so vivid and complex that it is hard to imagine that they serve any natural purpose. It is a popular misconception that the chameleon changes its colour to match that of the background.

The chameleon's specialized vision and a specialized tongue-projection system permit the capture of insects and even birds from a distance. The chameleon's eyes are very good at detecting and regulating light. The lens of a chameleon's eye is capable of focusing extremely rapidly, and it can enlarge visual images much like a telephoto lens. Although many other lizards also use the tongue to capture prey, most can expel it only a short distance. In contrast, chameleons can launch their tongues at great speed to a distance of more than twice their body length, and they can strike and capture their prey with great accuracy. The hydrostatic force resulting from rapid contraction of a ringed accelerator muscle is used to project the tongue toward the chameleon's prey. A sticky tongue tip adheres to the victim's body, and strong retractor muscles pull the tongue and prey back into the mouth.

Most species are egg layers. Typically, females descend from their shrub or tree to bury between two and 40 eggs in the soil or rotting logs, and incubation lasts about three months. Some species, such as the large Jackson's chameleon (*C. jacksonii*), bear their young live; however, they do this without a placenta between the mother and the developing young. All nutrients necessary for development are contained within the egg itself, which simply develops within the female's oviduct minus a shell.

In addition, the Madagascan chameleon, *F. labordi*, has been widely acknowledged as the vertebrate with the shortest life span. The eggs of *F. labordi* hatch in November, and the young chameleons grow extremely fast; they mature to adulthood just two months later. After an intense competition for mates, eggs are laid in February, and the entire adult population perishes.

GECKOS

A gecko is any lizard of the family Gekkonidae, which contains over 100 genera and nearly 1,000 species. Geckos are mostly small, usually nocturnal reptiles with a soft skin. They also possess a short stout body, a large head, and typically well-developed limbs. The ends of each limb are often equipped with digits possessing adhesive pads. Most species are 3 to 15 cm (1.2 to 6 inches) long, including tail length (about half the total). They have adapted to habitats ranging from deserts to jungles. Some species frequent human habitations, and most feed on insects. Presently, the gecko family is made up of five subfamilies: Aleuroscalabotinae, Diplodactylinae, Eublepharinae, Gekkoninae, and Teratoscincinae. Of these, the eublepharines, such as the banded geckos (*Coleonyx*) of the southwestern United States, and the aleuroscalabotines have movable eyelids.

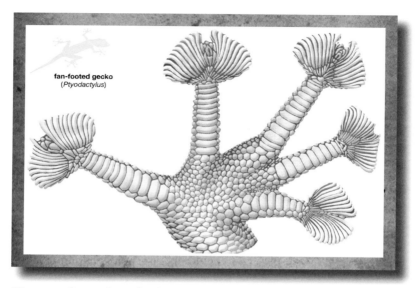

The toe fans of a fan-footed gecko (Ptyodactylus hasselquistii). Encyclopædia Britannica, Inc.

Most geckos have feet modified for climbing. The pads of their long toes are covered with small plates that are in turn covered with numerous tiny, hairlike processes that are forked at the end. These microscopic hooks cling to small surface irregularities, enabling geckos to climb smooth and vertical surfaces and even to run across smooth ceilings. Some geckos also have retractable claws. Like snakes, most geckos have a clear protective covering over the eyes. The pupils of common nocturnal species are vertical and are often lobed in such a manner that they close to form four pinpoints. The tails of geckos may be long and tapering, short and blunt, or even globular. The tail serves in many species as an energy storehouse on which the animal can draw during unfavourable conditions. The tail may also be extremely fragile and if detached is quickly regenerated in its original shape.

Geckos' colours are usually drab, with grays, browns, and dirty whites predominating, though *Phelsuma*, a genus made up of the day geckos of Madagascar, is bright green and active in the daytime. Unlike other reptiles, most geckos have a voice, the call differing with the species and ranging from a feeble click or chirp to a shrill cackle or bark. Most species are oviparous, the eggs being white and hard-shelled and usually laid beneath the bark of trees or attached to the underside of leaves. A few species in New Zealand give birth to live young.

Geckos are abundant throughout the warm areas of the world, and at least a few species occur on all continents except Antarctica. The banded gecko (*Coleonyx variegatus*), the most widespread native North American species, grows to 15 cm (6 inches) and is pinkish to yellowish tan with darker bands and splotches. The tokay gecko (*Gekko gecko*), the largest species, attains a length of 25 to 35 cm (10 to 14 inches). It is gray with red and whitish spots and bands. The tokay gecko, native to Southeast Asia, is frequently sold in pet shops.

IGUANAS

Iguanas are classified into eight genera and roughly 30 species of the larger members of the lizard family Iguanidae. The name *iguana* usually refers only to the members of the subfamily Iguaninae. The best-known species is the common, or green, iguana (*Iguana iguana*), which occurs from Mexico southward to Brazil. Males of this species reach a maximum length of over 2 metres (6.6 feet) and 6 kg (13.2 pounds). It is often seen basking in the sun on the branches of trees overhanging water, into which it will plunge if disturbed. The common iguana is green with dark bands that form rings on the tail; females are grayish green and about half the weight of males.

Food of the common iguana consists largely of leaves, buds, flowers, and fruits of fig trees (genus *Ficus*), although

Desert iguana (Dipsosaurus dorsalis). Encyclopædia Britannica, Inc.

many other trees are also fed upon. Whereas this lizard has a well-developed digestive system housing bacteria that ferment plant material, it also eats invertebrates when young and has been known to eat small birds and mammals.

During the rainy season, males become territorial, and mating pairs are established. At the end of the rainy season, eggs are fertilized and then laid in clutches of 30 or 50 in the ground during the early dry season. After 70–105 days, the 7.6-cm- (3-inch-) long hatchlings emerge. During this time, eggs and young are vulnerable to predators such as coatis and other omnivores. Adult iguanas have been used as food by humans for thousands of years and are threatened by hunting and habitat loss. In rural areas they are a major source of protein.

Other genera include the West Indian iguana (*Cyclura*) and the desert iguana (*Dipsosaurus*) of the southwestern United States and Mexico. Two genera inhabit the Galapagos Islands: the marine iguana (*Amblyrhynchus*) and a terrestrial form (*Conolophus*). The latter genus includes

HORNED TOADS

Horned toads, which are also called horned lizards (genus *Phrynosoma*), constitute about 14 species of lizards belonging to the family Iguanidae that are usually characterized by daggerlike head spines, or horns. A flattened oval body, pointed fringe scales along the sides of the body, and a short tail are typical features.

Ranging in length from less than 7.5 to more than 12.5 cm (3 to 5 inches), horned toads inhabit western North America from British Columbia southward to Guatemala and from Arkansas and Kansas westward to the Pacific coast. The usual habitat is desert or semidesert sandy country. Horned toads conceal themselves by colour-pattern change and by wriggling sideways into the sand until the entire body, except the head, is covered. They are food specialists, eating mainly ants. The horned toads include both egg-laying and live-bearing species.

Defense mechanisms include the ability to inflate the body quickly by gulping air, and (rarely) spurting blood from the eyes. They are often kept as pets but seldom live long in captivity because they slowly starve as a result of their specialized diet.

the pink iguana (*C. rosada*), which inhabits the slopes of Wolf Volcano on Isabela (Albemarle) Island. All iguanas are egg layers.

MONITORS

Monitors (family Varanidae) are any lizard of the genera *Varanus* or *Lanthanotus* in the family Varanidae. About 50 species of *Varanus* are recognized in the subfamily Varaninae. Most have an elongated head and neck, a relatively heavy body, a long tail, and well-developed legs. Their tongues are long, forked, and snakelike. They are found in Africa south of the Sahara, through southern and southeastern Asia, in Australia, and on islands in the southwestern Pacific.

The smallest monitor attains a full length of only 20 cm (8 inches), although several species grow to great size and length. Examples of large monitor species include the Komodo dragon (*V. komodoensis*) of Indonesia, the largest of all lizards, which grows to a length of 3 metres (10 feet); the two-banded, or water, monitor (*V. salvator*) of Southeast Asia, which grows to 2.7 metres (9 feet); the

KOMODO DRAGONS

Komodo dragon (Varanus komodoensis).
James A. Kern

The Komodo dragon (*Varanus komodoensis*) is the largest extant lizard species in terms of physical size. The dragon is a monitor lizard of the family Varanidae. It occurs on Komodo Island and a few neighbouring islands of the Lesser Sunda Islands of Indonesia. The popular interest in the lizard's large size and predatory habits has allowed this endangered species to become an ecotourist attraction, which has encouraged its protection.

The lizard grows to 3 metres (10 feet) in total length and attains a weight of about 135 kg (about 300 pounds). It digs a burrow as deep as 9 metres and lays eggs that hatch in April or May. The newly hatched young, about 45 cm (18 inches) long, live in trees for several months. Adult Komodo dragons eat smaller members of their own species and sometimes even other adults. They can run swiftly and occasionally attack and kill human beings. Carrion, however, is their main diet item, although they commonly wait along game trails to ambush pigs, deer, and cattle. They seldom need to capture live prey directly, since their venomous bite delivers toxins that inhibit blood clotting. It is thought that their victims go into shock from rapid blood loss. Komodo dragons often find their prey in the process of dying or shortly after death.

perentie (*V. giganteus*) of central Australia, which grows to 2.4 metres (8 feet); and *V. bitatawa* of the island of Luzon in the Philippines, which grows to 2.0 metres (about 7 feet). Partial fossils of *Megalania prisca*, an extinct Australian monitor that lived during the Pleistocene Epoch, suggest that it exceeded 7 metres (23 feet) in length and likely weighed nearly 600 kg (about 1,300 pounds).

All *Varanus* species except *V. bitatawa* and *V. olivaceus* (another monitor found on Luzon) are carnivorous and often consume large insects and spiders, other lizards, small mammals, and birds. *V. komodoensis* is known to capture much larger prey such as water buffalo (*Bubalus bubalis*). *V. olivaceus* eats fruits in addition to animal prey, whereas *V. bitatawa* appears to subsist primarily on fruit.

The earless monitor (*L. borneensis*), a rare and little-known lizard native to Borneo, is the only species in the subfamily Lanthanotinae. It too is elongate with a relatively long neck, but the limbs are small. It grows to a length of 40 cm (16 inches).

SKINKS

Skinks (family Scincidae) make up about 1,275 species of lizards, mostly secretive ground dwellers or burrowers, that are represented throughout most of the world but are especially diverse in Southeast Asia and its associated islands, the deserts of Australia, and the temperate regions of North America. The bodies of skinks are typically cylindrical in cross section, and most species have cone-shaped heads and long, tapering tails.

The largest species, the prehensile-tailed skink (*Corucia zebrata*), reaches a maximum length of about 76 cm (30 inches), but most species are less than 20 cm (8 inches) long. Ground-dwelling and burrowing skinks may show such adaptations as a transparent "window" scale in place of a movable lower eyelid. This adaptation allows the animal to see and protect its eyes from rough particles while burrowing. Other species of skinks may have such peculiarities as reduced or absent limbs and sunken eardrums. Some species are arboreal (tree-dwelling), and others are semiaquatic. Skinks eat insects and similar small invertebrates; large species are herbivorous and consume fruits of various kinds. Some species lay eggs, while others give birth to fully developed young.

Keeled skinks (*Tropidophorus*), which are semiaquatic, are found from Southeast Asia to northern Australia. Mabuyas (*Mabuya*), with about 105 species, are ground dwellers and are distributed worldwide in the tropics. Sand skinks (*Scincus*), also called sandfish, run across and "swim" through windblown sand aided by fringes of scales on their toes. Their countersunk lower jaw, scales that partially cover the ear openings, specialized nasal openings, and fringes on the eyelids allow them to move through sand without it entering their bodies. Sand skinks are native to the deserts of North Africa and southern Asia.

Slender skinks (*Lygosoma* and many other genera) and skinks of the genus *Plestiodon* (formerly *Eumeces*) also are common. Slender skinks are found throughout the Old World tropics, with a few species in the New World. They have thick tails and reduced legs, and their eyelids are often partially transparent. Most of the approximately 41 species from the genus *Plestiodon* have longitudinal stripes, although some, such as the Great Plains skink (*P. obsoletus*), have no stripes at all. In many of the striped skinks, such as the five-lined skink (*P. fasciatus*) and the broad-headed skink (*P. laticeps*), stripes fade after the skinks reach sexual maturity. *Plestiodon* is the dominant genus of skink in north temperate regions of the New World as well as Japan and surrounding areas; however, they are absent from Europe.

The broad-headed skink and, to a lesser degree, the five-lined skink have become model organisms for the study of behavioral ecology. As a result, both species have contributed greatly to the understanding of how lizards operate in the natural world. Skinks are part of a group of lizards that use chemical signals in social interactions and in finding prey. Their ability to discriminate chemical signals is influenced by sex hormones, and the same hormones influence some aspects of their morphology, particularly in males. During the breeding season, when levels of the male sex hormone testosterone are high, the heads of males become red in colour and muscles in the head increase slightly in size. Males become aggressive toward other males, and they pursue females in an attempt to mate with them.

Males can discriminate between sexes based on the chemical signals they pick up on their tongues and deposit in a highly receptive sensory organ called the Jacobson's organ (or vomeronasal organ) located in the roof of the mouth. This organ transmits signals to the lizard's brain. Males can also distinguish between sexually receptive and nonreceptive females using this system. During the non-breeding season when sex hormone levels are low, males are not aggressive toward other males and do not attempt to mate with females, and their heads are a dull brown colour. Sexual selection has favoured males with these traits, resulting in considerable differences between the sexes (sexual dimorphism).

Five-lined skinks and slender skinks have also been used in studies of tail loss as an antipredator mechanism. Like many other lizards, skinks can voluntarily release the tail when it is seized by a predator. Skinks often move or wave their tails in order to direct predators away from their bodies. Tails of many species are brightly coloured, enhancing the distraction effect. Once a predator has

Potential predators of the blue-tailed skink (Plestiodon skiltonianus) *are attracted to its tail, which can be shed at will.* E.S. Ross

grasped the tail, the skink contracts tail muscles and the tail is released. Energy stored in the tail is used to fuel rapid thrashing movements by the released tail, which further distracts the predator. The skink then walks away from the predation attempt. Tails are usually regenerated so that any other functions of the tail are regained. In some skinks, the lost tail itself has a high probability of escaping from the predator due to its violent thrashing. Five-lined skinks and slender skinks often return to the area and consume their released tails, thus regaining some of the lost energy.

Skinks have also contributed greatly to the understanding of reptile reproduction. Although most skink species deposit their eggs in nests and then abandon them, many are live-bearers (viviparous). Among the live-bearing species are some that have developed a complex placenta for transferring nutrients directly to the developing offspring. In one skink, the South American

SNAKE-EYED SKINKS

There are about 35 species of snake-eyed skinks. All snake-eyed skinks are found in two genera (*Ablepharus* and *Cryptoblepharus*) of the family Scincidae. They are extremely variable in colour.

Snake-eyed skinks lack eyelids and have transparent scales (spectacles) covering the eyes similar to those of snakes. Although the function of the spectacle remains unknown, it likely reduces water loss by evaporation from the head region. Spectacles in these two skink genera evolved independently and thus represent an example of convergent evolution. The spectacle is derived from the lower eyelid, which is fused to scales above the eye. They are the only skinks with a fixed plate (spectacle) on their eyes instead of a movable eyelid.

Members of the genus *Ablepharus*, often referred to as ocellated skinks, range from southeastern Europe to Pakistan. They have elongate bodies, long tails, and small limbs. They live within leaf litter or under rocks, twigs, or low vegetation. Members of the genus *Cryptoblepharus* are slender with long tails but with well-developed limbs. They occur in southeast Africa, Australia, the Indo-Pacific Islands and have been introduced to so many places that they may have the widest geographic distribution of any lizard genus. Excluding South America, *Cryptoblepharus* has a nearly worldwide distribution in the tropics, partially because it has either rafted on debris to islands or has been introduced to many islands by humans.

species *M. heathi*, the placenta is as developed and complex as that found in mammals.

UNUSUAL LIZARDS

Several lizards are notable for the unusual physical characteristics and behaviours they possess. Among them are lizards of the genus *Draco*, which are gliders. The Florida worm lizards are examples of amphisbaenians—a group of burrowing, limbless lizards with concealed ears and scale-covered eyes. Frilled lizards startle their potential predators by suddenly raising their neck frills.

DRACO LIZARDS

Draco is a genus of the lizard family Agamidae. Members of the genus are commonly referred to as flying lizards, because scaly membranes between the forelegs and hindlegs allow them to glide from tree to tree. There are more than 40 species of *Draco*. Most species are small, with a snout-vent length less than 8 cm (about 3 inches), and occur in the forests of Southeast Asia and the East Indies.

Draco species are usually dull-coloured, although their "wings" can be brightly coloured (e.g., orange with black spots). The membranes are supported by ribs that grow away from the body. At rest, the ribs and membranes fold against the sides of the body. To glide, these animals jump outward, spread their rib wings, and drift downward. A low-angle glide can carry the lizard as much as 50 metres (about 160 feet) to another tree or to the ground.

FLORIDA WORM LIZARDS

The Florida worm lizard (*Rhineura floridana*) is a pale or pinkish wormlike form characterized by the absence of limbs, external eyes, or ear openings, representing the only living member of the amphisbaenian family Rhineuridae. It is known only from the peninsula of Florida in the United States. However, fossils from the northern Plains indicate that the family had a much wider distribution in the past. *R. floridana* has a long wormlike body and a short stubby tail. It grows to a length of 18–38 cm (7–15 inches), and it preys on spiders, worms, and termites. It is an egg-laying species, and females deposit eggs from which tiny fully formed young emerge.

R. floridana burrows in soil, sand, and leaf mold and spends the greater part of its life underground. Tunnels are constructed by forcing the head into the soil and moving the head up and down to pack the soil away from the direction of movement. The animal then moves its body forward and repeats the process. When disturbed, it backs into its hole. Although they are difficult to find within their natural habitat, worm lizards are often discovered on roads following heavy rains.

FRILLED LIZARDS

The frilled lizard (*Chlamydosaurus kingii*) is a type of reptile found in Australia and New Guinea known for its ability to run standing up on its hind legs with its forelegs and

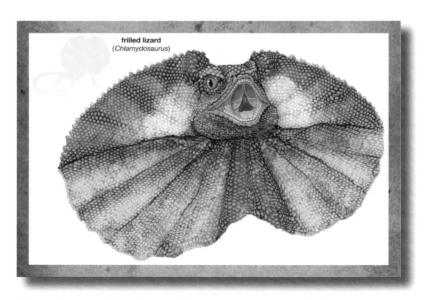

frilled lizard
(*Chlamydosaurus*)

The frill of a frilled lizard (Chlamydosaurus kingii). Encyclopædia Britannica, Inc.

tail in the air. The scaly membrane around its neck is used as a large part of the lizard's defensive posture. Normally, the neck frill, often as wide as the lizard is long, lies like a cape over the shoulders. When the lizard is irritated or threatened, it can raise the frill perpendicular to its body, enabling it to surprise its enemies by suddenly displaying a head several times its normal size.

Chlamydosaurus kingii averages 85 cm (33 inches) in length and spends most of its time in trees feeding on insects and small mammals.

ANOLES

Anoles (genus *Anolis*) make up more than 250 species of small tree-dwelling lizards. They are related to iguanas

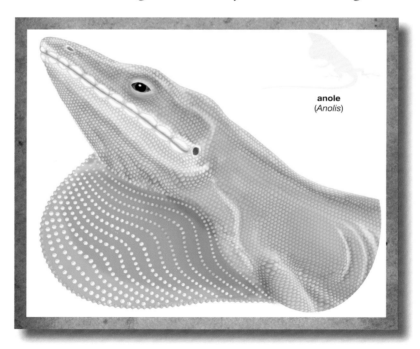

The dewlap of an anole (Anolis). Encyclopædia Britannica, Inc.

(family Iguanidae) and occur throughout the warmer regions of the Americas and are especially abundant in the West Indies. Like the gecko, most anoles have enlarged finger and toe pads that are covered with microscopic hooks. These clinging pads, together with sharp claws, enable them to climb, even over a smooth surface, with great speed and agility. Adult anoles may grow to 12 to 45 cm (5 to 18 inches) in length, and most species can change colour. The males have large throat fans, or dewlaps, that are often brightly coloured. The dewlap signals a male's possession of a territory and also serves to attract females for mating.

A familiar anole (*A. carolinensis,* or green anole, commonly but erroneously called the American chameleon) is native to the southern United States. Its colour varies at times from green to brown or mottled, but its colour-changing ability is poor compared with that of the true chameleons of the Old World. Green anoles reach a maximum length of 18 cm (7 inches) and have a pink dewlap.

GILA MONSTERS

The Gila monster (*Heloderma suspectum*) is one of two species of North American venomous lizards in the genus *Heloderma* of the family Helodermatidae. The Gila monster (*H. suspectum*) was named for the Gila River Basin and occurs in the southwestern United States and northern Mexico. It grows to about 50 cm (about 20 inches), is stout-bodied with black and pink blotches or bands, and has beadlike scales. A closely related species, the Mexican beaded lizard (*H. horridum*), is slightly larger (to 80 cm [about 32 inches]) and darker but otherwise similar in appearance.

During warm weather the Gila monster feeds at night on small mammals, birds, and eggs. Fat stored in the tail

Gila monster (Heloderma suspectum). Richard Weymouth Brooks/ Photo Researchers

and abdomen at this time is utilized during the winter months. Both species of *Heloderma* are slow, methodical predators. Their large heads and muscular jaws yield a strong bite that is held while venom seeps into the wound. Many teeth have two grooves that conduct the venom, a nerve poison, from glands in the lower jaw. Fatalities to humans are rare.

Glass Lizards

Glass lizards, which are also called glass snakes, constitute any lizard of the genus *Ophisaurus* in the family Anguidae. The reptile is so named because the tail is easily broken off. The Eastern glass lizard, *Ophisaurus ventralis,* occurs in southeastern North America and

Glass snake (Ophisaurus ventralis). Hal H. Harrison from Grant Heilman

grows to about 105 cm (41 inches). Together, the lizard's head and body account for only 30 to 35 percent of its total length. It has no legs but is easily distinguished from a snake by its ears, movable eyelids, nonexpandable jaws, and the fact that the scales on the lower and upper sides of the body are of equal size. It closely resembles the slender glass lizard, *O. attenuatus,* which has a broader distribution in southeastern North America northwestward into the upper Mississippi River valley. Unlike *O. ventralis,* which has a broad band along each lower side, *O. attenuatus* has narrow dark lines.

Both species live in loose soil, among leaves and grass, or under roots or stones. *O. apodus,* found over much of southeastern Europe, southwestern Asia, and northern Africa, grows to about 120 cm (47 inches) long (two-thirds of this length is tail). The glass lizards are egg

SLOWWORMS

The slowworm (*Anguis fragilis*), which is also called blindworm, is a legless lizard of the family Anguidae. It lives in grassy areas and open woodlands from Great Britain and Europe eastward to the Urals and Caspian Sea. Adults reach 40 to 45 cm (16 to 18 inches) in body length, but the tail can be up to two times the length from snout to vent. External limbs and girdles are absent, and only a remnant of the pelvic girdle persists internally. Its elongated body form, combined with an absence of limbs, gives the slowworm its snakelike appearance. Unlike snakes, however, slowworms have ear openings and eyelids.

The diet of *A. fragilis* is made up of snails, slugs, earthworms, other soft-bodied invertebrates, and some vertebrates. They are live-bearers that mate in spring and give birth to 8 to 12 young in late summer.

layers that produce modest clutches of 5–15 eggs. Each clutch is often attended by a female. Glass lizards principally inhabit grassland or open forest environments and eat a large variety of invertebrates.

CHAPTER 4

SNAKES

S nakes (suborder Serpentes), which are also called serpents, make up about 2,900 species of reptiles distinguished by their limbless condition and greatly elongated body and tail. Classified with lizards in the order Squamata, snakes represent a lizard that, over the course of evolution, has undergone structural reduction, simplification, and loss as well as specialization. All snakes lack external limbs, but not all legless reptiles are snakes. Certain burrowing lizards may have only front or hind limbs or be completely legless. Unlike lizards, snakes lack movable eyelids, which results in a continuous and often disconcerting stare. Snakes also lack external ear openings. Internally, they have lost the urinary bladder. The visceral organs are elongated, with reduction of the left member in relation to the right; the left lung is greatly reduced or even lost entirely. However, snakes possess increased numbers of vertebrae and have developed two novelties among vertebrates: a tracheal lung in the neck region and a venom-conducting system for subduing prey.

SNAKES AND HUMANS

Snakes are a misunderstood and often maligned group of animals, primarily out of ignorance about their true nature and position in the natural world. All snakes are predators, but venomous snakes have given an inaccurate reputation to the entire group, as most people cannot tell the dangerous from the harmless. Only a small percentage (fewer than 300 species) are venomous, and of those only about half are capable of inflicting a lethal bite. Although snakebite mortality worldwide is estimated at 30,000–40,000 people per year, the majority of deaths (25,000–35,000) occur in Southeast Asia, owing principally to poor medical treatment, malnutrition of victims, and a large number of venomous species. Although there are 8,000 venomous snakebites per year in the United States, the average number of annual fatalities is only a dozen or so per year—fewer than are attributed to bee stings and lightning strikes. In Mexico, 10 times as many people die annually from bee stings as from snakebites.

Snakes can control the amount of venom they inject and may bite aggressively for food or defensively for protection. They have a limited amount of venom available at any given time and do not want to waste it on nonprey organisms. As a result, about 40 percent of bites suffered by humans are defensive in nature and "dry" (without envenomation). Statistics show that the vast majority of snakebites occur while either catching and handling captive snakes or trying to molest or kill wild ones. In either case, the snake is only defending itself. Rattlesnakes, for example, are venomous, and large ones are quite dangerous owing to the amount of venom they can inject. However, most are shy and retreating, and none will attack a person unmolested. When approached or molested, they will coil up and rattle as a warning to be left alone, striking only as a last resort.

Most cases of reputed snake attack are based upon encroachment by a person into the snake's territory, which makes it feel trapped or cornered, or provocation of a snake during

Timber rattlesnake (Crotalus horridus).
Jack Dermid

the breeding season. Even in these scenarios, only two snakes have a reputation as dangerous aggressors: the black mamba (*Dendroaspis polylepis*) of Africa and the king cobra (*Ophiophagus hannah*) of Southeast Asia. Nevertheless, snakes are inoffensive under the vast majority of circumstances. People are rarely indifferent about them, generally exhibiting emotions that range from religious awe and superstitious dread to repulsion and uncontrollable fear.

It is interesting to note that, although most people profess to fear or hate snakes, one of the most visited areas of any zoo is the snake house — proof that snakes are mysterious and fascinating, even if they are loathed. Given their exquisite colours, patterns, and graceful movements as they crawl, swim, or climb, some snakes can be considered among the most beautiful animals.

Nearly every culture since prehistoric times (including various present-day cultures) has worshipped, revered, or feared snakes. Serpent worship is one of the earliest forms of veneration, with some carvings dating to 10,000 BCE. Although Satan is depicted as a serpent in the biblical account of the Creation, snakes are revered by most societies. Owing to ignorance, a vast global compendium of superstitions and mythologies about snakes has sprung up. Many stem from the snake's biological peculiarities: its ability to shed the skin is associated with immortality; the ever-open eyes represent omniscience; their propensity for sudden appearance and disappearance allies snakes with magic and ghosts; a phallic resemblance embodies procreative powers; and the ability to kill with a single bite engenders fear of any snakelike creature.

The hides of six snake species (especially pythons and wart snakes) are commonly bought and sold in the skin trade. The number of rattlesnakes used for their skins is minor in comparison. Hundreds of thousands of live snakes are collected for sale in the international pet trade.

Nearly 100,000 ball pythons and 30,000 boa constrictors are imported annually into the United States. The removal of such enormous numbers from the wild threatens the survival of these species, and many snake populations are in decline owing to capture and habitat destruction.

NATURAL HISTORY OF SNAKES

Most snakes do not spend much of their time doing anything but resting. A snake's primary activity is concerned with either thermoregulation or finding live food, which often involves passive waiting rather than active searching. The thermoregulation problem varies with latitude and altitude. The actions and reactions of a snake in temperate North America are distinct from those of one living in the American tropical lowlands but are similar to those of another living at higher altitudes in the Andes of Ecuador. No matter where they live, snakes are subjected to pressures from the living (biotic) parts of the environment as well as from the physical, nonliving (abiotic) parts. But the amount or degree of challenge to the snake from different segments of the environment changes drastically depending upon the region it inhabits. An individual living in the hot, humid tropics of Africa, with comparatively constant temperatures close to optimum throughout the year and ample moisture from both rainfall and the surroundings, faces environmental problems that are overwhelmingly biotic, involving competition with other members of its own species for food, the challenge from other species of snakes and perhaps other vertebrates for possession of the ecological niche, and constant pressure of the predators that find it a tasty morsel. On the other hand, the common adder, or European viper (*Vipera berus*), living north of the Arctic Circle in Europe, is the only snake present in the area and lives practically unchallenged in its niche.

However, its survival is challenged continually by its physical environment, and death from overheating, freezing, or dehydration is a repetitive threat. These differences between animals from different parts of the world are reflected in their life histories, and it is neither possible nor legitimate to speak of the "life history of the snake" unless one speaks of only a single region or species.

DORMANT PERIODS

In the tropics, life continues at approximately the same activity level throughout the year. The only break in the rhythm comes in the dry season—and this only when the dry season is not just a period of slightly less rainfall. At such times, snakes may enter a short period of dormancy, which is at least in part a consequence of the effect that the dry season has upon their prey. This dormant period is similar to hibernation in winter by temperate-area snakes, although little is known about physiological changes that may or may not take place in tropical dormancy. At higher latitudes and altitudes, during periods of maximum stress (which for most snakes are the cold months), the animals must seek out a place where they can be completely inactive and nonreactive, where their inability to respond to the stimulus of danger is compensated for by the absence of danger, and where the surrounding extremes of low temperature and low humidity remain within tolerable limits. Such places are few and far between, and good hibernacula (dens used for hibernation) are recognized over generations and are utilized year after year, with snakes of several different species often sharing a den. It is likely that snakes, like sea turtles, can migrate by using celestial or geomagnetic cues. Scent trails, most commonly laid down by females during the breeding season, are also used. Many of the changes that occur in the individual snake after arriving at the hibernaculum are direct results of its dependence upon the environment. As the body cools, the heartbeat and respiration slow almost to a stop, and there is no muscular activity, little digestion, and no defecation. Physiological changes that are not correlated with or responsive to the surroundings also take place, but not to a degree comparable to those occurring in a hibernating mammal, and there is no "alarm system" to stir the snake into activity if a tolerance limit is passed. In such a case, the snake simply dies.

At the end of the cold season, the snake is totally dependent upon the changes in its surroundings to bring it back to activity; it cannot rouse itself. The stimuli are felt by all almost simultaneously, and snakes emerge by the dozens or even by the hundreds from some denning places. In some species, copulation takes place immediately after enough of the sun's rays have been absorbed to permit the development of an interest in the surroundings; in others, copulation is the final act before entering hibernation, and the sperm remain dormant in the hibernating female. Fertilization of the egg can take place immediately after copulation, but, in at least some species, the female can store the sperm for several years, using them to fertilize successive batches of eggs.

INTERACTIONS BETWEEN INDIVIDUALS

Snakes in both tropical and temperate regions tend to be solitary in their habits. The denning and mating aggregations are, for the most part, the only social events of the season. Sea snakes (subfamily Hydrophiinae) differ in this respect, sometimes being seen traveling in large troops, which seems to indicate an urge to aggregate. Female sea snakes also congregate in large numbers in seawall caves at parturition time, but this may have no social significance, since it seems to be a consequence of availability of a safe place for the young to be born rather than aggregational behaviour per se. There is some tendency for females of certain species in temperate areas to use a single site for egg deposition. Hunting of food is strictly an individual act for snakes; there are no known instances of cooperative hunting, as seen in some mammal and bird species. Hiding places and basking sites are occasionally shared; this again is a consequence of availability, and in the tropics, where hiding places abound, it is rare to find more than one snake at a time under a log or a rock. Except for these few weak instances, there is no development of social behaviour in snake populations—no establishment of social hierarchies, no territoriality, and perhaps no dominance. While combat dance certainly establishes a dominant individual temporarily, there is no indication that awareness of this dominance is retained by either snake. A dominance that must be reestablished at every encounter does not contribute to a social structure.

REPRODUCTION

The reproductive process in snakes varies by species. Snakes share many of the same kinds of reproductive characteristics and behaviours with lizards, and many snake species engage in very elaborate courtship and competitive displays. In some species, eggs are retained within the body of the mother for the duration of her pregnancy. However, in other species, eggs are laid in nests and even incubated. The degree of parental care also varies between species.

MATING

The occurrence of mating immediately after emergence from hibernation allows snakes to take advantage of the fact that the females are accessible, concentrated, and receptive. The males are equally concentrated, so pair formation and copulation are a simple matter. Males of some species have nuptial tubercles on various parts of the body, used to stroke or massage the female and, presumably, to arouse her sexually. Even when obvious tubercles are absent, the male uses a rubbing technique to stimulate the female, and in some species a muscle ripple moving along the male's body will provide a lateral caress. There are many descriptions in the literature of courtship dances done by snakes, in which the bodies are entwined and as much as one-third lifted off the ground, the coils ebbing and flowing with silent grace. Unfortunately, in many of these reports, the snakes were not captured and sexed, and the observer simply assumed that a male and female were involved. The combat dance engaged in by two males is believed to be a competitive behaviour for the acquisition of females during the breeding season. As in the courtship dance, the front of the bodies entwine and are raised higher and higher off the ground until finally one snake overthrows the other. It has been suggested that the combat dance is essentially a homosexual encounter, with each male attempting to copulate with the other. In any event, copulation is achieved after a comparatively brief courtship through the insertion of a hemipenis in the female's cloaca (a common urogenital chamber, lying just anterior to the anus). The hemipenis is one of a pair of mirror-image intromittent organs lying in the base of the male's tail, posterior to the anus, and strictly reserved for mating, for the urinary passages empty directly into the cloaca of the male. Either hemipenis can be used in copulation and must be everted through a process of turning itself inside out. This is achieved primarily by engorgement of the organ with blood.

The everted organ is heavily armed with spines, spinules (minute spines), flounces, calyxes, and other ornaments, all of which appear to play a role in ensuring that the male is securely attached to the female for the entire period until the sperm have been deposited. The sperm pass along a deep groove in the hemipenis, which, although open along one margin when examined in a dead snake, clearly forms a tubular passage as a result of the pressures of the engorged margins of the groove. After release, the sperm may immediately move up the oviducts and fertilize eggs just released from the ovary, or they may be stored by the female and released later to achieve fertilization.

EGG FORMATION AND LAYING

Once fertilization has occurred, the egg begins to accumulate additional layers from the shell glands in the oviduct. In some species, this continues until a firm yet pliable leathery shell has been formed, permeable to both gases and liquids but capable of retaining much of its liquid content unless in a very dry place. The female then deposits the entire clutch of eggs in a protected damp, warm, and usually dark place, often along with clutches from other females of the same species, for the same stimuli that lead snakes to congregate for hibernation also take them to the same places for egg laying. Many species immediately abandon the eggs; some remain with the clutch and certainly appear to be protecting them from external danger; and a very few actually assume the role of a brood hen, maintaining a body temperature measurably higher than the surroundings and presumably assisting in incubation. In certain species, additional layers of membranous material are deposited around the embryo, but the calcareous (calcium-containing) shell does not form. Instead, the embryo is retained in the oviduct and continues its development there. This is termed ovoviviparous development, since it is simply an egg retained in the oviduct, in contrast to viviparous, the condition seen in mammals, where the fetus develops in the uterus and establishes a placental connection with the uterine wall to permit exchange of materials with the maternal circulation. But, while an umbilical connection does not develop, there is considerable evidence of an exchange of materials between mother and fetus across their contiguous, highly vascularized membranous surfaces.

Regardless of the devices used to provide it with protection, the snake fetus is always brought to term before the onslaught of environmental conditions that could result in its death. The embryonic turtle can sleep away its first winter in the egg and hatch the following spring none the worse for the experience, but there is as yet no evidence that snakes can do the same. The contrast may result from the fact that the female turtle can scoop out a hole deep enough for freezing temperatures not to affect her brood, but the female snake is restricted, both by her limblessness and by the nature of the egg itself, to egg laying on or near the surface, where below-freezing temperatures are unavoidable. In the tropics, evidence is scant, but it would appear that there is an endogenous (i.e., controlled from within) rhythm there as well, since young are not produced throughout the year.

EARLY DEVELOPMENT AND GROWTH

The young snake, whether from an egg or born alive, comes equipped with a sharp cutting device on its upper lip, the egg tooth. It slashes its way out of the rubbery eggshell with this tooth or, in the case of the live-born, cuts its way out of the soft membranes and is instantly competent to cope with its surroundings. Almost invariably, the first act of a newborn snake is to extend its tongue and taste the surroundings, conveying to the Jacobson's organ (a sensitive region in the roof of the mouth) chemical information perhaps more significant than the visual cues picked up by the pair of very inexperienced eyes. Young snakes begin to feed immediately after hatching, displaying considerable ability in the capture and consumption of prey. Venomous snakes are born with functional venom glands and fangs and are capable of imme-diate utilization of their most formidable weapons. Some of the viperid snakes are born with a bright green tail tip (con-trasting strongly with the rest of the body colour), which they are capable of waving and shaking in a way that attracts the attention of possible prey. Within a very short time after birth, the first sloughing of the skin takes place, and the egg tooth is shed at about the same time.

The rate of growth is correlated with availability of food and temperatures high enough to permit full meta-bolic activity. When all factors are optimal, snakes grow surprisingly fast. A brood of California rosy boas (*Charina trivirgata*) doubled their length in a nine-month period, growing to only a few inches shorter than their mother, an adult close to maximum length for the species. It has been suggested that all snakes grow rapidly until they reach sexual maturity, after which time growth slows but very seldom stops completely. Snakes have indeterminate growth, which means there is no terminal point in time or size for growth in their lifetime, but they can continue to increase in length until they die. Sexual maturity is reached in about two years by many snakes. In the larger species, sexual maturity comes later, after four or five years or more.

In terms of total length, the reticulated pythons (*Python reticulatus*)—which inhabit Southeast Asia, Indonesia, and the Philippines—are the largest, growing to more than 7 metres (23 feet) as adults. In contrast, adults of the spe-cies *Leptotyphlos carlae*, a type of worm snake found on the island of Barbados, average only 10 cm (4 inches) long.

MOLT

A regularly recurrent event during the activity period of all snakes is the shedding, or molting, of the skin. Dormant individuals do not shed, but quite often this is one of the first events to take place after the end of dormancy. The integument of all animals represents the primary buffer between internal structures and the environment, and it is constantly subject to wear, tear, and other damage. The first line of defense against damage, especially when the skin is completely broken, is the formation of a blood clot or a scab, cellular reorganization, and scar formation. The second line of defense is the constant production of new cells in the deeper layers of the skin to replace cells lost or worn away from the surface. In snakes, the replacement procedure has been modified to a considerable degree. The replacement cells are not constantly produced independently of one another but grow on the same cycle and cohere into a complete unit. When this unit is functional, the old skin lying external to it becomes a threat to continued good health. At this point, the snake's eyes become a milky blue, an indication of a physiological loosening of the skin that forms the eye cap. This loosening is duplicated all over the body, although not so obviously. Shortly, the eyes clear, and the snake rubs loose the skin around the mouth and nose and crawls out of it completely, leaving a new, functional skin resplendent in fresh, bright colours. The rattlesnake sheds its skin in the same fashion as all other snakes, but the process is highly modified at the tail tip, where successive layers of keratinized, hardened epidermis are interlocked, or nested, to form the rattle, a device used to ward off large mammals. The use of the rattle is reasonably successful with buffalo, cattle, or horses but spectacularly unsuccessful with man because, through this advertising, the rattling snake precipitates either its death or its capture but seldom its escape.

LOCOMOTION

The snake has overcome the handicap of absence of limbs by developing several different methods of locomotion, some of which are seen in other limbless animals, others being unique. The first method, called serpentine locomotion, is shared with almost all legless animals, such as some lizards, the caecilians, earthworms, and others. This is the way most snakes move and has been seen by any zoo visitor. The body assumes a series of S-shaped horizontal loops, and each loop pushes against any resistance it can find in the environment, such as rocks, branches, twigs, dust, sand, or pebbles. The environment almost always provides sufficient resistance to make movement possible, and many snake species never use any other method of locomotion. Such species, when placed on a surface providing no resistance, such as smooth glass, are unable to move, whipping and thrashing around without progress. Snakes, like fishes and eels, swim by lateral undulation, which is essentially identical to serpentine locomotion. The sea snakes, however, possess a distinct anatomy in the form of a flattened, oarlike tail.

Other methods of terrestrial movement also involve at least some resistance by the environment but usually less than the first. One of these is known as "concertina" locomotion, because the snake in action resembles the opening and closing of an accordion or a concertina. First the tail and the posteriormost part of the body are securely anchored, and then the head and the rest of the body are extended as far forward as possible from that secure base. At the maximum extension, the head and the forepart of the body are anchored and the posterior part drawn up as close as possible in the accordion-like folds. A second cycle follows the first, and the snake progresses. Tree snakes, such as *Imantodes* and *Oxybelis*, modify this technique to move from branch to branch and have a strongly compressed body that permits surprising lengths of it to be stiffened and extended, using a modified I-beam effect for rigidity.

The third method is called "caterpillar" or "rectilinear" locomotion, because the body moves in a straight line, using a flow of muscle contractions along the sides that looks like a caterpillar in motion. The body musculature is used for sequential lifting, anchoring, and pushing against individual ventral scales, which results in an inching along. It is used by large, heavy-bodied snakes, such as the boas and some of the vipers.

The fourth method is the least dependent on friction with the surface and is called sidewinding. This mode characterizes snakes living in the desert (though some non-desert dwellers also use it), where the sand simply gives way under any kind of push. The sidewinder does not progress forward when in motion but actually goes sideways. The snake, lying extended on the sand, lifts the anterior part of the body, moves it several centimetres to the side, and rests that part on the sand, maintaining the rest of the body as a lifted loop. This loop is then progressively shifted along the body to the end of the tail, at which time the entire snake has moved to the side from its previous position. By the time the first loop has reached the end of the tail, a new loop has already lifted the head and started down the body, and the snake looks like a coiled spring rolling across the

Blunt-headed tree snake (Imantodes cenchoa). Dade W. Thornton—The National Audubon Society Collection/Photo Researchers

sand. There is no rolling involved, however, since the ventral surface is always in contact with a substrate and usually leaves its impression behind in the sand, like a footprint. Sidewinding allows minimal contact of the body with hot sand and thereby allows the snake to be active at a time when surface travel would be lethal.

FORM AND FUNCTION

The most characteristic aspect of the snake form is the elongate body and tail and the absence of limbs. There is no snake in which the limb remnants still retain a function in locomotion, but complete or reduced elements of the pelvis and femur remain in many snake families, including the boa and python families. The body is usually slender, although there are some comparatively short and thick-bodied species. The body shape is correlated with activity level, with the slender species moving about all the time and the heavy forms leading a sedentary life. The pit vipers, for example, while not always long, are often big. It seems likely that these snakes evolved in the direction of heaviness only after the development of a heat-sensitive depression, the loreal pit, located between the eye and the nostril, and the venom apparatus, which enabled them to stay in one place and wait for their prey, rather than engaging in a continuous active search for food. Similarly, some of the largest nonvenomous snakes (boas, anacondas, and pythons) have labial pits that function in the same way as the loreal pit of the vipers, so they too can be sedentary and grow fat.

Arboreal snakes are the most elongated and slender of all, with the tail (the region posterior to the anus) approaching half the length of the entire body. The body is often strongly compressed laterally, which permits greater rigidity of the body frame while crawling from

East African green mamba (Dendroaspis angusticeps). E.S. Ross

branch to branch. Burrowing (fossorial) snakes are seldom large, and the true burrowers, the Typhlopidae and Leptotyphlopidae, living all their lives like earthworms, are the tiniest snakes of all. The burrowers have almost no tail, although some of them retain a spiny tail tip, which probably serves the animal as an anchoring point when crawling through the soil. The tail of sea snakes is flattened to form an oar, used to scull through the water. Sea snakes are almost totally helpless on land, locomoting only with the utmost difficulty.

VERTEBRAE

The vertebral column of snakes is highly elongated and has more vertebrae than any other living animal—up to 600 in the Australian python (*Morelia oenpelliensis*). Since there are no limb girdles associated with the skeleton, there are no good delimiters of regions, but snakes are generally regarded as having only two kinds of vertebrae: body (precaudal) and tail (caudal). There are 100–450 vertebrae in the body and 10–205 vertebrae in the tail. A pair of ribs is associated with each body vertebra except for a few immediately behind the head. By definition, there are no ribs on the tail vertebrae. Each vertebra articulates with its neighbour at five different points: first, at the contact point between the main, central bodies of the bones (centra), which is a ball-and-socket joint; then at two projections (prezygapophyses and postzygapophyses) from the centra, with articulating surfaces that lie above and below; and finally the zygosphenes and zygantra, found almost exclusively in snakes, the zygosphene being a projecting shelf on the upper part of the vertebra and the zygantrum being a pocket into which the zygosphene fits and within which it can swivel. These five points permit lateral and vertical rotation while preventing almost entirely any twisting of the vertebral column, thus achieving both flexibility and rigidity. The vertebra may bear on its ventral surface a long posteriorly directed projection called a hypapophysis. The presence or absence of this structure on the vertebrae of the posterior third of the body has been of considerable importance in snake classification because large groups of species show this as a common characteristic. In the egg-eating snakes (subfamily Dasypeltinae), the hypapophyses of a series of vertebrae a short distance behind the head have developed anteriorly directed tips that have a distinct coating of an enamel-like substance. These serve as eggshell breakers, projecting through a gap in the dorsal intestinal wall, where they can rip into a swallowed egg when the snake constricts the muscles of the body. The crushed shell is regurgitated, and the contents of the egg pass on to the stomach. The vertebrae of the tail tip in the rattlesnake are highly modified to form a "shaker" for the hollow rattle segments.

THE SKIN

Snakes are covered with scales, which are cornified folds in the epidermal layers of the skin. These scales are usually arranged in rows along the body, the numbers and arrangement of which are characteristic of the species. The scales may be large and shield-shaped, in which case the number of rows is low (from 10 to 30), or they may be very small, rounded, and occasionally with the centre raised, in which case the number of rows can be as high as 180. A single scale may be very smooth and shiny (as in the rainbow snakes), have a raised ridge (keel) along its centre, be heavily striated, or even have a raised spine in the centre, as in the Javanese wart snake. The scales in some species have sensory structures on the posterior margins called apical pits, and all scales have various micro-ornamentations, consisting of hairlike projections, holes, spinules (small spines), and other specializations visible only through an electron microscope. The scales on the ventral surface of the body are modified into broad plates in the majority of species and are used in locomotion. The ventral scales of sea snakes (Hydrophiinae), worm snakes, and blind snakes are small, as on the dorsal surface, and there are several other species, including boas and pythons, that have partly enlarged ventral scales.

COLORATION

The colours and colour patterns seen in snakes are often bright and occasionally spectacular. Snake colours are produced in two ways, either by pigment deposited in the skin or by differential diffraction of light as a consequence of the physical properties of the skin itself. When seen on a unicolour or uniform background, most snakes are obvious, and their colour patterns seem bold and prominent. When the animals are placed in their natural habitat, however, the significance of the colour patterns becomes obvious. The many lines running at sharp angles to the elongated lines of the body, the triangles or rectangles of colour, the blotches, spots, bands, or lozenges—all become highly disruptive to the eye, and the snake disappears into its surroundings. Blotched or spotted snakes tend to be sedentary and heavy-bodied, while striped and the occasional unicolour snakes are usually active species. In both cases, the coloration is protective, since a coiled sedentary snake has its body outline completely obscured by the overlapping patterns, while the stripes on a crawling snake eliminate the sensation of motion until they suddenly narrow at the tip of the tail and the snake disappears.

Although in most snakes the colours are such that they help the animal to hide, there are some species that seem to be advertising their presence rather than trying to hide it. Their patterns are aposematic, or warning, in nature, and they let a possible enemy or predator know that it runs some risk in an encounter with the snake. The warning is effective, of course, only if the intruder is knowledgeable concerning its significance and can take heed. This implies a teaching and learning sequence, with

Scarlet snake (Cemophora coccinea). Hal H. Harrison/Grant Heilman Photography

the dangerous snake as "teacher" and the predator as "student." For this reason, it has been suggested that the bright colours of the highly (and often fatally) venomous coral snakes did not evolve as warnings of the snakes' own poison but as mimics of some other venomous species, less dangerous but still able to teach the predator the significance of the warning coloration.

There is no evidence that avoidance of aposematic species is instinctive; on the contrary, naive predators readily attempt to take aposematic forms. A predator that dies in its first encounter with a dangerous species cannot act as a selective force favouring the coloration of that species. There are quite a few mildly poisonous rear-fanged snakes, brightly banded in red, black, and yellow (colours found in the coral snakes), that can make a predator suffer a sufficiently painful lesson that it will avoid contact with all similarly coloured snakes, including the fatally venomous coral snakes and the completely harmless milk snakes (*Lampropeltis*) and scarlet snake.

SKULL AND SENSE ORGANS

Snakes rely on several senses to inform them of their surroundings. The pits, found in the region between the nostril and the eye in the pit vipers (the viperid subfamily Crotalinae) and in the scales of the lip line in some boas and pythons, are sensitive to very slight changes in temperature. These snakes feed almost exclusively on animals, such as birds and mammals, that maintain a constant body temperature and can therefore be located by the snake through the reception of the heat of the warm body. The heat lost by even a small rodent is sufficient to alert a waiting viper and enable it to direct a fast strike at the animal as it passes by. Death follows rapidly, and the snake follows the dying animal at a leisurely pace, perhaps in full awareness that it will not go far. The boids use the same technique for detecting warm prey, but after striking they retain the grip, killing by constriction.

The eye of the snake is lidless and covered by a transparent cap of epidermis, which is shed with the rest of the skin at each molt. Animals active during the day usually have round pupils, while the nocturnal species have a vertical or slit pupil that opens up in the dark, as does that of a cat, but closes more effectively in bright light, protecting the sensitive, dark-adapted retina. The eye has been almost completely lost in the burrowing families, in which it is visible only as a black spot and may be covered with a scale or flesh. Arboreal snakes often have a bulging, laterally placed eye, which permits them to see activities directly below as well as above and around them. The structure of the eye in snakes indicates that their lizard ancestor was probably a burrower and that all aboveground activity by snakes is a secondary invasion from an ancestral life underground.

The reception of sound is entirely by bone conduction within the skull. The snake has no external ear, but it still retains a few vestiges of the internal ear, which are connected to other skull bones in such a way as to permit transmission of some earth-borne, and perhaps a few aerial, sound waves of low frequency.

The skull of snakes is characterized by mobility. It is light, with a reduced number of bones, and there are hinge joints at several levels that permit slight rotation or movement of one segment upon another. The only compact unit is the central braincase, with all other skull bones little more than attachments held in place by ligaments and muscles. In most snakes, the six bones of the upper jaw (left and right of the maxilla, palatine, and pterygoid) can move forward and back as well as sideways. The flexibility of the skull and the jawbones attached to it is a major compensation for the loss of limbs and allows a snake to swallow prey that is several times the diameter of its head.

To swallow prey, the skulls of snakes move in a variety of ways, ranging from a lizardlike "inertial-feeding" mode, whereby the upper and lower jaws are both engaged

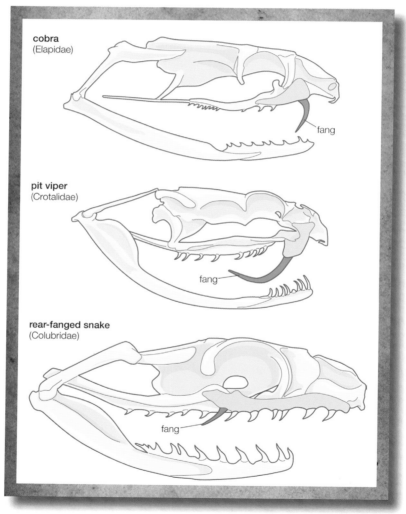

Skulls of representative poisonous snakes. Drawing by M. Moran

forward over the prey items, to a "walk feeding," whereby each of the four jaw arches moves independently of the others. Inertial feeding is found in the primitive blind snakes and thread snakes (infraorder Scolecophidia). In shieldtail snakes and their relatives (superfamily Anilioidea), a solid skull and limited movement of the jawbones allow "snout-shifting," where one entire side of the head is moved forward in relation to the other side, which clamps the prey. Boas and pythons (superfamily Booidea) are more advanced and utilize a "walk-feeding" method in which one jaw arch is disengaged and moved forward, while the three other arches hold fast. The "walk" progresses by moving the jaw arches in order: upper left, upper right, lower left, lower right, and so on.

In most snakes, the upper jaw is connected to the lower jaw by a joint that acts as a pivot point, and, when eating, all toothed bones on one side of the mouth move forward as a unit. In the slug- and snail-eating snakes (the colubrid subfamilies Dipsadinae and Pareatinae), the connection between the upper jaw and the quadrate is lost, and there are four independent units rather than two. This jaw modification permits them to hold their food with three jaws while the fourth is advanced. The maxillary bone (the main bone of the upper jaw) of most snakes is elongated, with many teeth, but, in the Viperidae (Old World vipers, New World rattlesnakes, and other pit vipers), only one functional fang remains, on a short, blunt, rotatable maxillary. The position usually occupied by the maxillary has been taken by the pterygoid bone. In the Elapidae (cobras and relatives), the maxillary bears a single fang in a fixed position, sometimes followed by a few smaller, solid teeth. In several different evolutionary lines of snakes, the posterior one or two teeth on the maxillary have enlarged and changed, usually in the direction of developing a groove or canal on the anterior edge to conduct a flow of venom. These are the rear-fanged snakes, usually (although not always) nonlethal to man.

Snake teeth are usually long, slightly recurved, and needle-sharp. This facilitates swallowing and prevents loss of food, because the only direction in which a food item, which may be alive when swallowed, can go to escape the teeth is down the throat. Modifications in food habits have often been accompanied by changes in tooth structure or the loss of teeth. The egg-eating snakes, for example, have only a few peglike teeth left. The burrowing blind snakes have very reduced dentition and often have lost the teeth of one jaw entirely.

UROGENITAL SYSTEM

The urogenital system in snakes is not very distinctive from that of other vertebrates. The testes and ovaries tend to be staggered as a consequence of the elongation of the body, with the right usually lying anterior to the left. Snakes do not have a urinary bladder, and kidney wastes are excreted in a solid state as uric acid. As mentioned in the section Mating, the male snake has two separate intromittent organs, the hemipenes. This structure is not homologous with the penis of mammals but seems to represent a completely different solution to the problem of internal fertilization. It is a saclike structure that must be turned inside out to be inserted in the cloaca of the female and can be removed only by turning it back inside, because to draw it out directly would damage the female considerably. The hemipenis is extremely variable in its overall appearance and structure; the cloaca of the female is often similarly constructed, which thus prevents cross-fertilization by males of related species.

VENOM

Venom is the poisonous secretion of an animal, produced by specialized glands that are often associated with spines, teeth, stings, or other piercing devices. The venom apparatus may be primarily for killing or paralyzing prey or may be a purely defensive adaptation. Some venoms also function as digestive fluids. The venom poisoning of humans is primarily a problem of rural tropical regions, though it occurs worldwide. Many thousands of human deaths due to venom poisoning occur each year.

Most venoms injure humans only when introduced into the skin or deeper tissues, usually through a sting or bite. Venoms are mixtures of toxic enzymes and various other proteins that act on the body in different ways. Neurotoxin venoms act on the brain and nervous system and can cause either nervous excitation (characterized by such symptoms as muscle cramps, twitching, vomiting, and convulsions) or nervous depression (with such symptoms as paralysis and weakening or arrest of respiration and heartbeat). Hemotoxins affect the blood or blood vessels: some destroy the lining of the smaller blood vessels and allow blood to seep into the tissues, producing local or widespread hemorrhages, while others render the blood less coagulable or cause abnormally rapid clotting, leading to circulatory collapse that can be fatal. Still other venoms produce the symptoms of an allergic reaction, resulting in wheals, blisters, and violent inflammation, often followed by death of tissue and muscle spasms.

Most major animal phyla contain venomous species, but relatively few come into harmful contact with humans. These few include certain snakes (e.g., cobras, mambas, vipers, pit vipers, coral snakes, and rattlesnakes); certain fishes (e.g., stingrays, weevers, spiny sharks, scorpion fish, ratfish, and certain catfish); a few lizards (Gila monster); some scorpions and several spiders (e.g., the black widow and brown recluse); some social insects (e.g., the bee, wasp, and certain ants); and various marine invertebrates, including some sea anemones, fire corals, jellyfish, cone shells, and sea urchins. Snakes and spiders inject venom into their victims with their fangs; fishes use venomous spines and scorpions and many insects use stings.

Venom attacks can range in severity from a simple localized inflammation of the skin to almost immediate death, depending on the animal involved and the potency and mode of action of its venom. An attack's severity also depends on the victim's age (children are more severely affected than are adults) and the location of the injury (a venom wound on an arm or leg is usually less serious than a similar one on the head or trunk).

Specializations for Securing Food

The most essential and time-consuming activity for a snake during nondormant periods, regardless of its habitat, is the pursuit, capture, and digestion of food. Most snakes consume one prey item and then rest before eating again. There are many morphological and behavioral modifications to be observed in snakes that facilitate food gathering. Some of these changes are widespread and found in practically every kind of snake. Jacobson's organ, for example, is located in the roof of the mouth and is capable of detecting minute quantities of various chemical substances when they are picked up externally on the delicate double-tipped tongue and thrust into the organ for analysis. It is so significant and useful that it has never been lost by any snake species. While important primarily in trailing and recognition of prey, the Jacobson's organ is also used in detection of enemies, in trailing other snakes of the same species, and in courtship.

Some snakes have specialized salivary glands that elaborate a potent venom, along with either grooved or tubular teeth to permit internal injection of the venom. This device for rapid immobilization of prey has proved successful whenever it has occurred, and several different lines of evolution can be detected both in the type of injector tooth and in the chemical composition or mode of action of the venoms. The types of injector tooth include the long tubular fang of the viperids, the short hollow fang on a fixed maxillary seen in the elapids, and the several kinds of grooved tooth on the posterior end of the maxillary. In the latter case, there is little doubt but that the development of grooving has taken place several different times in different places. As for the venom, it is true that the terms *neurotoxic*, *hemotoxic*, and *cardiotoxic*, once used to describe the different effects, are clearly misleading and are too simple for accurate statements concerning venom composition. Nevertheless, it is still accurate to say that some components of venom cause changes in red blood cells, coagulation defects, and blood-vessel injury, while others produce deleterious changes in sensory and motor functions and in respiration, and still others have a direct effect on the heart. Some venom kills very rapidly, such as that of the golden fer-de-lance (*Bothrops insularis*) of Queimada Island, off the Brazilian coast, which would lose as prey most of the birds it bites if they could fly very far away. Other venoms kill more slowly, and the snake bites, retires, and waits, finally trailing the bitten prey, using the tongue and the Jacobson's organ until it finds the already stiffening body. Some snakes, in particular the rear-fanged species, bite, chew, and hold on, eventually bringing the hindmost maxillary teeth into play, which permits the injection of toxin.

Other feeding specializations are not so widespread among species, and some are restricted to a single group. Nearly all boids and many colubrids utilize a constriction method for killing their food. The prey is struck and held by the teeth, and a series of body coils are rapidly thrown around it. These coils tighten until respiration is impossible and suffocation results, but very seldom are bones crushed or broken. The snail-eating snakes have a series of modifications of the teeth, the toothed bones, and the lower jaw that permit insertion of the lower jaw into a shell to pull out the snail's body. One genus of sea snakes, *Microcephalophis*, has a tiny head and a long neck with the same diameter as the head, which can be inserted deeply into very narrow holes inhabited by its prey. An Asian water snake, *Erpeton tentaculatus*, has a sizable pair of tentacles on its snout, the purpose of which is uncertain. There is a great correlation between the difficulty in catching a particular kind of prey and the development of morphological and behavioral devices to help solve the problem. The blind snake living in a termite nest needs no more than its tongue and Jacobson's organ to permit it to recognize the soft-bodied, defenseless termites, so its eyes and most of its teeth have been lost. But the rattlesnake, seeking the most elusive prey of all in agile, aware, and sensorially acute small mammals, has a full armament of equipment, including the facial pit, the venom gland, the rotatable maxillary bone, the tubular fang, and two functional eyes.

EVOLUTION

The origin of snakes has been debated since the mid-19th century. On the basis of unique shared derived features (such as paired copulatory organs and the Jacobsen's organ), it is clear that snakes and lizards are close relatives. However, it is not known whether snakes evolved from (1) a prelizard group, (2) a common ancestor of both lizards and snakes, or (3) a lizard group. The last hypothesis is currently in favour, but the specific group (living or extinct) is uncertain. Concerning habitat type, it has been thought that snakes evolved from (1) an aquatic ancestor (such as mosasauroids), (2) a burrowing ancestor (such as the amphisbaenian worm lizards or the blind lizards), or (3) a secretive ancestor. Each of these is consistent with the morphological changes observed in modern snakes as compared with lizards (loss of limbs, lengthening of body, absence of movable eyelids and external ear opening).

The discovery of three marine snake fossils with hind limbs (*Hassiophis*, *Pachyrhachis*, *Podophis*) from the

Cretaceous Period (144 million to 65 million years ago) of the Middle East has sparked renewed controversy over the origin of snakes. The interpretation and analysis of these fossils vary among researchers. Some classify them as the most primitive serpents in a sister group to all snakes, whereas others suggest they are a more advanced group related to boas and pythons. The latter interpretation, if correct, would mean either that the hind limbs were re-evolved in these snakes or that the snakes represent an independent evolutionary line that never lost the hind limbs. This debate may be resolved only with the discovery of additional fossils and further analysis.

The evolutionary history of snakes can be characterized as the transition from the lizardlike "inertial-feeding" mode of the primitive Scolecophidia (worm snakes and blind snakes), whereby the upper and lower jaws are both engaged forward over the prey items, to "walk feeding." Although the fossil record of snakes is poor and fragmentary compared with other vertebrates, much is known about the evolution of living and extinct groups. The oldest fossils are found in South America, Africa, and Madagascar from the time when these continents were joined as Gondwanaland. The earliest undisputed snake (*Lapparentophis*) was terrestrial. Found in Africa, it dates to 120 million years ago, but it can be assumed that snakes originated farther back in time, probably during the Late Jurassic Epoch (159 million to 144 million years ago). The initial dichotomy among living snakes occurred between the specialized, burrowing Scolecophidia (worm snakes and blind snakes) and the generalized Alethinophidia (ancient and modern snakes). Given present distribution, it is likely that the Scolecophidia originated in Gondwanaland; the fossil record clearly indicates a Gondwana origin for the superfamilies Anilioidea and Booidea. Some of the more advanced snakes (families

Viperidae, Elapidae, and Colubridae) originated in the ancient continent of Laurasia, their earliest fossils being from North America and Europe.

The burrowing Anilioidea of South America and Southeast Asia is the most primitive group of alethinophidians. The Aniliidae of the Amazon probably most closely represent the ancestral snake condition. They are moderate-sized, with a lizardlike skull, barely enlarged ventral shields, and a vestigial left lung. Fossil anilioids are known from the Cretaceous of South America to the Eocene Epoch (54.8 million to 33.9 million years ago) of Europe.

The anilioids gave rise to the booids, a primitive but more generalized group of boas and pythons. The fossil record of the extinct terrestrial Madtsoiidae extends from about 80 million years ago to the Pleistocene Epoch (2,600,000 to 11,700 years ago) of Europe, Africa, Madagascar, South America, and Australia. The two most primitive living booid families, Xenopeltidae and Loxocemidae, are small ground-dwelling snakes. The Boidae and Pythonidae are the first snakes to have moved aboveground and diversified into terrestrial, arboreal, and aquatic habitats. Their success was probably due to increased size and changes in the feeding apparatus (loosening of the skull's jaw bones, increased dentition on the four jaw arches, expandable skin between scales) that permitted them to subdue large warm-blooded mammals and birds by constriction.

Boas and pythons are large, heavy, and slow-moving and include the largest living serpents, with some reaching 6 to 10 metres (20 to 33 feet) in length. During the Late Cretaceous, a land bridge connecting South America to North America allowed anilioid and booid snakes to invade the northern supercontinent of Laurasia from Gondwanaland. These two groups then spread from North America eastward to Europe and possibly westward into Asia. The fossil record indicates that the height of booid evolution and diversity occurred in the Eocene, when they dominated the world's snake fauna, after which time they diminished in numbers. Between the end of the Cretaceous and the middle of the Eocene, the largest terrestrial vertebrate in the world was a booid snake (*Titanoboa cerrejonensis*). Known from a single fossilized vertebra, *Titanoboa* probably weighed 1,135 kg (about 2,500 pounds) and reached a length of 13 metres (about 43 feet).

The most advanced snake group, the superfamily Colubroidea, evolved during the Eocene in Laurasia. These snakes were smaller and faster and possessed more flexible jaws than the booids, and several groups developed venom glands and fangs for subduing prey. The fossil record indicates that colubroids outcompeted the booids, which today number fewer than 80 species, as opposed to some 2,200 colubroids. The Oligocene Epoch (33.7 million to 23.8 million years ago) was a transitional period, with the booids and anilioids diminishing in numbers and the colubroids increasing. The Miocene Epoch (23.8 million to 5.3 million years ago) was a period of great expansion of colubroids in North America, Europe, and Asia. The first venomous snakes evolved in the Early Miocene, with the Viperidae appearing in North America, Europe, and Asia and the Elapidae in North America and Europe. It was during the Miocene that Africa was invaded by the Colubridae, Elapidae, and Viperidae from Europe. The diversification and expansion of the Colubridae as the dominant snake group began in the Miocene and has continued to the present. During Australia's long separation and isolation from Gondwanaland and other continents, only four families existed there, three of which survive today (Typhlopidae, Pythonidae, and Elapidae) and one of which became extinct in the Pleistocene (Madtsoiidae).

CHAPTER 5
TYPES OF SNAKES

O ne way to differentiate among snakes is to examine the ways in which they obtain nourishment. Snakes embrace several different types of hunting strategies when capturing their prey. Some species deliver a poisonous bite to their victims, whereas others simply rely on the force of their bite alone. Constrictor snakes apply crushing and asphyxiating force by coiling their bodies around their prey.

The snakes described in this chapter are classified by how they capture their prey. The first group contains descriptions of cobras, rattlesnakes, and other groups that are known for their venom. The second group provides examples of relatively harmless, nonpoisonous snakes, while the third group provides examples of snakes that use constriction to subdue their prey.

POISONOUS SNAKES

Only about five percent of all snake species are capable of killing a human being. A sampling of venomous snakes from the families Colubridae, Elapidae, and Viperidae are described below.

ADDERS

Adders make up several groups of venomous snakes of the viper family, Viperidae, and the Australo-Papuan death adders, viperlike members of Elapidae, the cobra family. The name *adder* may also be applied to certain other snakes, such as the hognose snake (*Heterodon*), a harmless North American genus. Among the adders of the viper family are the European common adder (*Vipera berus*), the puff adders (9 or 10 species of *Bitis*, including *B. arietans*), and the night adders (four species of *Causus*).

The European common adder, or European viper (*V. berus*), a serpent often mentioned in works of literature, is a stout-bodied snake that is widely distributed across Europe and Asia. It even ranges north of the Arctic Circle in Norway. It grows to a maximum length of approximately 85 cm (33 inches) and is usually gray to brown with a dark zigzag band on the back and spots on the sides. The common adder eats frogs, young birds, and small mammals. It bears its young alive, and 6–20 are born in August or early September. Its bite is rarely fatal to humans.

The puff adder (*B. arietans* and others) is a large extremely venomous snake found in the semiarid regions of Africa and Arabia. It is so named because it gives warning by inflating its body and hissing loudly. The puff adder is about 1 to 1.5 metres (3 to 5 feet) long and is coloured gray to dark brown with thin yellow chevrons on its back. It is a thick-bodied snake with a potentially lethal bite, and it tends to stay put, rather than flee, when approached.

Night adders (*Causus*) are small relatively slender vipers found south of the Sahara and are typically less than 1 metre (3 feet) long. They are active at night and feed nearly exclusively on frogs and toads.

Although death adders (*Acanthophis*) are related to the slender-bodied cobras, they are viperlike in appearance, with thick bodies, short tails, and broad heads. They are about 45 to 90 cm (18 to 35 inches) long and are gray or brownish with darker crosswise bands. Death adders typically occupy habitats ranging from desert to rainforest in Australia and New Guinea however, *A. antarcticus* occurs near the more-temperate and maritime eastern and southern coasts of Australia. While their taxonomy is uncertain, death adders from New Guinea have been assigned to three species

(*A. praelongus*, *A. laevis*, and *A. rugosus*). The desert death adder (*A. pyrrhus*) is found only in arid areas of Australia.

As a group, death adders are sedentary predators that prey on frogs, lizards, and small mammals. They are

VIPERS

Vipers (family Viperidae) account for more than 200 species of venomous snakes belonging to two groups: pit vipers (subfamily Crotalinae) and Old World vipers (subfamily Viperinae), which are considered separate families by some authorities. They eat small animals and hunt by striking and envenomating their prey. Vipers are characterized by a pair of long, hollow, venom-injecting fangs attached to movable bones of the upper jaw (the maxillaries) that are folded back in the mouth when not in use. Their eyes have vertical pupils, and their scales are keeled. Vipers range in length from less than 25 cm (10 inches) in the Namaqua dwarf viper (*Bitis schneideri*) of southern Africa to more than 3 metres (10 feet) in the bushmaster (*Lachesis muta*) of the Amazon basin and Central America.

The pit vipers are found from desert to rainforest, primarily in the New World. This group includes copperheads, rattlesnakes, and fer-de-lances (genus *Bothrops*), among others. They may be terrestrial or arboreal. Some, such as the moccasins (genus *Agkistrodon*), are aquatic. Except for the egg-laying bushmaster, all pit vipers are live-bearers (viviparous).

Pit vipers are distinguished by a temperature-sensitive pit organ located on each side of the head midway between each nostril and eye. This structure is sensitive to infrared radiation, which enables the snake to "see" heat images of warm-blooded prey. As a pair, they provide a form of binocular vision that helps the snake accurately aim its strike at warm-blooded prey. At least some Old World vipers have infrared receptors in the same area as the pit organs, although there is no external evidence of them. Some boas and pythons have similar infrared organs located in pits between the lip scales.

Old World vipers live in desert to forest habitats of Europe, Asia, and Africa. They are typically slow, stocky, and broad-headed. Many, such as the European viper, or common adder (*Vipera berus*), and the Gaboon viper (*Bitis gabonica*) are terrestrial, but tree vipers (genus *Atheris*) are slender, prehensile-tailed, and arboreal. Some species lay eggs; others produce live young.

live-bearers, giving birth to perhaps as many as 10 to 30 young. Death adders are dangerous snakes that produce a potent venom that causes death in about one-half of untreated cases.

BOOMSLANGS

The boomslang (*Dispholidus typus*) is a venomous snake of the family Colubridae, one of the few colubrid species that is decidedly dangerous to humans. This moderately slender snake grows to about 1.8 metres (6 feet) in length and occurs in savannas throughout sub-Saharan Africa. When hunting, it lies in wait in a bush or tree for chameleons and birds; the forepart of the body often extends motionless into the air.

Its body and eye colour are extremely variable, and camouflage is excellent. In defense the boomslang inflates the neck, showing the dark skin between the scales; it then may strike. It is rear-fanged, but the fangs are set relatively far forward in the mouth. The venom causes hemorrhages and can be fatal to humans in small amounts.

Boomslang (Dispholidus typus). Dade Thornton—The National Audubon Society Collection/Photo Researchers

BUSHMASTERS

The bushmaster (genus *Lachesis*) is the longest venomous snake in the New World, found in scrublands and forests from the Amazon River basin north to Costa Rica. Three species of bushmaster (*L. muta*, *L. stenophrys*, and *L. melanocephala*) are known to exist, and they normally measure about 1.8 metres (6 feet) long but may grow to as long as 3 metres (10 feet). These large snakes are reddish brown to pinkish gray in colour, matching their forest floor habitats, and they may bear x-like or diamond patterns across the back. Although seldom encountered, the bushmaster is dangerous, with a potentially lethal venom.

The bushmaster is a pit viper (subfamily Crotalinae). Infrared pits, located between the eyes and nostrils, are used to "smell" prey, which consists mostly of small rodents. Prey is swallowed head-first, but the snake will bite and then release larger or more dangerous prey. In this type of attack, their eyes and pits are well protected by folds of skin.

A bushmaster may coil for several weeks at one site, waiting to ambush prey along routes of travel, such as fallen limbs, buttresses of trees, or trails along the ground. This snake can survive on fewer than 10 large meals per year. It is the only pit viper in the Americas to lay eggs (instead of bearing live young), and females may remain with the eggs for a time before they hatch.

Common tropical American vipers (family Viperidae) related to the bushmaster include the eyelash viper (*Bothriechis schlegelii*), the fer-de-lances (*Bothrops*), and the hog-nosed vipers (*Porthidium*).

Bushmaster (Lachesis muta). Dade Thornton from The National Audubon Society Collection—Photo Researchers

CAT SNAKES

Cat snakes are made up of any of several groups of arboreal or semiarboreal rear-fanged snakes in the family Colubridae with eyes having vertically elliptical pupils similar to those found in felines. Cat snakes are nocturnal hunters that become active at twilight. By day their pupils are contracted to narrow vertical slits, but as night falls the pupils expand to a nearly circular shape to let in as much light as possible. The body is thin and laterally compressed, and the head is triangular and distinct from the neck. Their short rear fangs can deliver a mild venom that is not dangerous to humans. Representatives occur on all continents except Antarctica. Some of the major groups are listed below.

Eurasian cat snakes (*Telescopus*) inhabit dry regions of southeastern Europe, southwestern Asia, and northern Africa. About 12 species are known; they feed entirely upon lizards, and females lay between 4 and 12 eggs to a clutch. European cat snakes (*T. fallax*) occur in six subspecies. They are moderately sized at 0.5–0.7 metre (1.6–2.3 feet) long, though some may reach 1.3 metres (about 4 feet). Clutch sizes in this species range from four to six eggs.

Other Old World cat snakes include *Boiga*, which is mainly distributed through Southeast Asia and the East Indies, with more than 35 species ranging from Pakistan to Australia. Two species (*B. blandingii* and *B. pulverulenta*) occur in Africa. This large and diverse group ranges in size from 0.5 to 2 metres (1.6 to 6.5 feet), though some can grow to be 2.8 metres (about 9 feet) long. They feed on birds, mammals, lizards, frogs, and other snakes, as well as the eggs of these animals. Breeding females of this genus lay between 3 and 15 eggs. One of the largest and most spectacular species is the black-and-yellow mangrove snake, or gold-ringed cat snake (*B. dendrophila*), a shiny black snake with a yellow crossbar pattern on its body. It ranges from the Malay Peninsula to the Philippines and can reach 2.5 metres (about 8 feet) in length.

In addition to *B. blandingii* and *B. pulverulenta*, African cat snakes also include members of the genus *Dipsadoboa*. This genus is made up of 11 or more species that are primarily restricted to rainforests and open woodlands south of the Sahara; they are uniformly green to brown in colour, with yellow or orange eyes. African cat snakes are slender and grow to about 0.5–0.7 metre (1.6–2.3 feet) in length, though some may grow to 1.4 metres (about 4.5 feet). They feed upon frogs, toads, and tadpoles, and females lay 2–8 eggs in a clutch.

Often classified separately, cat-eyed snakes (*Leptodeira*) of the New World tropics are superficially similar to Old World cat snakes. Ten species of cat-eyed snakes occur in dry habitats from Mexico to Argentina. The most common species is the banded cat-eyed snake (*L. annulata*), which is found over the entire range of the genus. These snakes are light brown in colour with dark brown spots or blotches on the back, and they typically grow to 0.5–0.8 metre (1.6–2.6 feet), though specimens of 1.1 metres (about 3.6 feet) have been found. Banded cat-eyed snakes feed mainly upon frogs, but they also eat lizards. Breeding females deposit clutches of 3–12 eggs.

COBRAS

Cobras constitute various species of highly venomous snakes, most of which expand the neck ribs to form a hood. While the hood is characteristic of cobras, not all of them are closely related. Cobras are found from southern Africa through southern Asia to islands of Southeast Asia. Throughout their range, different species are favourites of snake charmers, who frighten them into assuming the upreared defense posture. The snake sways in response to the movement and perhaps also to the music of the charmer, who knows how to avoid the relatively slow strike and who may have removed the snake's fangs. The short fangs at the front of the mouth have an enclosed groove, which delivers the venom. Cobra venom generally contains neurotoxins active against the nervous system of prey—primarily small vertebrates and other snakes. Bites, particularly from larger species, can be fatal depending on the amount of venom injected. Neurotoxins affect breathing, and although antivenin is effective, it must be administered soon after the bite. Thousands of deaths occur each year in South and Southeast Asia.

The world's largest venomous snake is the king cobra, or hamadryad (*Ophiophagus hannah*). Found predominantly in forests from India through Southeast Asia to the Philippines and Indonesia, it preys chiefly on other snakes. Maximum confirmed length is 5.6 metres (18 feet), but most do not exceed 3.6 metres (12 feet). King cobras guard a nest of 20 to 40 eggs, which are laid in a mound

Black-necked cobra (Naja nigricollis). E.S. Ross

of leaves gathered by the female. The guarding parent will strike if a predator or a person approaches too closely. Not all cobras are egg layers.

The Asian cobra (*Naja naja*) was formerly considered a single species with much the same distribution as the king cobra. Recently, however, biologists have discovered that nearly a dozen species exist in Asia, some being venom spitters and others not. They vary both in size (most ranging between 1.25 and 1.75 metres [4–5.7 feet]) and in the toxicity of their venom. Spitters propel venom through the fangs by muscular contraction of the venom ducts and by forcing air out of the single lung.

In Africa there are also spitting and nonspitting cobras, but the African cobras are not related to the Asian cobras, nor are they related to each other. The ringhals, or spitting cobra (*Hemachatus haemachatus*), of southern Africa and the black-necked cobra (*Naja nigricollis*), a small form widely distributed in Africa, are spitters. Venom is accurately directed at the victim's eyes at distances of more than 2 metres (about 7 feet) and may cause temporary, or even permanent, blindness unless promptly washed away. The Egyptian cobra (*N. haje*) — probably the

ASPS

Asp, which is an anglicized form of *aspis*, is the name used in classical antiquity for a venomous snake, probably the Egyptian cobra, *Naja haje*. It was the symbol of royalty in Egypt, and its bite was used for the execution of favoured criminals in Greco-Roman times. Cleopatra is said to have killed herself with an asp.

European aspic vipers (*Vipera aspis*) of France, Switzerland, Spain, and Italy are often referred to as asps. Adult aspic vipers may reach 50 cm (20 inches) in total length, although most are smaller. They live in a variety of habitats ranging from sea level to high-altitude environments near 2,600 metres (8,500 feet) in the Swiss Alps. These animals prey on small vertebrates and give birth to a litter of 5–16 young.

asp of antiquity—is a dark, narrow-hooded species, also about 2 metres long, that ranges over much of Africa and eastward to Arabia. Its usual prey consists of toads and birds. In equatorial Africa there are tree cobras (genus *Pseudohaje*), which, along with the mambas, are the only arboreal members of the family Elapidae.

COLUBRIDS

A colubrid is any member of the most common family of snakes, Colubridae, characterized by the complete absence of hind limbs, the absence or considerable reduction of the left lung, and the lack of teeth on the premaxilla and usually having a loose facial structure, relatively few head scales, and ventral scales as wide as the body. There are more than 1,600 species of colubrids, and they account for about two-thirds of the world's snakes. Most have solid and conical teeth; some have grooved teeth at the rear of the upper jaw and produce a venom that induces paralysis. A few have short, erect fangs in the front half of the mouth. For most of the venomous colubrid species, a bite unaccompanied by chewing is rarely harmful to humans. In a few species with fangs, a single bite can be dangerous and possibly fatal.

Colubrids lay eggs, but some (especially the aquatic forms) are live-bearing. Colubrids occur in virtually all habitats.

COPPERHEADS

Copperheads include any of several unrelated snakes named for their reddish head colour. The North American copperhead *Agkistrodon* (also spelled *Ancistrodon*) *contortrix* is a venomous species found in swampy, rocky, and wooded regions of the eastern and central United States. Also called highland moccasin, it is a member of the viper family (Viperidae) and is placed in the subfamily Crotalinae (pit vipers) because it has the characteristic small, sensory pit between each eye and nostril. It is usually less than 1 m (3 feet) long and is a pinkish or reddish snake with a copper-coloured head and reddish brown, often hourglass-shaped, crossbands on its back. It takes both cold- and warm-blooded prey and is important in rodent control. Many snakebites by it have been reported, but the venom of this snake is relatively weak and rarely fatal.

The Australian copperhead (*Denisonia superba*), a venomous snake of the cobra family (Elapidae) found in Tasmania and along the southern Australian coasts, averages 1.5 metres (about 5 feet) long. It is usually coppery or reddish brown. It is dangerous but is unaggressive when left alone. The copperhead of India is a rat snake, *Elaphe radiata*.

CORAL SNAKES

Coral snakes constitute about 90 species of small, secretive, and brightly patterned venomous snakes of the cobra family (Elapidae). New World coral snakes range in size from 40 to 160 cm (16 to 63 inches) and are classified in three different genera; they are found mainly in the tropics. Five additional genera of related snakes live in Asia and Africa. Most species are tricoloured (rarely bicoloured), with various combinations of red, black, and yellow or white rings; width of the rings varies. All have thin cylindrical bodies, smooth scales, and a short tail. Short hollow fangs deliver a potent neurotoxic venom.

Sixty-five species of American coral snakes (genus *Micrurus*) range from the southern United States to Argentina. Only two species live in the United States. The eastern coral snake, or harlequin snake (*M. fulvius*), is about a metre (3.3 feet) long and has wide red

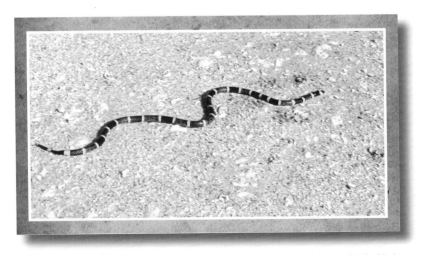

Eastern coral snake (Micrurus fulvius). Luther C. Goldman/U.S. Fish and Wildlife Service

and black rings separated by narrow rings of yellow. The Arizona coral snake (*Micruroides euryxanthus*) is a small (40–50-cm [15.75–19.7 inches]) inhabitant of the American Southwest. The rhyme "Red on yellow, kill a fellow, red on black, venom lack" distinguishes coral snakes from similar North American snakes. There are 50 genera of coral snake mimics such as false coral snakes (the king snake and the scarlet snake, among others), and nearly one-third of all American species have some coral snake pattern.

Most coral snakes prey on other snakes, particularly worm snakes and blind snakes, with lizards being a secondary food source. New World coral snakes lay from 1 to 13 eggs. The longevity record for *Micrurus* in captivity is 18 years.

Coral snakes belong to the family Elapidae, which also includes cobras and various other venomous snakes. Old World coral snakes include eight species of *Calliophis* and five species of *Sinomicrurus* in Asia, plus the single *Hemibungarus* species of the Philippines. In the two East Indian species of *Maticora*, the venom glands extend more than one-third of the way down the body. Two African coral snakes (*Homoroselaps*) are orange, black, and yellow.

MANGROVE SNAKES

Mangrove snakes (genus *Boiga*), which are also called cat-eyed snakes or cat snakes, constitute about 30 species (family Colubridae) of weakly venomous, rear-fanged snakes, ranging from South Asia to Australia. They are at home on the ground and in trees; many catch birds at night. Because they have elliptical pupils and may be green-eyed, they are sometimes referred to as cat or cat-eyed snakes. The head is broad and triangular, and the body ranges from long and slender to moderately stout.

The black-and-yellow mangrove snake (*B. dendrophila*) of the Malay Peninsula to the Philippines is black, with narrow yellow bars and yellow lips and throat. It may grow to a length of 2.5 metres (about 8 feet). Most *Boiga* species attain lengths of 1.5 metres (about 5 feet) and are strongly arboreal, although they are also highly mobile on the ground. Juveniles commonly prey on lizards, and adults regularly prey on rodents. Birds are the main prey for some species. Mangrove snakes are egg layers that produce modest clutches of 4–12 eggs.

MOCCASINS

Moccasin (genus *Agkistrodon*) is the common name for either of two venomous aquatic New World snake species of the viper family (Viperidae): the water moccasin (*Agkistrodon piscivorus*) or the Mexican moccasin (*A. bilineatus*). Both are pit vipers (subfamily Crotalinae), so named because of the characteristic sensory pit between each eye and nostril.

The water moccasin inhabits marshy lowlands of the southeastern United States. It is also known as the cottonmouth, because it threatens with the mouth open, showing the white interior. It measures up to 1.5 metres (5 feet) in length and is brown with darker crossbands or completely black. A dangerous snake with a potentially lethal bite, the cottonmouth tends to stand its ground or move slowly away when alarmed. It eats almost any small animal, including turtles, fish, frogs, and birds.

The Mexican moccasin, or cantil, is found in lowland regions from the Rio Grande to Nicaragua. It is a dangerous snake and is brown or black with narrow irregular whitish bars on its back and sides. It is usually about 1 metre (3.3 feet) long. Moccasins are live-bearers (viviparous) rather than egg layers.

RATTLESNAKES

Rattlesnakes constitute 33 species of venomous New World vipers characterized by a segmented rattle at the tip of the tail that produces a buzzing sound when vibrated. Rattlesnakes are found from southern Canada to central Argentina but are most abundant and diverse in the deserts of the southwestern United States and northern Mexico. Adults usually vary in length from 0.5 to 2 metres (1.6 to 6.6 feet), but some can grow to 2.5 metres (8.2 feet). A few species are marked with transverse bands, but most rattlesnakes are blotched with dark diamonds, hexagons, or rhombuses on a lighter background, usually gray or light brown. Some are various shades of orange, pink, red, or green.

The most common species in North America are the timber rattlesnake (*Crotalus horridus*) of the eastern United States, the prairie rattlesnake (*C. viridis*) of the western United States, and the eastern and western diamondbacks (*C. adamanteus* and *C. atrox*). These are also the largest rattlers. Twenty-six other species also belong to the genus *Crotalus*, including the small North American sidewinder (*C. cerastes*). The other three species belong to a more primitive genus, *Sistrurus*, which includes the North American massasauga (*S. catenatus*) and pygmy rattler (*S. miliarius*). These rattlesnakes have nine large scales on the upper surface of their heads.

Rattlesnakes are not aggressive and will not attack humans if unprovoked; in fact, they are quite shy and timid. However, they are venomous and can be dangerous if molested or handled. With improved methods of treatment and the abandonment of folk cures (many of which presented more danger than benefit to the victim), a rattlesnake bite is no longer the threat to life that it once was, but medical assessment should always be sought after any bite. A rattlesnake bite is very painful, and that of a snake more than 1 metre (3.3 feet) long can be fatal. The snake should be killed and brought in for identification, even for "dry" bites, in which venom is not injected. A person with a "dry" bite should not be treated with antivenin because many people

Eastern diamondback rattlesnake (Crotalus adamanteus). Jack Dermid

are allergic to the horse serum used in its production. The allergic reaction can result in shock and death.

The most dangerous species are the Mexican west coast rattlesnake (*C. basiliscus*), the Mojave rattlesnake (*C. scutulatus*), and the South American rattlesnake, or cascabel (*C. durissus*). Their venom attacks the nervous system more strongly than that of other rattlesnakes. The South American rattlesnake has the largest distribution of any rattlesnake; it ranges from Mexico to Argentina and is the only rattlesnake found throughout Central and South America.

Rattlesnakes are pit vipers (subfamily Crotalinae of the family Viperidae), a group named for the small heat-sensing pit between each eye and nostril that aids in hunting. The pits provide the snake with stereoscopic heat "vision," enabling them to detect and accurately strike a living target in complete darkness. Most rattlesnakes live in arid habitats and are nocturnal, hiding during the day but emerging in the evening or at twilight to hunt for prey, which consists primarily of small mammals, especially rodents. Young and small rattlesnakes feed largely on lizards.

A rattlesnake fang is similar to a curved hypodermic needle. At the top it meets with the end of the venom duct. Soft tissue surrounds the end of the venom duct and the base of the fang, providing a seal against leakage. Large venom glands at the base of the jaws are responsible for the distinctly triangular shape of the head. Fangs are periodically lost owing to wear and breakage. Each fang has a series of seven developing fangs behind the functional fang, each smaller and less developed than the one preceding it. Fang length depends on the species and size of the snake, but large rattlers can have fangs 10–15 cm (4–6 inches) long. When the snake's mouth is closed, the fangs are folded back and lie parallel to the roof of the mouth. Linkages of bones in the upper jaw allow the fangs to be deployed into a vertical position for stabbing and biting.

Like other reptiles, rattlesnakes cannot tolerate extreme heat or cold. During the heat of the day, rattlesnakes hide themselves underground in burrows or under rocks. In the fall they congregate in rock slides or crevices for their winter hibernation in dens that may shelter hundreds of individuals of several different species. Upon emerging in the spring, the males mate with females and then disperse from the den site to spend the summer in surrounding countryside. In the fall they all return to the same den.

Rattlesnakes give birth to young that develop from eggs retained inside the mother (ovoviviparous). In the late summer, broods of 1–60 are produced; average broods number 4–10 young. Newborn rattlesnakes have functioning fangs and venom glands. Their venom is more potent but of lesser quantity than that of their mother, a condition that helps ensure that the young can secure food. The newborn babies are also equipped with a single button on the end of the tail. After the first shedding of their skin (within a week of birth), they will have two rattle segments. Once the third rattle segment has been obtained, the young snake can buzz like an adult. The rattle, presumably a warning device, is composed of horny, loosely connected hollow segments, one of which is added every time the snake sheds its skin. The age of a rattlesnake cannot be determined from the number of its rattle segments, as rattlesnakes usually shed three or four times a year. In captivity, 10 species have lived from 20 to 30 years.

Every year in the United States, an estimated 5,000 rattlesnakes are collected and destroyed in about 30 highly commercialized "rattlesnake roundups." Supposedly conducted to save the lives of people and cattle, these spectacles may only reduce rattlesnakes' valuable service in the control of rodent pests and in maintaining the natural balance of desert ecosystems.

SEA SNAKES

Sea snakes consist of 61 species of highly venomous marine snakes of the cobra family (Elapidae). There are two independently evolved groups: the true sea snakes (subfamily Hydrophiinae), which are related to Australian terrestrial elapids, and the sea kraits (subfamily Laticaudinae), which are related to the Asian cobras. Although their venom is the most potent of all snakes, human fatalities are rare because sea snakes are not aggressive, their venom output is small, and their fangs are very short.

Of the 55 species of true sea snakes, most adults are 1–1.5 metres (3.3–5 feet) long, though some individuals may attain 2.7 metres (8.85 feet). They are restricted to coastal areas of the Indian and western Pacific oceans, except for the yellow-bellied sea snake (*Pelamis platurus*), found in open ocean from Africa eastward across the Pacific to the west coast of the Americas. All other species live mainly in waters less than 30 metres (100 feet) deep, as they must dive to the seafloor to obtain their food among coral reefs, among mangroves, or on the ocean bottom. Some species prefer hard bottoms (corals), while others prefer soft bottoms (mud or sand) in which to hunt their prey. Most sea snakes feed upon fishes of various sizes and shapes, including eels. Two primitive groups (genera *Aipysurus* and *Emydocephalus*) eat only fish eggs; *Hydrophis* specializes in burrowing eels.

In adaptation to marine life, true sea snakes have a flattened body with a short oarlike tail, valvular nostrils on top of the snout, and elongated lungs that extend the entire length of the body. Their scales are very small and usually not overlapping (juxtaposed), abutting against one another like paving stones. The belly scales are reduced in size in the primitive species, whereas in the more advanced forms they are absent. As a result, the advanced species cannot crawl and are thus helpless on land. When swimming, a keel is formed along part of the belly, increasing surface area and aiding propulsion, which occurs by lateral undulation. Sea snakes can remain submerged for several hours, possibly as much as eight or more. This remarkable feat is partly due to the fact that they can breathe through their skin. More than 90 percent of waste carbon dioxide and 33 percent of their oxygen requirement can be transported via cutaneous respiration. Sea snakes give birth in the ocean to an average of 2–9 young, but as many as 34 may be born. The 54 species in subfamily Hydrophiinae belong to 16 different genera.

The six species of sea kraits (genus *Laticauda*) are not as specialized for aquatic life as the true sea snakes. Although the tail is flattened, the body is cylindrical, and the nostrils are lateral. They have enlarged belly scales like those of terrestrial snakes and can crawl and climb on land. The typical colour pattern consists of alternating bands of black with gray, blue, or white rings. The yellow-lipped sea krait (*L. colubrina*) is a common species that possesses this pattern and has a yellow snout. Sea kraits are nocturnal, feeding primarily on eels at depths of less than 15 metres (49 feet). They go ashore to lay their eggs, climbing up into limestone caves and rock crevices, where they deposit 1–10 eggs. Adults average 1 metre (3.3 feet) in length, but some grow to more than 1.5 metres (about 5 feet). The longevity record in captivity is seven years.

SIDEWINDERS

Sidewinders, which are also called horn vipers, make up four species of small venomous snakes that inhabit the deserts of North America, Africa, and the Middle East, all of which utilize a "sidewinding" style of crawling. The North American sidewinder (*Crotalus cerastes*) is a rattlesnake. This pit viper (subfamily Crotalinae) has small horns above each eye, possibly to keep sand from covering the eyes when the snake is buried. It is a nocturnal inhabitant of the southwestern United States and northwestern Mexico, where it feeds upon rodents. Adults average slightly more than 50 cm (20 inches) but can attain 80 cm (31.5 inches). Sidewinders give birth to 5–18 young in the fall. Some individuals have lived nearly 20 years in captivity.

The three species of Old World sidewinders are pitless vipers (subfamily Viperinae) of the genus *Cerastes*. Two of them (*C. cerastes* and *C. vipera*) live in the Sahara. The third (*C. gasperetti*) is found in the Middle East and Arabia. All are short (50 cm) and stout with broad heads; some individuals have a hornlike scale over each eye. Their coloration is light, resembling the desert sands of their environment—shades of tan, pink, orange, or gray—with darker spots on the back. During the day they hide beneath the sand or rocks; at night they emerge to hunt for rodents, birds, and lizards. Instead of giving birth to

North American sidewinder (Crotalus cerastes). Anthony Mercieca/ Root Resources

live young, these sidewinders lay from 8 to 23 eggs. In captivity *C. cerastes* has lived up to 17 years.

Sidewinders are noted for their unique method of locomotion, which leaves a characteristic j-shaped trail. Loops of the body are thrown obliquely across the sand so that only two points are in contact with the ground at any time. This prevents the snake from overheating due to excessive contact with the desert sand. Although they are venomous, their bite is usually not fatal to humans.

NONVENOMOUS SNAKES

Most of the planet's 2,900 snakes are nonvenomous. Some nonvenomous groups, such as the racers, rely on their speed when hunting, whereas others, such as the egg-eating snakes, seek out stationary prey.

BLIND SNAKES

Blind snakes (superfamily Typhlopoidea) are any of several nonvenomous snakes characterized by degenerate eyes that lie beneath opaque head scales. Blind snakes belong to the families Anomalepidae, Leptotyphlopidae, and Typhlopidae in superfamily Typhlopoidea. Since these three families are the only ones classified within infraorder Scolecophidia, blind snakes are sometimes called "scolecophidian snakes." Blind snakes are mainly small with blunt heads, cylindrical bodies, and short tails. Their bodies are encased in smooth, shiny scales. All are fossorial (that is, subterranean or burrowing) and are regularly associated with termite and ant nests. Individuals can be found on the ground surface at night or after heavy rains. They are occasionally found high in trees, presumably having reached these heights by using termite galleries. Blind snakes primarily feed on the eggs and larvae of both termites and ants; they also eat other soft-bodied arthropods and their eggs. All reproduce by laying eggs.

Anomalepids (early blind snakes) and leptotyphlopids (threadsnakes and wormsnakes) are slender, and species of both families are seldom more than 30 cm (12 inches) long from snout to vent and grow to a maximum of 40 cm (16 inches) in total length. The anomalepids are made up of 15 species belonging to four genera that inhabit the forests of Central and South America. In contrast, the leptotyphlopids are more widespread, occurring in Southwest Asia and in tropical and subtropical regions of Africa and the New World. Leptotyphlopids are represented by approximately 90 species belonging to two genera (*Leptotyphlops* and *Rhinoleptus*).

The typhlopids (true blind snakes) are even more diverse, with over 200 species in six genera. They occur naturally throughout the tropics; however, one species, the flowerpot snake (*Ramphotyphlops braminus*), now occurs on many oceanic islands and all continents except Antarctica. It gained its worldwide distribution through its presence in the soil of potted plants and because of parthenogenesis, a form of reproduction that does not require fertilization to produce offspring. *R. braminus* is an all-female species, and its eggs do not require a male's sperm to fertilize them, as development is self-activated. Thus, only a single individual is required to found a new population. *R. braminus* and most other typhlopids are small; adults may reach 14 to 30 cm (5.5 to 12 inches) in total length, though a few individuals may grow to be nearly 1 metre (3.3 feet) long. Typhlopids are also more diverse in appearance, with darker pigmentation and rounded, pointed, or flattened heads. They occupy a wider range of habitats than anomalepids and leptotyphlopids; true blind snakes can be found in habitats ranging from semiarid grasslands to forests.

EGG-EATING SNAKES

Egg-eating snakes are small, fairly slender, harmless African snakes that feed exclusively on birds' eggs. Egg-eating snakes are notable for their ability to eat the contents of whole eggs several times larger than their head. The egg-eating snake is classified in the genus *Dasypeltis* of the colubrid family, Colubridae. The five species in this genus are mainly nocturnal tree climbers of savanna and woodlands. Their days are spent under rocks or in old logs. Adults range in length from 60 to 76 cm (24 to 30 inches). The head is small with flared jaws. The eyes are large, and the pupils are vertical slits in daylight. Coloration is buff gray to brown with rows of irregular patches. Scales are heavily ridged. The egg-eaters resemble vipers — some populations of egg-eaters mimic vipers when threatened.

To engulf an egg, the snake braces the egg against its body, widens its jaws, and slowly stretches the skin of its head around the shell. At the back of the throat, protruding through the esophagus, are sharp projections of the snake's vertebrae. These projections saw through the shell until it collapses inward and releases the egg contents. The empty shell is then expelled from the mouth.

All egg-eating snakes are oviparous — that is, they lay eggs. These snakes scatter their eggs rather than lay them in a clutch. The most common species, *D. scabra*, is gray with dark patches and is the most likely to be sold as a terrarium pet. A rare Indian egg-eating snake, *Elachistodon westermanni*, closely parallels the African types, with the same spinal adaptation for egg-sawing. Some authorities place it in the same subfamily, Dasypeltinae.

FLYING SNAKES

There are five species of flying snakes—nonvenomous snakes constituting the genus *Chrysopelea* of the family Colubridae. These slender arboreal snakes are found in South Asia and the Indonesian archipelago. They are able to glide short distances through the air by drawing up their ventral scales to make their undersides concave. Flying snakes make an undulatory motion to maintain their balance as they descend.

They are active by day, capturing rodents, bats, birds, and lizards. *Chrysopelea ornata* of India and Sri Lanka, sometimes called golden treesnake, is up to 100 cm (40 inches) long and usually black or greenish, with yellow or reddish markings.

GARTER SNAKES

There are more than a dozen known species of garter snakes (genus *Thamnophis*). They are nonvenomous snakes having a striped pattern suggesting a garter: typically, one or three longitudinal yellow to red stripes, between which are checkered blotches. Forms in which the stripes are obscure or lacking are often called grass snakes. Authorities differ as to the number of species, since garter snakes show only slight differences in their scales but considerable geographic differences in coloration. In many areas from Canada to Central America, they are the most common serpent. Western forms are associated with water more than eastern forms.

Garter snakes are small to moderate in size—usually less than 100 cm (39 inches) long—and quite harmless. If handled they struggle and discharge a foul secretion from the anal gland; some will strike. Among the

Garter snake (Thamnophis). Leonard Lee Rue III

more defensive species is the common garter snake (*Thamnophis sirtalis*), probably North America's most widely distributed reptile. The ribbon snake (*T. sauritus*), small and slender, is a strongly striped form. Garter snakes live chiefly on insects, earthworms, and amphibians; the ribbon snake is especially fond of frogs. They do not lay eggs but generally breed in early spring and give birth in late summer.

HOGNOSE SNAKES

Hognose snakes (genus *Heterodon*) are nonvenomous snakes found in North America that belong to the family Colubridae. There are three known species. Hognose snakes are named for the upturned snout, which is used for digging. These are the harmless but often-avoided puff adders, or blow snakes, of North America. When threatened, they flatten the head and neck, then strike with a loud hiss — rarely biting. If their bluff fails, they roll over, writhing, and then feign death with mouth open and tongue lolling.

Hognose snakes live chiefly on toads and are capable of neutralizing the toad's poisonous skin secretions physiologically. They lay 15 to 27 eggs underground. The widely distributed species are the eastern (*Heterodon platyrhinos*) and western (*H. nasicus*). Both are heavy-bodied and blotchy; their usual length is about 60 to 80 cm (24 to 31 inches).

RACERS

Racers are any of several large, swift nonvenomous snakes belonging to the family Colubridae. Racers of North

Hognose snake (Heterodon platyrhinos)*, playing dead.* Jack Dermid

America belong to a single species, *Coluber constrictor*, and several species of the genus *Elaphe* in Southeast Asia are called racers. Blue racers are the central and western North American subspecies of *C. constrictor;* they are plain bluish, greenish blue, gray, or brownish, sometimes with yellow bellies. The eastern subspecies is called black snake; it is all black except for a patch of white on its chin and throat. The young of all subspecies are blotched or spotted.

C. constrictor ranges from southern Canada to Guatemala. Despite its scientific name, *C. constrictor* does not kill by constriction; it holds down its prey—usually a small warm-blooded animal—by the weight of its coils, then swallows it.

North American racers are slender and long-tailed, with big eyes and smooth scales. Some are 1.8 metres (about 6 feet) long. They are active by day and are among the fastest of snakes, moving at a speed of about 5.6 km (3.5 miles) per hour on the ground and through bushes. If cornered they vibrate the tail and strike repeatedly. In the western United States, colour phases of the coachwhip are called red racers and western black racers.

SHIELDTAIL SNAKES

Shieldtail snakes (family Uropeltidae) are any of 45 species of primitive burrowing snakes endemic to southern India and Sri Lanka. There are eight genera of shieldtail snakes. Of the 30 Indian species, 18 are members of the genus *Uropeltis*, and of the 15 species found in Sri Lanka, eight are members of the genus *Rhinophis*. Shieldtail snakes are small, typically growing to between 25 and 50 cm (10 and 20 inches) in length—although some may grow to 90 cm (35 inches). They are harmless, specialized snakes that have narrow, pointed heads with tiny eyes beneath head shields. Shieldtails are named for their unique tails, which are heavily keeled and terminate in disklike shields or multiple spines in most species. Most species appear black, purple, or brown, but some are coloured with red, orange, or yellow spots and bars; all are highly iridescent.

Shieldtails are nocturnal and live at higher elevations in loose soil, among plant roots, under decaying vegetation, and in agricultural beds. They dig their own tunnels, which are plugged by their disked tails that provide a purchase when tunneling. This practice prevents other predatory snakes from attacking them from behind. When they are handled, their defensive behaviour is defecation. Their diet is principally made up of earthworms; however, some species also consume arthropods. Shieldtails are completely inoffensive and never bite. They give birth to 3–9 living young.

CONSTRICTOR SNAKES

To capture and immobilize their victims, constrictor snakes often bite and hold before coiling their bodies around their prey. Their victims are then asphyxiated by the crushing pressure of contracting muscles before being devoured. The largest extant snake species, anacondas and pythons, are constrictor snakes.

ANACONDAS

Anacondas (genus *Eunectes*) make up either of two species of constricting, water-loving snakes found in tropical South America. The green anaconda (*Eunectes murinus*), also called the giant anaconda, sucuri, or water kamudi, is an olive-coloured snake with alternating oval-shaped black spots. The yellow, or southern, anaconda (*E. notaeus*) is much smaller and has pairs of overlapping spots.

Green anacondas live along tropical waters east of the Andes Mountains and on the Caribbean island of Trinidad. The green anaconda is the largest snake in the world. Although anacondas and pythons both have been reliably measured at over 9 metres (30 feet) long, anacondas have been reported to measure over 10 metres (33 feet) and are much more heavily built. Most individuals, however, do not usually exceed 5 metres (16 feet).

Green anacondas lie in the water (generally at night) to ambush caimans and mammals such as capybara, deer, tapirs, and peccaries that come to drink. An anaconda seizes a large animal by the neck and almost instantly throws its coils around it, killing it by constriction.

Giant anaconda (Eunectes murinus). © Z. Leszczynski/Animals Animals

Anacondas kill smaller prey, such as small turtles and diving birds, with the mouth and sharp backward-pointing teeth alone. Kills made onshore are often dragged into the water, perhaps to avoid attracting jaguars and to ward off biting ants attracted to the carcass. In the wild, green anacondas are not particularly aggressive. In Venezuela, they are captured easily during the day by herpetologists who, in small groups, merely walk up to the snakes and carry them off.

Green anacondas mate in or very near the water. After nine months, a female gives live birth to 14–82 babies, each more than 62 cm (24 inches) in length. The young grow rapidly, attaining almost 3 metres (10 feet) by age three.

Anacondas are members of the boa family (Boidae).

BOAS

Boa is a common name for a variety of nonvenomous constricting snakes. About 40 of the 64 species are true boas (family Boidae). Other boas are the Mascarene, or split-jawed, boas (family Bolyeriidae) and dwarf boas (ground and wood boas of the family Tropidophiidae); these two families are not closely related to each other or to the true boas.

The true boas are divided into two subfamilies, Boinae and Erycinae. Boinae includes the boa constrictor (*Boa constrictor*), tree boas (genus *Corallus*), and anacondas (genus *Eunectes*) of the American tropics; two other genera are found on Madagascar and islands of the southwestern Pacific. Members of Boinae range from 1 metre (3.3 feet) long in some species to commonly more than 4 metres (13 feet) in the giant, or green, anaconda. The boa constrictor occupies a variety of habitats from coastal northern Mexico and the Lesser Antilles to Argentina; though seldom more than 3.3 metres (11 feet) long, some have grown to more than 5 metres (16 feet). One subspecies, the red-tailed boa (*Boa constrictor constrictor*), is particularly popular in the pet trade. Several tree boas possess sizable teeth used for catching birds. An example is the 1.8-metre (6-foot) emerald tree boa (*Corallus caninus*) of tropical South America; the adult is green above, with a white dorsal stripe and crossbars, and yellow below. The rainbow boa (*Epicrates cenchria*) of Costa Rica to Argentina is not strongly patterned but is markedly iridescent. Except for the anacondas, most boines are terrestrial to strongly arboreal. The young often move from the trees to the ground as they get older and larger. Most species have labial (lip) pits with heat-sensing organs that complement their sense of smell and excellent vision. Mammals and birds are common prey, which is usually captured by a bite-grasp followed by constriction.

Subfamily Erycinae includes 10 Asian, Indian, and African species of sand boa (genus *Eryx*) and the West African earth python (*Charina reinhardtii*), in addition to two North American species. Erycines are live-bearers (as opposed to egg layers) that have stout cylindrical bodies, blunt heads, and short tails. Most measure less than 70 cm (28 inches). These terrestrial snakes are often subterranean, and most live in arid and semiarid habitats, where they prey on lizards and small mammals. The brown, 45-cm (18-inch) rubber boa (*Charina bottae*) of western North America is the most northerly boa and is a burrower that looks and feels rubbery. The 90-cm (35-inch) rosy boa (*Charina trivirgata*), ranging from southern California and Arizona into Mexico, usually is brown- or pink-striped.

Except for two egg-laying Asian species (genus *Xenophidion*), the 24 dwarf boas of family Tropidophiidae bear live young and live in the West Indies, Central America, and northern South America. They are predominantly terrestrial, occasionally foraging in low trees and bushes to hunt small vertebrates, especially amphibians and lizards.

The single surviving species of family Bolyeriidae (*Casarea dussumieri*) lives on Mauritius and Round Island. It is unique among snakes in that the lower jaw is hinged in the middle, which enables the snake to grasp hard-bodied skinks with a firm ratchetlike grip. It is a 0.8–1.4-metre- (2.6–4.6-foot-) long egg layer. *Bolyeria multocarinata* was similar and went extinct owing to human introduction of rats and other predators.

One extinct relative of modern boas (*Titanoboa cerrejonensis*) lived between the end of the Cretaceous Period (some 65.5 million years ago) and the middle of the Eocene Epoch (about 40 million years ago). At the time it was the largest terrestrial vertebrate in the world. Known from a single fossilized vertebra, *T. cerrejonensis* probably weighed 1,135 kg (about 2,500 pounds) and reached a length of 13 metres (about 43 feet).

BULL SNAKES

Bull snakes (*Pituophis catenifer*) are North American constrictor snakes of the family Colubridae. These snakes are called bull snakes over much of their range; however, in the western United States they are often called gopher snakes. Bull snakes are rather heavy-bodied, small-headed, and may reach 2.5 metres (8 feet) in length. Typical coloration is yellowish brown or creamy, with dark blotches. The nose shield is enlarged for digging.

They are related to pine snakes (*P. melanoleucus*) of the eastern and southern United States and the Mexican bull snake (*P. deppei*) of north central and western Mexico.

Bull snakes can be found in sandy, open country and in pine barrens, where they eat mainly rodents but also prey on birds and lizards. In defense they hiss loudly and thrash about while vibrating their tail. Bull snakes are therefore frequently mistaken for rattlesnakes. Bull snakes may bite, but they are not venomous. They are egg-layers.

PYTHONS

Pythons make up about 28 species of nonvenomous snakes native to the Old World tropics and subtropics. All but one are found in these regions. Most are large, with the reticulated python (*Python reticulatus*) of Asia attaining a maximum recorded length of 9.6 metres (31.5 feet).

Eight species of genus *Python* live in sub-Saharan Africa and from India to southern China into Southeast Asia, including the Philippines and the Moluccas islands of Indonesia. Other related genera inhabit New Guinea and Australia. Some Australian pythons (genus *Liasis*) never grow much longer than one metre (3.3 feet), but some pythons of Africa (*P. sebae*), India (*P. molurus*), New Guinea (*L. papuanus*), and Australia (*L. amethistinus*) regularly exceed 3 metres (10 feet). Despite their large size, some of these species survive in urban and suburban areas, where their secretive habits and recognized value as rat catchers par excellence serve to protect them.

Most pythons are terrestrial to semiarboreal, and a few, such as the green tree python (*Morelia viridis*) of Australia and New Guinea, are strongly arboreal. Terrestrial pythons are regularly found near water and are proficient swimmers, but they hunt and eat almost exclusively on land. Larger pythons prey mainly on mammals and birds; smaller species also eat amphibians and reptiles. Pythons have good senses of smell and sight, and most can also detect heat. Pits lying between the lip scales have receptors that are sensitive to infrared radiation and enable pythons to "see" the heat shadow of mammals and birds even during the darkest night. Prey is captured by striking and biting, usually followed by constriction.

Pythons are egg layers (oviparous) rather than live-bearers (viviparous). Females of most, if not all, species coil around the eggs, and some actually brood them. Brooders select thermally stable nesting sites, then lay their eggs and coil around them so that the eggs are in contact only with the female's body. When the air temperature begins to drop, she generates heat by shivering in a series of minuscule muscle contractions and thus maintains an elevated and fairly constant incubation temperature.

Taxonomists divide the family Pythonidae into either four or eight genera. The only New World python (*Loxocemus bicolor*) is classified as the sole member of the family Loxocemidae. It is an egg layer found in forests from southern Mexico to Costa Rica. Usually less than 1 metre (3.3 feet) long, it is reported to reach nearly 1.5 metres (about 5 feet). It seems to be predominantly nocturnal, foraging on the ground for a variety of small vertebrates. The so-called earth, or burrowing, python (*Calabaria reinhardtii* or *Charina reinhardtii*) of West Africa appears to be a member of the boa family (Boidae).

RAT SNAKES

Rat snakes (genus *Elaphe*) are members of the family Colubridae. The 40 and 55 species that are known occur in North America, Europe, and Asia east to the Philippines. Most are found in woodlands and around farm buildings. They hunt rats and mice and kill them by constriction. They also eat eggs, and some species raid poultry yards and are sometimes called chicken snakes. Some hunt birds in trees and have the ventral scales keeled (ridged), for climbing. These rather large, nonvenomous, egg-laying snakes are normally slow and docile, but in self-defense they vibrate the tail, discharge a foul liquid from the anal gland, and strike from an upreared position.

The black rat snake, or pilot black snake (*Elaphe obsoleta obsoleta*), of the eastern United States usually is about 1.2 metres (about 4 feet) long but may exceed 2.5 m (8 feet). It is black, with whitish chin and throat—like the true black snake—but has slightly keeled dorsal scales. Other races of *E. obsoleta* are tan, gray, yellow, reddish, or brown, and some are blotched or striped.

The corn snake (*E. guttata*) ranges from New Jersey and Florida to Utah and northeastern Mexico. In the east it is yellow or gray, with black-edged red blotches, and is often referred to as the red rat snake. In the west it usually is pale gray, with black-edged brownish or dark gray blotches.

The fox snake (*E. vulpina*), chiefly of farmlands of Wisconsin to Missouri, is yellowish or pale brown above, with strong dark blotches, and yellow below, with black checkering. Its head may be quite reddish.

One of Europe's largest serpents is the four-lined snake (*E. quatuorlineata*), which may be 1.8 m (about 6 feet) long. It ranges from Italy to the Caucasus and Turkey and is grayish, with two dorsal and two lateral stripes. The Aesculapian snake (*E. longissima*), plain and dark coloured, is native to southeastern Europe and Asia Minor. In ancient times it was sacred to Aesclepius, god of medicine; the present isolated populations in Germany and Switzerland are descended from specimens conveyed to health resorts there by the Romans. The leopard snake (*E. situla*) of the eastern Mediterranean region to the Caucasus has large round red markings.

Chicken snake is the usual name in southeastern Asia for two slender greenish species, *E. prasina* and *E. oxycephala;* both are strongly arboreal. The copperhead of India is *E. radiata.* The Oriental rat snake (*Zaocys carinatus*) of southeastern Asia may be the largest member of the family Colubridae; one specimen measured 3.7 m (12 feet). The Indian, or greater, rat snake (*Ptyas mucosus*) may be more than 2.5 m (8 feet) long.

CHAPTER 6
TURTLES AND TUATARAS

The orders Testudines (turtles) and Rhynchocephalia (tuataras) contain reptiles that are very different from one another. Turtles are very diverse and globally distributed, whereas the two species of living tuataras are restricted to the northern part of New Zealand. Structurally, turtles and tuataras differ from one another. The most prominent structural feature of a turtle is its shell. In contrast, the tuatara, whose body structure resembles that of lizards and snakes, possesses a parietal eye (third eye) on the top of its head.

TURTLES

A turtle (order Testudines) is a reptile with a body encased in a bony shell. This category also includes tortoises. Although numerous animals, from invertebrates to mammals, have evolved shells, none has an architecture like that of turtles. The turtle shell has a top (carapace) and a bottom (plastron). The carapace and plastron are bony structures that usually join one another along each side of the body, creating a rigid skeletal box. This box, composed of bone and cartilage, is retained throughout the turtle's life. Because the shell is an integral part of the body, the turtle cannot exit it, nor is the shell shed like the skin of some other reptiles.

There are about three hundred species of turtles living on land in all continents except Antarctica and in both salt water and fresh water. Tortoises (family Testudinidae) live exclusively on land and have anatomic features distinguishing them from other turtles, but the term *tortoise* has long been used to refer to other terrestrial testudines as well, such as the box turtle and the wood turtle. Similarly, *terrapin* is sometimes used to describe any aquatic turtle but is now largely restricted to the edible diamondback terrapin (*Malaclemys terrapin*) of the eastern United States.

Despite turtles' broad distribution, there is not and never seems to have been a great many species of turtles at any time over the course of their long evolutionary history. The small number of species, however, does not equate to a lack of diversity. There are turtles with carapace lengths (CL, the standard way to measure turtles) of less than 10 cm (4 inches), as in the flattened musk turtle (*Sternotherus depressus*), and of more than 1.5 metres (about 5 feet), as in the leatherback sea turtle (*Dermochelys coriacea*). Some species live in seasonally cold climates

European pond turtle (Emys orbicularis). Joe B. Blossom/Photo Researchers

with growing seasons of only about three months; others live in the tropics and grow year-round. Some tortoises rarely see water, while other turtles spend virtually their entire lives in it, be it in a single small pond or traveling the vast open ocean.

Both common and rare turtles are kept as pets. In the Western Hemisphere, pond turtles such as the red-eared slider (*Trachemys scripta*) and cooters (*Pseudemys* species) are very often seen in pet stores. The ornate shells that make some species valuable as pets also make them vulnerable to extinction in the wild, since these turtles frequently are found only in small geographic areas or do not breed in captivity.

Before the advent of plastics, tortoiseshell from the hawksbill sea turtle (*Eretmochelys imbricata*) was used in eyeglass frames and decorative items. Turtles and their eggs have long been eaten in many parts of the world, and they continue to be in great demand commercially. In some areas, local populations and even entire species have been hunted to extinction.

Such exploitation is not a recent phenomenon. For example, the Native Americans who settled Florida quite possibly ate its giant tortoises to extinction. The first colonists of Madagascar soon eliminated that island's giant tortoise (*Geochelone grandidieri*), and European settlers and sailors eliminated giant tortoises from the islands of Mauritius and Réunion. Every sea turtle species has long been killed for meat, with its eggs being harvested from beach nests as soon as they are laid. This practice now endangers many populations of sea turtles. Before 1969, for example, more than three thousand female leatherback sea turtles emerged from the ocean annually to nest on the beaches of Terengganu, Malaysia. In the 1990s only 2 to 20 females appeared each year. Their disappearance resulted from years of excessive egg harvesting and the capture and slaughter of juveniles and adults during their migratory search for food.

Overharvesting is not confined to large species. In China, turtles large and small are used for both food and medicine. By the early 1990s, many local populations of turtles had disappeared within the country, so turtles began to be imported from around the world. Some species, such as the three-striped box turtle, or golden coin turtle (*Cuora trifasciata*), are so popular for traditional Chinese celebrations that aquaculturists raise them and can sell individual turtles for more than $1,000 (U.S.), an amazing price for a reptile less than 20 cm (about 8 inches) long.

FORM AND FUNCTION

The turtle's shell is an adaptation that protects it from predators. The carapace and plastron each arose from two types of bone: dermal bones that form in the skin and endochondral bone derived from the skeleton. Evolution has intricately linked these two types of bone to produce the shell of modern turtles. The carapace consists of 10 trunk vertebrae and their ribs, which are overlain by and fused to dermal plates. Another series of dermal plates forms the perimeter of the carapace. The plastron usually contains four pairs of large plates and a single one centred near the front (the anteromedial plate); these plates are large dermal bones, although the anterior ones may contain parts of the shoulder girdle. The shell is variously modified and shaped to meet the needs of defense, feeding, and movement.

Most tortoises have high, domed shells, the major exception being the pancake tortoise (*Malacochersus tornieri*) of southeastern Africa. The pancake tortoise lives among rocky outcroppings, where its flat shell allows

(A) Plastron and (B) carapace, showing the relationship between bony and horny parts of the shell of a freshwater turtle. Shaded areas indicate parts of horny shell; dark lines indicate joints in underlying bone. (C) Relationship between the dermal bones (plastron and carapace) and the axial skeleton in a marine turtle. Encyclopædia Britannica, Inc.

it to crawl into crevices to rest. Once in a crevice, the pancake tortoise can inflate its lungs, thus expanding the shell and lodging itself so securely that a predator cannot pull it free. The domed shell of other tortoises and land turtles such as box turtles (*Cuora, Terrapene*) seems to be an adaptation that makes the shell difficult for a predator to hold in its mouth and crush. Among aquatic turtles, some groups are swimmers and usually have streamlined shells; streamlining is best-developed in the sea turtles. Other aquatic turtles, such as the matamata and snapping turtles, are bottom-walkers. Their shells are less streamlined and often have ridged carapaces that may assist in camouflage.

The manner in which the neck folds is the main criteria for differentiating the two main groups (suborders) of turtles. All turtles, no matter how long or short their necks, have eight cervical vertebrae, but those that fold their neck vertically can withdraw the head into the shell.

Gulf Coast box turtle (Terrapene carolina major). John H. Gerard

These are the so-called S-necked, or vertical-necked, turtles of the suborder Cryptodira (which means "hidden neck"). Turtles that cannot withdraw the head belong to the suborder Pleurodira, meaning "side neck."

In addition to differences in the neck, skulls vary in size and shape between the two groups, though all are made up of the same bony elements. The pleuro-diran and cryptodiran turtles differ fundamentally in lower jaw architecture and musculature. This difference typically yields a flatter and broader skull in the pleurodires—an architecture that may have allowed the evolution of the gape-and-suck feeding mechanism seen in many pleurodires and best developed in the South American matamata (*Chelus fimbriatus*). This turtle can quickly enlarge the cavity of its mouth and throat when striking at passing prey. As the turtle's head nears its victim, the greatly enlarged cavity acts like a vacuum, sucking water and prey into the mouth. As the throat area is compressed, the mouth is opened to allow water to escape but not the prey. Most carnivorous turtles use a head strike to capture their prey and when scavenging.

No present-day turtles have teeth; rather, the upper and lower jaws bear keratinous sheaths that fit onto the skull like a pair of false teeth. The edges (occasionally with serrations) are sharp and allow turtles to cut pieces of flesh from carcasses and quickly kill small prey. The cutting edges are also effective in chopping vegetation into bite-size pieces. Turtles do not chew. Those that eat mollusks crush them with a broad, thick sheath inside the mouth.

All the turtle's senses are well-developed, and they are used in avoiding predators and in finding and capturing food. The eyes have the typical anatomy of other vertebrates having good vision. Aquatic turtles have eyes that quickly adjust for aerial or aquatic vision, seeing well in both situations. Tortoises appear to have colour vision, but colour vision is untested for most turtles. Turtles, particularly aquatic ones, are not strongly olfactory, but all are capable of smelling. Some aquatic species have protuberances on the chin in the form of tubercles and papillae. These appear to be mainly tactile, although some may be chemosensory. The turtle ear has an eardrum flush with the surface of the head. A single bone, the stapes, transmits sound to the inner ear.

NATURAL HISTORY OF TURTLES

Owing to their adaptability to different environments, turtles are among the most successful and widely distributed of reptiles. There are some species that specialize on one particular food item or another. The survival of these species is often tied to the availability of their food source. Most turtles, however, eat more than one type of food, which allows them to switch from scarce food types to more abundant types when appropriate. Turtles have adopted individualist lifestyles. They are not social and do not provide parental care to their offspring, but they are often ranked among Earth's longest-lived animals.

HABITATS

Turtles have adapted to a remarkable variety of environments, but the greatest number of species occur in southeastern North America and South Asia. In both areas, most species are aquatic, living in bodies of water ranging from small ponds and bogs to large lakes and rivers. A few are strictly terrestrial (tortoises), and others divide their time between land and water. Although turtles as a group are broadly distributed, each species has a preferred habitat and is seldom found elsewhere. For example, both the gopher tortoise (*Gopherus polyphemus*) and the Eastern box turtle (*Terrapene carolina*) live in the southern United States and are equally terrestrial, but they are not usually found together, as the box turtle prefers moist forest and the gopher tortoise open woodlands on sand ridges. The eastern mud turtle (*Kinosternon subrubrum*) is commonly considered an aquatic turtle, yet it spends the summer months in dormancy, estivating beneath vegetation in woodlands adjacent to its pond and stream habitats. The alligator snapping turtle (*Macrochelys temmincki*) lives in the deep, slow-moving streams and backwaters of the U.S. Gulf Coast. Map turtles (*Graptemys*), on the other hand, select the faster-flowing waters of those same streams. The saltwater terrapin (*Malaclemys terrapin*) lives in brackish coastal estuaries and marshes from Cape Cod, Mass., to Padre Island, Texas. In some instances, juvenile sea turtles share these estuaries; larger and older sea turtles swim offshore in coastal waters to the mid-continental shelf.

A comparable range of species and preferred habitats is observed among the South Asian turtles. South Asia

has a broad range of habitats and environments, ranging from desert to rainforest and from shallow tropical
seas to frigid mountain forest. Turtles are found in most
of these habitats, though mostly at low elevations and in
waterways. Softshell turtles (family Trionychidae) have
their greatest diversity in Asia and occur in most waters,
from tiny ponds to large rivers. The Indian and Burmese
flapshell turtles (genus *Lissemys*) are ubiquitous in slow-
moving streams and rice paddies. Their mud colouring
and relatively small size (carapaces up to 28 cm [11 inches])
make them inconspicuous and more likely to be overlooked in cultures that view all turtles as harvestable for
food or medicine. On the other hand, their giant cousins, the narrow-headed softshells (genus *Chitra*) and the
Asian giant softshells (genus *Pelochelys*), are inhabitants of
large, deep rivers and attain shell lengths of over 1 metre
(3.3 feet). They are poorly protected from habitat loss and
harvesting, and some are now critically endangered. All
softshell turtles are predominantly carnivores, though the
flapshells eat some plant matter.

The Asian pond or river turtles (family Geoemydidae)
show more diversity than their North American relatives
(Emydidae). The six to eight species of Asian box turtles
(genus *Cuora*) tend to be more aquatic than the American
box turtles, spending much of their time in forest ponds
and streams. As with the softshell turtles, Asia has two
of the largest species of pond turtles—the Asian river
turtle, or batagur (*Batagur baska*), and the painted terrapin
(*Callagur borneoensis*)—with shell lengths to a half-metre
(about 20 inches) and weights to 25 kg (55 pounds). Both
are tidal-river species, tolerating salinities up to about half
that of marine salt water, and both include large amounts
of fruits and leaves from waterside vegetation in their diet.

Asia has a few tortoises, the most widespread being
the elongate tortoise (*Indotestudo elongata*), which is found

in a variety of open woodland habitats. Although it is predominantly a herbivore, it consumes invertebrates and is not averse to eating carrion.

Turtles can be very common in some habitats, although in many places human activities have reduced their populations. Turtles also can attain surprisingly high densities, reaching 300 per hectare (120 per acre) in the red-eared slider. In contrast, the North American bog turtle (*Clemmys muhlenbergi*) lives in isolation, each bog containing only a dozen or fewer adults. The Aldabra giant tortoise (*Geochelone gigantea*) of the Indian Ocean has received modest protection, and as a result it has attained a total population of about 100,000, with densities in some areas of 30 to 160 individuals per hectare (12 to 64 per acre).

FEEDING BEHAVIOUR

Turtles are not social animals. Although members of the same species may be observed congregating along a stream or basking on a log, there is usually little interaction between individuals. Several species may inhabit the same river or lake, but each has different foods, feeding behaviours, and likely different activity periods. For example, a small lake in Georgia may be home to at least seven turtle species: snapping turtles, red-eared sliders, eastern cooters, common mud turtles, loggerhead musk turtles, stinkpots (common musk turtles), and spiny softshell turtles. The snapper is strongly carnivorous and will catch fish, frogs, snakes, and small aquatic birds. The softshell, musk, and mud turtles, meanwhile, will pursue many of the same small aquatic animals but with different preferences. For instance, the softshell hunts mainly fish and crayfish, the stinkpot eats mainly snails, insect larvae, and carrion, and the mud turtle primarily feeds on insects, mollusks, and carrion. The slider and cooter, on the other hand, have a mixed diet, the cooter's being more heavily vegetarian.

Like the Georgia turtles, most turtles eat a variety of foods. Tortoises (family Testudinidae) are herbivores that regularly eat a variety of plants and plant parts as available. Green sea turtles prefer marine grasses but, if these are not available, will eat algae. Many of the large river turtles are also herbivorous—for example, the yellow-spotted Amazon River turtle (*Podocnemis unifilis*), the Asian river turtle, or batagur (*Batagur baska*), and the Suwannee cooter (*Pseudemys suwanniensis*). Commonly, juvenile aquatic herbivores are insectivores and become herbivorous as they approach adulthood. There are some dietary specialists, however. For example, the Asian black marsh turtle (*Siebenrockiella crassicollis*), the American loggerhead musk turtle (*Sternotherus carinatus*), and the African Zambezi flapshell turtle (*Cyclanorbis frenatum*) eat only mollusks. The leatherback sea turtle predominantly consumes gelatinous prey in the form of jellyfish and salps, apparently timing its movements into different areas to coincide with the seasonal blooms of prey.

Turtles, in turn, are prey for a variety of animals, mainly as eggs and hatchlings. Sharks will attack even adult sea turtles, alligators and other crocodilians can crush the shell of most freshwater turtles, and mammalian predators can kill adult turtles on land.

REPRODUCTION

All turtles lay their eggs on land, and none show parental care. Amid this apparent uniformity, however, there is a variety of reproductive behaviours, ecologies, and physiologies.

Reproductive Age and Activity

The age at which turtles first reproduce varies from only a few years to perhaps as many as 50, with small species typically reaching sexual maturity sooner. Female false map turtles (*Graptemys pseudogeographica*) of the central United States, for example, are about 8 cm (3.2 inches) long and become sexually mature at two to three years. The eastern (U.S.) mud turtle (*Kinosternon subrubrum*) is somewhat larger and spends three to four years as a juvenile. The much larger common snapping turtle (*Chelydra serpentina*), at nearly 30 cm (one foot), takes 10 to 12 years to mature, and the slightly larger Mexican tortoise (*Gopherus flavomarinatus*) matures at 14 to 15 years. Age at maturity is also tied to a turtle's rate of growth, which relates to both the quantity and quality of food. Along Florida's Atlantic coast the metre-long (3.3-foot) green sea turtle (*Chelonia mydas*) takes 24 to 28 years to mature, but in Hawaii it takes 30 to 34 years, and some Australian populations near the southern end of the Great Barrier Reef take more than 40 years.

Reproductive activity is generally seasonal, and for most species it occurs in conjunction with a major annual weather change. For most turtles living in temperate regions, reproductive activity can occur with increasing day length and temperature (i.e., in springtime), whereas for many tropical species it may occur late in the dry season or early in the rainy season. Egg laying coincides with periods favourable for the development and emergence of hatchlings—for instance, times of abundant food or of optimal weather conditions.

Courtship and Copulation

Courtship and copulation require cooperation because of the turtles' shells. Mating can occur only with entwined tails, thus placing the male and female vents together for insertion of the penis. Courtship patterns range from a seemingly abusive interaction to a titillation routine that entices the female's cooperation. Many male tortoises

(*Geochelone* species) compete with one another in a series of head bobs and ramming charges. A male then uses the same behaviour along with biting to force the female into immobility and submission. In contrast, male sliders (*Trachemys*) and cooters are more subtle in their approach. These freshwater turtles have exceptionally long and straight claws. Depending upon the species, the male swims above or backward in front of the female with his forelimbs extended and his claws brushing the sides of the female's head. His forefeet vibrate, and the rapid, light touch of the claws titillates the female. In a few species, including the Asian river turtle, or batagur (*Batagur baska*), and the Argentine side-necked turtle (*Phrynops hilarii*), the male develops bright head and trunk colours that signal his reproductive readiness and possibly elicit a female's cooperation.

Nesting and Egg Laying

Leatherbacks and other sea turtles are migratory in that they traverse hundreds of kilometres from their main feeding areas to nest on the beaches where they hatched. Annual migration also occurs in some river-dwelling turtles, including the South American arrau (*Podocnemis expansa*) and the Asian river turtle (*Batagur baska*). These turtles move tens of kilometres along rivers in order to find large sandbars on which to nest. The females of all aquatic species must leave the water to find nesting sites. Some merely move to the banks adjacent to the streams they live in, others travel hundreds of metres across land to find appropriate nesting conditions. Nesting is an arduous affair that exposes females to increased predation.

The number of eggs in a single clutch is variable both within and between species. Small species typically lay few eggs—only one or two in the Asian black marsh turtle or the pancake tortoise. The number of eggs increases with body size among species and occasionally within a species. However, the largest turtle, the leatherback sea turtle, produces fewer eggs (average 50–90 eggs per clutch) than do smaller sea turtles such as the hawksbill (140–160 eggs) and olive ridley (105–110). Similarly, the large Aldabran tortoise (60–80 cm [24–32 inches]) lays 12–14 eggs, yet the common snapping turtle (20–35 cm [8–14 inches]) lays 20–30 eggs, and the Suwanee cooter (14–28 cm [5.5–11 inches]) lays 15–20 eggs.

In most species, eggs are laid annually; a few species lay every other year, and some lay twice in one nesting season. The sea turtles generally nest in three- to four-year cycles, the female usually laying multiple clutches of eggs during each nesting season. Within the season, cycles of egg laying occur about two weeks apart, allowing the female time to rest from the energy-demanding excursion ashore and for ovulation and shelling of the eggs. Turtle eggshells can be leathery, as in sea turtles, or brittle, as in many tortoises. Calcium carbonate is a constituent of both types of shells; the leathery ones simply have less.

Nest digging is a fixed behavioral pattern in all but a few species. Most turtles dig chambers in which the eggs are laid. Once the female finds a desired nesting site, she begins to dig the chamber with alternate scooping movements of the hind limbs. As one hind limb supports the rear half of the body, the other one moves inward under the tail and, with a semicircular twist of the foot, spades into the soil and makes a quick sideward flip, dropping the soil to the outside as the hind foot locks into its supportive position. The opposite foot repeats the pattern, and in a slow, steady alternation the nest is dug. Digging stops when the female has reached a depth equal to the length of her outstretched hind limbs. Then, bracing herself on both hind limbs and with the tail centred over the nest, she drops her eggs into the hole. After she has expelled all of her eggs, the hind limbs resume their alternate movement, but now they drag the loose soil back into the nest. The female departs when the nest is filled. A few species, such as the stinkpot, or common musk turtle (*Sternotherus odoratus*), dig a shallow nest with both the fore- and hind feet.

EGG DEVELOPMENT AND HATCHING

The rate of development inside the egg is temperature-dependent, with warmer temperatures speeding development and cooler temperatures slowing it. As a result, incubation time is variable. For the majority of turtles, incubation ranges between 45 and 75 days. A few species, including the scorpion mud turtle (*Kinosternon scorpioides*) of Central and South America and the northern snake-necked turtle (*Chelodina rugosa*) of Australia, have embryonic diapause, in which development stops soon after an egg is deposited. Diapause is usually triggered by an environmental stimulus, and development resumes when a contrasting stimulus (temperature and moisture) occurs. Incubation with diapause can be as long as 12 months from egg laying to hatching.

In most turtles, sex is determined by temperature. Within a narrow range of temperatures (centred at 28 °C [82 °F]), a clutch of eggs yields nearly equal numbers of females and males. Above that range all hatchlings are female, and below it all are male. The critical period for sex determination is during the second trimester of incubation, and the critical temperature seems to be the average during this period rather than the maximum or minimum.

Hatching consists of two separate events: exiting the egg and emerging from the nest. Hatchlings have a small, pointed, keratinous bump (caruncle) on the tip of the snout. This structure is analogous to the egg tooth possessed by hatchling birds and some other reptiles. The caruncle is pushed against the inner surface of the egg-shell, breaking it. The hatchling then tears a larger opening and climbs out of the shell. After a pause to uncurl its body and shell from the cramped conditions within the egg, the hatchling begins to dig upward. This may be an individual effort, but usually several hatchlings dig together, helping one another. In sea turtles a collective effort is required because a single hatchling lacks the energy and time to do it alone. Upon reaching the surface, hatchlings of aquatic species move to the water; terrestrial ones make their way into leaf litter or dense vegetation to avoid predators. Eggs and hatchlings are the most vulnerable life stages, and many become a meal for almost any predator in their habitat.

LONGEVITY

The long lives of turtles are often proclaimed as fact, but reliable evidence is lacking for many of the claims. In some cases of exceptional longevity, written records reveal that the individual has mysteriously changed sex or species from beginning to end, hinting at a surreptitious replacement. Even so, if an individual survives to adulthood, it will likely have a life span of two to three decades. In the wild, American box turtles (*Terrapene carolina*) regularly live more than 30 years. Obviously, sea turtles requiring 40 to 50 years to mature will have life spans reaching at least 60 to 70 years. The giant tortoises of the Galapagos Islands and Aldabra (*Geochelone elephantopus* and *G. gigantea*, respectively) have lived more than 60 years in zoos.

On occasion it has been reported that individuals of a few tortoise species have lived in captivity for 100 to 250 years. In many of these cases, the reported sex of the supposedly long-lived tortoise, or the species, or even both, have mysteriously changed during captivity, making it difficult to accept the reliability of such reports. It is

Galapagos tortoise (Geochelone elephantopus). Francisco Erize/Bruce Coleman Ltd.

likely that 100 years is not the maximum for a few species, especially sea turtles and giant tortoises, but, in order to surpass this age, an extremely nurturing, protective environment would be required.

ORIGIN AND EVOLUTION

The earliest turtles known date to 220 million years ago. The oldest and most primitive, *Odontochelys semitestacea*, a fossil species, possesses a complete plastron, broad dorsal ribs, and a series of neural plates; however, it lacks a fully developed carapace. Authorities contend that this species is evidence that the carapace evolved after the plastron. This evidence also suggests that the carapace of later turtles arose from neural plates that hardened over time to become flat sections of bone (osteoderms) supported by wide dorsal ribs. In addition, despite the fact that both the upper and lower jaws of *Odontochelys* have teeth, there is no question that it is a turtle.

A slightly younger fossil species, *Proganochelys quenstedi*, also has teeth, but the teeth are located on the roof of the mouth, not on the upper or lower jaw. In contrast to *Odontochelys*, the shell of *Proganochelys* has most of the features of modern turtles, and it completely encases the shoulder and pelvic girdles.

Although *Odontochelys* and *Proganochelys* offer insight into early anatomy, the origin of turtles remains a strongly debated issue. The two main hypotheses on turtle ancestry are very different. The parareptile hypothesis suggests that turtles arose within an ancient and basal group of reptiles called the Parareptilia. These early reptiles have no other modern survivors. The diapsid hypothesis suggests that turtles arose as an early divergence from the group (Diapsida) that would subsequently include dinosaurs, pterosaurs, crocodilians, birds, and lizards. Existing evidence does not overwhelmingly support either hypothesis.

Proterocheris is another ancient fossil turtle that lived at the same time as *Proganochelys*. *Proterocheris* has many features that suggest that it is a side-necked turtle. If this is true, the two major taxonomic groups of living turtles, suborders Pleurodira (side-necks) and Cryptodira (hidden necks), had their origins in the Middle Triassic (some 230 million years ago) at the latest, making turtles an extremely ancient group. *Proterocheris* and two later-appearing Triassic genera are likely not true side-necks but turtles that share some pleurodire characteristics. Unquestionable pleurodires do not appear until the Early Cretaceous (about 145 to 100 million years ago), and the first modern side-neck families do not appear until the Late Cretaceous (some 100 to 65 million years ago).

In tracing back the history of the other turtle suborder, Cryptodira, *Kayentachelys aprix* of the Late

Jurassic (some 150 million years ago) is almost assuredly a cryptodire; it is also the oldest known North American turtle. Other cryptodires are known from the Late Jurassic, although they are not representative of existing families. Softshell turtles (family Trionychidae) are the first modern turtles found in the fossil record, appearing in the Cretaceous Period. The oldest sea turtle (*Santanachelys gaffneyi*) is known from the mid-Cretaceous. It is a member of the Protostegidae, a likely sister group of modern leatherback sea turtles. *S. gaffneyi* had a stream-lined shell of about 1.5 metres (5 feet) and forelimbs well along the evolutionary path to becoming flippers.

TUATARAS

Tuataras are either of two species (genus *Sphenodon*) of moderately large, lizardlike reptiles endemic to New Zealand. The two species of extant tuataras, *Sphenodon guntheri* and *S. punctatus*, and possibly other now-extinct species, inhabited the main islands before the arrival of the Maori people and the kiore—the Polynesian rat (*Rattus exulans*). *S. guntheri* lives on a few islets in the western Cook Strait, and *S. punctatus* inhabits the North Island and about 30 islets off the island's northeast coast. *Tuatara* is the Maori word for "peaks on the back."

Tuataras are the sole survivors of an ancient group (order Sphenodontida) of reptiles that first appeared in the fossil record of the Late Triassic Period, approximately 220 million years ago. *Sphenodon*, the only extant genus of tuataras, has no fossil history; many of the oldest known fragments of these animals are less than 10,000 years old. The absence of fossils suggests that *Sphenodon* has never been very diverse and has likely possessed a limited distribution. Tuataras are distantly related to the reptiles of order Squamata (lizards, snakes, and amphisbaenians [worm lizards]).

NATURAL HISTORY OF TUATARAS

Tuataras are largely, but not exclusively, nocturnal animals. They regularly bask during daylight hours at the mouth of their burrows; however, they become much more active at night, foraging in and around their burrows and interacting with other tuataras. While capable of digging their own burrows, tuataras often use those of the fairy prion (*Pachyptila turtur*), a burrow-nesting seabird. These settings provide tuataras with protection and food. Excreta from the birds supply a large arthropod community, and the tuatara prey on the diverse array of arthropods and smaller lizards that use this resource. Tuataras may also prey on fairy prion eggs and chicks.

The burrow systems are often made up of a network of interconnected tunnels. Each tunnel may be several metres long and possess multiple entrances. Although tuataras are solitary and territorial, as many as five or six tuataras may occupy the same system; however, they will not share the same tunnel segment, and individuals will often use more than one tunnel system. The social structure of tuataras is similar to that of iguanian lizards (iguanas, anoles, agamas, chameleons, and others) in that territorial defense and courtship behaviours are established through body display and colour changes.

Beginning in January and lasting through March, following the reproductive season of the fairy prion, the mating season for the tuatara occurs. During this period, social interactions between tuataras increase. A male defends his territory by inflating his body, erecting the crest on his head and neck, and shaking his head. Close encounters between males result in a sequence of mouth-gaping behaviours that can lead to chases. These pursuits may culminate in forceful biting if both males are initially unwilling to yield. Males often make croaking sounds during these intense confrontations, but these "vocalizations" are seldom heard at other times and are most likely the by-product of chest compression.

During courtship the male approaches the female, inflates his body, and erects his spines. This body enlargement is accentuated by his stilted, stately walk toward the female and around her. A male may circle a female several times before copulation occurs. If the female remains stationary, the male will approach her, step over her back, and move forward. Since tuataras have rudimentary hemipenes, they cannot truly copulate. To compensate, both participants position their cloacal vents as close as possible to one another, and sperm is transmitted from the male's cloaca to the cloaca of the female.

For most females, egg deposition occurs on a four-year cycle and not until late October to mid-December. Each female lays 8–15 eggs, which are promptly buried. Each egg requires 11–16 months of incubation in the ground before hatching occurs. The growth of the juveniles is also slow, and individuals require 9–13 years to attain sexual maturity in most populations. Tuataras commonly live 60 years or more, and many individuals are capable of reproduction well into their 20s and 30s; a few can even reproduce after 60 years of age.

The tuatara's largely nocturnal habits conceal it from many potential predators, but occasionally it is preyed upon by hawks, gulls, or kingfishers. The kiore, or Polynesian rat, preys heavily on eggs and the young, and the tuatara may be regarded as seriously threatened with extinction on islands where rats and other mammals, such as cats and pigs, have been introduced.

FORM AND FUNCTION

Physically, *S. guntheri* and *S. punctatus* are quite similar to one another. From the snout to the tip of the tail, adults average 50 cm (20 inches) in length and weigh between 0.5 and 1 kg (1 and 2 pounds). Males tend to be larger, often approaching 60 cm (24 inches) in length, and generally weigh twice as much as females. Both species have robust lizardlike bodies with a large head, well-developed limbs, and a stout tail. The snout is distinct because of the presence of fused toothless premaxillary bones that give it a beaklike appearance. The entire body is covered with scales. The body is mottled, and coloration ranges from dirty tan to olive-green to slaty gray. Body colour can change over the animal's lifetime. Males and females possess a series of broad spines, which are derived from scales, that extend down the midline of the back from the nape onto the tail. The largest spines occur on the neck and trunk.

The eyes are well developed with vertical pupils and a retinal structure adapted for low-intensity light. Tuataras also have a third, or parietal, eye on the top of the head. Although this eye has a rudimentary lens, it is not an organ of vision. It is thought to serve an endocrine function by registering the dark-light cycle for hormone regulation. Tuataras display no ear openings; however, they do have a middle ear cavity with a stapes (a small bone that conducts sound vibrations). They are most sensitive to sounds in the 100–800 Hertz range.

Tuatara (Sphenodon punctatus). M.F. Soper/Bruce Coleman Inc.

Tuataras are one of the few groups of reptiles that are active at low body temperatures. Their internal temperatures are typically less than 22 °C (72 °F) and usually hover around 18–19 °C (64–66 °F). They can even remain active when their body temperatures dip as low as 13–14 °C (55–57 °F). While they bask in the sun to elevate their body temperatures, life in the burrows and their nocturnal activity expose them to lower temperatures and conditions where thermoregulation is impossible. Through an evening's activity cycle, their body temperatures will regularly fluctuate across a range of 3–4 °C (5–7 °F). Their reduced activity at low temperatures might also be an adaptation to reduce water loss. To further stem water loss, tuataras excrete uric acid—like their distant reptilian relatives, the squamates.

Evolution and Classification

Order Sphenodontida is the sister group to the order Squamata, and sphenodontids share numerous traits with squamates. Both groups possess a transverse cloacal opening (the vent), teeth that are attached superficially to the jawbones, and fracture planes in the tail vertebrae. Sphenodontids and squamates also undergo ecdysis, the periodic shedding or molting of the skin to allow growth. Sphenodontids differ from squamates by the presence of gastralia (abdominal ribs), enclosed temporal fossae (depressions) in the skull, and the unique replacement of premaxillary teeth by a beaklike extension of the premaxillary bones. This latter characteristic is also seen in the earliest known sphenodontid, *Brachyrhinodon taylori* from a Late Triassic deposit in Virginia.

The sphenodontids were never very diverse; however, one small group of aquatic species, the pleurosaurs, radiated into a small number of genera and species between the Early Jurassic and Early Cretaceous periods (approximately 200–100 million years ago). The pleurosaurs had an elongate body and tail and a streamlined head that suggested an active fish-eating lifestyle. After the Jurassic the presence of sphenodontids in the fossil record declined, and as yet none have been reported from the Cenozoic Era.

Formerly, order Sphenodontida was widely known as order Rhynchocephalia, but the taxonomic changes associated with a better- known fossil history caused the latter name to fall out of favour. Rhynchocephalia is sometimes used to label the group containing current members of the order Sphenodontida and a few early fossil taxa that have since gone extinct. It is also used to label the group that includes only the earliest sphenodontids.

CHAPTER 7

TYPES OF TURTLES

A handful of Earth's roughly three hundred extant turtles is presented below. Many species, such as the musk turtles, pond turtles, and Blanding's turtle, inhabit freshwater areas. Others, such as the sea turtles, live in marine environments.

BLANDING'S TURTLE

Blanding's turtle (*Emydoidea blandingii*) is a freshwater turtle in family Emydidae that is found in southern Canada and the north-central to northeastern United States. The upper shell (carapace) of Blanding's turtle averages about 20 cm (8 inches) in length; it is smooth, rounded, and elongate with yellow markings on a blackish

*Box turtle (*Terrapene carolina). John H. Gerard

ground colour. The chin of the turtle is bright yellow, and the lower shell (plastron) is hinged in the centre and can be drawn up to protect the head, legs, and tail.

Blanding's turtle is usually found in ponds, quiet streams, and other shallow bodies of water with thick vegetation and soft bottoms. It is an omnivore but prefers crustaceans. Although a strongly aquatic turtle, it regularly basks in the sunlight during the spring. Females often travel long distances overland to find suitable nesting sites and typically deposit clutches of 6–21 eggs in early summer. Hatchlings emerge from their eggs by August or early September. They often overwinter in the nest and disperse during the early spring the following year.

BOX TURTLES

Box turtles have been assigned to any of two groups, Asian and North American, of terrestrial and semi-aquatic turtles. Box turtles have a high, rounded upper shell (carapace), a flattened bottom shell (plastron) with a transverse hinge, and ligamentous connections (instead of the bony bridge typical of most turtles) between plastron and carapace. Their common name is presumably derived from their ability to draw their head and limbs completely within the shell and close themselves up like a box. The presence of a hinge and ligamentous bridges permits this flexibility. Their high, domed shell makes them too large for many predators to consume whole, and the tight closure that occurs when all external parts are drawn into the shell makes box turtles difficult to crack open. The Asian and North American box turtles are not closely related in spite of their overall similarity. *Cuora*, the Asian genus, is part of family Geoemydidae, and *Terrapene*, the North American genus, is part of family Emydidae.

Cuora contains nine or more species that occur within subtropical and tropical regions of Asia from northeastern India to southeastern China and southward into the Sunda Islands and the Philippines. Asian box turtles are omnivorous, largely semiaquatic turtles that, depending on the species, have carapace lengths of 13–20 cm (5–8 inches) as adults. Each clutch size is typically two eggs, although two to four clutches are often deposited during a single nesting season.

Terrapene is largely found in cool to warm temperate regions east of the Rocky Mountains from southernmost Canada to the Gulf Coast of the United States and into Mexico. It is strongly terrestrial, although the Coahuilan box turtle (*T. coahuila*) is semiaquatic. The four species of *Terrapene* have the same range of shell sizes as *Cuora* and similarly share an omnivorous diet; however, they tend to lay larger clutches of eggs. The eastern box turtle (*T. carolina carolina*) lays a maximum of eight eggs in a clutch, although clutches of three or four eggs are more typical.

CHICKEN TURTLES

The chicken turtle (*Deirochelys reticularia*) is an edible freshwater turtle (family Emydidae) found in the southeastern United States. The chicken turtle has an exceptionally long neck and a finely grooved upper shell covered with an open network of yellowish lines on a brownish background. Shell length is usually about 10 to 15 cm (4 to 6 inches).

The chicken turtle inhabits quiet bodies of water and probably feeds on both animal and vegetable material. It frequently leaves the water and travels about on land.

CLEMMYS

The genus *Clemmys* is made up of small, terrestrial or semi-aquatic turtles in the family Emydidae. The genus contains four species, all restricted to North America. Earlier classifications included several European and Asian species that are now placed in the genus *Mauremys*.

Clemmys females lay fewer than a dozen eggs in early summer that hatch by fall. Three of the species occur in the eastern United States and one in the Pacific coast region. The bog turtle (*C. muhlenbergi*) is an officially recognized threatened species.

The spotted turtle (*Clemmys guttata*) is a small freshwater turtle (family Emydidae) found from southern Canada to the southern and central United States. The spotted turtle has a shell about 10 cm (4 inches) long. The upper shell is smooth, with round, bright-yellow or orange spots on a brown background; the lower shell is blackish, with orange or yellow markings.

The spotted turtle is a rather slow-moving reptile. It lives in shallow bodies of water, such as ponds, bogs, and ditches, and it commonly basks in groups in the sun.

MUD TURTLES

Mud turtles (genus *Kinosternon*) make up a group of about 18 species of semiterrestrial freshwater turtles belonging to the family Kinosternidae. Mud turtles are found in North and South America from New England to northern Argentina. Like the related musk turtles (*Sternotherus*), they are small animals (usually 15 cm [6 inches] or less in shell length) with fleshy barbels on the chin and the ability to exude a strong, musky odour. They differ from musk turtles by having a broad lower shell with a hinged section at either end. The hinged portions of the shells of some species can be pulled up to cover and protect the head, legs, and tail of the turtle.

Mud turtles occur in a variety of habitats that range from clear forest brooks to intermittent desert streams and ponds. Although highly aquatic in many respects—feeding is almost exclusively so—they are generally poor swimmers and instead prefer to walk along the bottoms of ponds and streams. In addition, some species, such as the striped mud turtle (*K. baurii*), survive drought periods through estivation (dormancy) under a shallow layer of mud.

Mud turtles are omnivores with a preference for animal matter, such as arthropods, worms, small fishes, and fish eggs. The clutch sizes of mud turtles vary from a single egg to nearly a dozen, depending on the female's size and health.

MUSK TURTLES

Musk turtles (genus *Sternotherus*) make up a group of four species of small freshwater turtles belonging to the

Stinkpot, or common musk turtle (Sternotherus odoratus). Alvin E. Staffan—The National Audubon Society Collection/Photo Researchers

family Kinosternidae. Musk turtles are named for the strong, musky odour they emit when disturbed. They are found in eastern North America, usually in slow-moving waters. Highly aquatic animals, they seldom emerge onto land. Similar to small snapping turtles in appearance and pugnacious temperament, musk turtles are characterized by a small lower shell and by small, fleshy barbels on the chin. Their upper shell is oval, dull in colour, and usually about 8–13 cm (3–5 inches) long.

The stinkpot, or common musk turtle (*S. odoratus*), is the only member of the genus found in both the northeastern and southern United States. The diet of the musk turtle includes plants, mollusks, small fish, and insects. Mating occurs underwater, and females may lay up to nine eggs.

PAINTED TURTLES

Painted turtles (*Chrysemys picta*) are brightly marked North American turtles (family Emydidae) found from southern Canada to northern Mexico. It is a smooth-shelled reptile with a shell about 14 to 18 cm (5.5 to 7 inches) long in adults. The upper shell, which is relatively flat, is either black or greenish brown with red and yellow markings along the margins.

The painted turtle usually lives in quiet, shallow bodies of fresh water, especially those with thickly planted mud bottoms. It feeds on plants, small animals, and some carrion. It often basks in large groups on logs and other objects, and in many areas it hibernates during the winter.

From mid-spring to mid-summer, the female painted turtle typically lays 2 to 20 eggs, depending upon her size, in a nest near the water. The eggs hatch in 60 to 80 days. Hatchlings that emerge from eggs laid during mid-summer remain in the nest until early spring.

PITTED SHELL TURTLES

The pitted shell turtle (*Carettochelys insculpta*)—which is also called fly river turtle, New Guinea plateless turtle, or pig-nosed turtle—belongs to the turtle family Carettochelyidae. The species lives in rivers in southern New Guinea and in a limited region in northern Australia. A combination of characteristics separates *C. insculpta* from other turtles, including a piglike nose, a shell with no scutes, and flipperlike forelimbs. It is a large turtle reaching carapace lengths of 55 cm (22 inches).

It is an omnivorous species that feeds heavily on nuts and fruits when they fall into the water, but it also preys on aquatic invertebrates and vertebrates. Toward the end of the dry season, when falling rivers expose sandbars for nesting, females deposit clutches of 15 to 30 eggs.

POND TURTLES

Pond turtles are any of several freshwater turtles of the families Emydidae and Bataguridae. Two of the best known are emydids: the Pacific, or western, pond turtle (*Clemmys marmorata*) and the European pond turtle (*Emys orbicularis*).

The Pacific pond turtle is one of the few turtles native to western coastal North America. Found from southern Canada to southern California, it usually inhabits ponds and other quiet waters. It once was widely sold for food in California. The smooth, broad upper shell of the Pacific pond turtle is about 15–25 cm (6–10 inches) long and is brown or blackish with yellow spots and streaks. The lower shell is yellow and black. The Pacific pond turtle is a highly aquatic, wary reptile. It feeds on plant and animal material and basks in the sun.

The European pond turtle, also known as the swamp turtle, or swamp tortoise, is found from the Ural Mountains through Europe and in northwestern Africa. It is primarily aquatic and omnivorous. The upper shell, which reaches a length of about 12–13 cm (5 inches), is brownish or blackish with yellow speckling and sometimes resembles that of the Pacific pond turtle. Unlike the latter species, the European pond turtle has a hinged plastron, although it is usually unable to close its shell completely.

SEA TURTLES

Sea turtles make up any of the species of marine turtles belonging to the families Dermochelyidae (leatherback sea turtles) and Cheloniidae (green turtles, flatback sea turtles, loggerhead sea turtles, hawksbills, and ridleys). Both families are highly aquatic, and most species only appear on coastal beaches for egg laying; however, the green turtle (*Chelonia mydas*) occasionally basks in terrestrial environments. Adult sea turtles are mainly denizens of tropical and subtropical seas, but the juveniles of both families occur naturally in more temperate waters.

Dermochelyids and cheloniids are distantly related; their divergence from one another took place between 100 million and 150 million years ago. Nevertheless, both groups have streamlined shells, forelimbs modified as flippers that propel their bodies through the water, figure-eight swimming strokes, and large, fully webbed hind feet as rudders. Cheloniids are hard-shelled sea turtles with a bony carapace (top shell) and plastron (bottom shell) with epidermal scutes (scales). In contrast, the leatherback shell of dermochelyids has a greatly reduced bony architecture, and the bones are less firmly articulated; scutes appear in hatchlings, but they are quickly shed, so the bony shell is covered with a thick, leathery skin.

Size varies greatly among the seven species; however, commonalities exist in diet and habitat. With some exception, most sea turtles are carnivorous and prefer warm, coastal marine environments. The leatherback sea turtle (*Dermochelys coriacea*) inhabits pelagic (open ocean)

Leatherback sea turtle (Dermochelys coriacea*).* Jane Burton/Photo Researchers

environments. Apparently following the blooms of its jellyfish prey, it moves widely throughout the oceans. The shell lengths of few individuals exceed 1.6 metres (5 feet), although some reportedly reach 2.4 metres (8 feet). Adult and juvenile olive ridleys (*Lepidochelys olivacea*) are also largely pelagic, but they are known to frequent coastal regions such as bays and estuaries. The olive ridley and its relative, the Kemp's ridley sea turtle (*L. kempii*), are small with wide rounded shells. As adults, both species have shells about 58–78 cm (23–31 inches) long. Leatherbacks and ridleys are largely carnivorous and consume a wide variety of crustaceans and mollusks.

Loggerhead (*Caretta caretta*) and green (*Chelonia mydas*) sea turtles have adult shell lengths between 0.9 and 1.2 metres (3 and 4 feet) long. The loggerhead is

Green sea turtle (Chelonia mydas). © Corbis

carnivorous and prefers coastal marine environments. It has the proportionately largest head of the sea turtles; this feature may be an adaptation that increases its jaw strength in order to crush the shells of large mollusks such as whelks. The green turtle is found in warm coastal waters around the world; however, unlike other sea turtles, it is predominantly herbivorous and feeds on algae or marine grasses.

The hawksbill sea turtle (*Eretmochelys imbricata*) is largely tropical and common in coral reef habitats, where it feeds on sponges and a variety of other invertebrates. The flatback sea turtle (*Natator depressa*) occurs in the seas between Australia and New Guinea; it also feeds on a variety of invertebrates. The shells of adults of both species range from 90 to 100 cm (35 to 39 inches).

While reproductive behaviours and timing vary among populations and species, a general pattern is shared among all sea turtles. All are egg layers, and females must come ashore to bury their eggs in sandy environments. Except for *Lepidochelys*, which has a nesting cycle of 1–3 years, females nest only every third or fourth year; however, they often nest multiple times during a nesting season. While most species usually have two to four egg-laying events per nesting season, the loggerhead has up to seven. The female emerges from the surf at night, ponderously crawls to sandy areas above the high tide line, and digs a nest. The nest or egg chamber is dug exclusively with the hind limbs, the tail is positioned over the centre of the nest opening, and eggs are deposited. The nest is then filled in with sand, and the female returns to the sea. Each nest is created 12 to 14 days apart, and clutch size varies among species and populations; about 100 eggs per nesting event are common.

Eggs incubate for about 50 to 60 days. Development is temperature-dependent, so a warmer nest brings about an earlier hatching. Within a given nest, hatching is nearly synchronous. Because of the depth of the nest, emergence requires that several hatchlings dig upward together. Hatchlings typically emerge from the ground at night and can instinctively recognize the horizon over the open ocean, although they can be confused by artificial lighting behind or along the beach. Once in the surf, the hatchlings swim outward into the open ocean, and those of most species enter the gigantic oceanic gyres. The young sea turtles are pelagic, likely for 5 to 10 years, before returning to warm nearshore waters to continue their growth.

Most species of sea turtles are threatened or endangered. They are typically slow to mature, long-lived, and migratory; before reaching sexual maturity, many are captured—either intentionally or accidentally—in coastal fisheries and killed. The minimum time from hatching to first reproduction appears to be about 10 to 15 years, a characteristic shared by the largest species, *D. coriacea*, and the smallest species, *L. kempii* and *L. olivacea*. Others, such as *Chelonia mydas*, require over 20 years to reach sexual maturity and reproduce for the first time.

SIDE-NECKED TURTLES

The name "side-necked turtle" refers to any species of turtle belonging to the families Chelidae, Pelomedusidae, and Podocnemididae in the suborder Pleurodira. The common name is derived from the animal's defensive posture. Instead of retracting the head and neck into the shell for protection, turtles of this group lay the head and neck to the side, beneath the margins of the shell. Other defining characteristics of pleurodires include the presence of a mesoplastron (a section of bone set into the plastron, or the bottom shell) in most forms and the fusion of the pelvic girdle to the plastron.

Pleurodires are an ancient group of turtles whose first members appeared in the late Triassic Period, about 220 million years ago. Today sidenecks occur in the Southern Hemisphere in Africa, Madagascar, Australia, South America, and a few islands in the Indian Ocean. All living species are aquatic to semiaquatic; however, during the Paleogene and Neogene periods, one group occurred in marine and estuarine environments in the Northern Hemisphere. Pleurodires are predominantly omnivores, but herbivory and carnivory occur among the more than 70 species of sidenecks. Similarly, there is a diversity of shell shapes and sizes ranging from 12 cm (about 5 inches), such as in the African dwarf mud turtle (*Pelusios nanus*), to more than 90 cm (35 inches) long, such as in the giant South American river turtle, or arrau (*Podocnemis expansa*).

SNAKE-NECKED TURTLES

Snake-necked turtles make up about 16 species of turtles belonging to the genera *Chelodina* and *Macrochelodina* in family Chelidae. They are characterized by long necks that can bend and move in a serpentine fashion. Snake-necked turtles are a group of side-necked turtles with necks that range from nearly as long as to slightly longer than the shell. They inhabit the waterways of Australia and southern New Guinea and possess the longest neck of any group of turtles in the world. The neck is so long that it cannot be retracted completely beneath the margin of the shell.

All snake-necked turtles appear to be strongly aquatic and prefer to walk along the bottom of streams and other water bodies rather than swim. They are carnivores and prey on fish. When hiding from predators or stalking prey, the neck is folded against the body. When prey is close, the neck and head lunge forward, and the animal opens its mouth and throat to create a vacuum. Water and prey are sucked into the mouth, which snaps shut. The mouth may then open slightly to allow water, but not the prey, to escape.

All snake-necked turtles are egg layers, and one species, the northern snake-necked turtle (*Macrochelodina rugosa*), lays its eggs in nest chambers beneath the water. Immediately after the eggs are deposited, the embryos go into diapause (a period of dormancy) and resume development only when the nesting chamber dries during the dry season. They hatch 9 to 10 months after egg deposition and just as the rainy season begins.

SNAPPING TURTLES

Snapping turtles, named for their method of biting, consist of several species of freshwater turtles (family Chelydridae). Snapping turtles are found continuously in

Common snapping turtle (Chelydra serpentina). Walter Dawn

North America from eastern Canada and New England to the Rockies, and they are also found in pockets from Mexico and Central America to Ecuador. Snapping turtles are noted for their large size and aggressive nature. They are tan to black in colour and have a rough upper shell, a small cross-shaped lower shell, a long tail, and a large head with hooked jaws. The female in both species lays clutches of 20 to 40 eggs; the young at hatching have shells about 2.5–4 cm (1–1.5 inches) long. Snapping turtles have long been valued as food.

The distribution of the common snapping turtle (*Chelydra serpentina*) is widespread from Canada to the west coast of northern South America. *C. serpentina serpentina* is the subspecies found throughout southern and eastern Canada and in the eastern half of the United States. It is distinguished by a saw-edged crest on the upper side of its tail and averages 20–30 cm (8–12 inches) in shell length and 4.5–16 kg (10–35 pounds) in weight. When young it has three longitudinal ridges on the upper shell; these become worn down with time. The common snapping turtle is often found buried in mud in shallow water. It is omnivorous, although it prefers animal prey. It is usually unaggressive in the water; however, it may lunge and snap while on land. Three other snapping turtle subspecies—*C. serpentina osceola* of Florida, *C. serpentina rossignoni* of Central America, and *C. serpentina acutirostris* of Ecuador—are also recognized. The latter two are generally smaller than *C. serpentina serpentina*.

The alligator snapping turtle, *Macrochelys* (or sometimes *Macroclemys*) *temminckii*, is the largest freshwater turtle in the United States. It is found in southern and central regions and is a sedentary turtle with three prominent longitudinal ridges on the upper shell. Shell length is about 40–70 cm (16–28 inches); weight ranges from about 18 to 70 kg (40 to 155 pounds) with a record of about 100 kg (220.5 pounds). The alligator snapping turtle has a wormlike appendage on the floor of its mouth. It often lies quietly on the bottom, mouth open, and lures fishes within reach by means of this structure. It also eats plants. Fossil snapping turtles have been found in Miocene deposits in Europe and North America.

SOFTSHELL TURTLES

Softshell turtles make up about 30 turtle species (family Trionychidae) characterized by a flattened shell. The shell lacks the epidermal scutes (large scales) characteristic of most turtles, as in the leatherback sea turtle (*Dermochelys coriacea*), and the bony architecture of the shell is reduced. Softshells have long necks and streamlined heads with elongated proboscis-like snouts bearing the nostrils at the tips. They often lie buried in mud, sand, and shallow water. By extending the head and neck so that the snout just breaks the surface, they can breathe in a snorkel-like manner. All softshells are mainly carnivorous. They actively search for and pursue prey or capture it by ambush. The flattened shape seems a strange one for an active animal, but apparently it is hydrodynamically efficient. Propelled by all four limbs—both forefeet and hind feet are strongly webbed—softshells are rapid swimmers.

The 14 genera of softshells are divided into two evolutionary groups: the subfamily Cyclanorbinae of southern Asia, northeastern Africa, and sub-Saharan Africa; and the subfamily Trionychinae of southeastern North America, southern Asia, and Africa. The cyclanorbine softshells are made up of two African genera

Softshell turtle (family Trionychidae). E.R. Degginger

(*Cyclanorbis* and *Cycloderma*) and a single genus (*Lissemys*) of Indian and Burman flapshelled turtles. The trionychine softshells are more biologically diverse. The three species of North American softshells (*Apalone*) are moderately sized, and adult males grow to about two-thirds the size of females. Adult female carapace lengths range from 17 cm (7 inches) in *A. mutica* and *A. spinifera* to 63 cm (25 inches) in *A. ferox*. The largest trionychine softshells are the narrow-headed softshell (*Chitra indica*) and the Asian giant softshell (*Pelochelys bibroni*) of Southeast Asia; the shells of both species reach lengths of more than 1 metre (3.3 feet).

Softshells can lay as few as two eggs, as in young females of the genus *Lissemys*, or more than 100 eggs, as in a large-bodied *Trionyx triunguis*. Embryonic development time varies from as few as 30 days to nearly 300 days, depending upon species and environmental conditions in the nest. Using their hind limbs, softshells dig nests in friable soil usually in areas adjacent to water.

TERRAPINS

Terrapin is a word formerly used to refer to any aquatic turtle but now restricted largely, though not exclusively, to the diamondback terrapin (*Malaclemys terrapin*) of the turtle family Emydidae. Until the last third of the 20th century, the word *terrapin* was used commonly in the United Kingdom and the Commonwealth countries as well as the United States.

The diamondback terrapins inhabit salt marshes and coastal waters of North America from New England to the Gulf of Mexico. They are moderate in size, with shell lengths of 10–14 cm (4–6 inches) in males and 15–23 cm (6–9 inches) in females. In addition, females often have

Diamondback terrapin (Malaclemys terrapin). Leonard Lee Rue III

a proportionately larger head, which may be associated with a heavier diet of mollusks. In general, terrapins are omnivores; they capture a variety of invertebrate prey and occasionally eat plant matter. Like sea turtles, terrapins must find egg-laying sites on beaches above the high-tide line. Most adult females nest annually from April through July, depending on latitude. Clutch sizes vary from 4 to 18 eggs, and incubation typically lasts 80 to 90 days.

The terrapin has been acclaimed as a "gourmet's delight," particularly during the late 19th and early 20th centuries, and this gustatory popularity resulted in the overcollection and near extinction of many coastal populations. Efforts were made to develop a hatchery-farming system in the early 20th century. This project never attained commercial success, but harvesting pressure was reduced by the Great Depression and World War II, and terrapin populations largely recovered. At the present time, the popularity of the blue crab (*Callinectes*) and its manner of harvest present a new threat to terrapin populations. Terrapins enter submerged crab traps to catch the crabs and baitfish, ensnare themselves, and drown because they cannot reach the surface to breathe.

TORTOISES

Tortoises are any member of the turtle family Testudinidae. Formerly, the term *tortoise* was used to refer to any terrestrial turtle. The testudinids are easily recognized because all share a unique hind-limb anatomy made up of elephantine (or cylindrical) hind limbs and hind feet; each digit in their forefeet and hind feet contains two or fewer phalanges. With the exception of the pancake tortoise (*Malacochersus tornieri*), the shell is

Leopard tortoise (Geochelone pardalis). © Digital Vision/Getty Images

high-domed. Shells of some species are nearly spherical with a flattened base.

Tortoises are exclusively terrestrial and occur on all continents except Australia and Antarctica. They also inhabit many islands, although numerous island populations and species are now extinct because of human occupation. There are at least 15 genera of living tortoises; one genus, *Geochelone*, is distributed from South America to Africa and Asia. There are about 49 species of tortoises, and they range in size from the padlopers (*Homopus*) of southern Africa, with shell lengths of 10 to 15 cm (4 to 6 inches), to the giant tortoises (*Geochelone*) of the Aldabra and Galapagos islands, with shells over 1 metre (3.3 feet) long. Tortoises live in a variety of habitats, from deserts to wet tropical forests. Most tortoises are vegetarians and eat foliage, flowers, and fruits; some tortoise species from moist forest habitats are more opportunistic and consume animal matter.

Copulation can be a precarious issue for male tortoises, because they must balance themselves on the high-domed shell of females to fertilize them. The majority of tortoise species lay small clutches of eggs, typically fewer than 20, and many small-bodied species lay fewer than five. Even though tortoises possess columnar hind limbs and stubby hind feet, they dig their nests with alternating scooping movements of their hind limbs, like most other turtles.

WOOD TURTLES

The wood turtle (*Clemmys insculpta*), a woodland streamside turtle of the family Emydidae, is found from Nova Scotia through the northeastern and north-central United States. The rough upper shell of the wood turtle is about 15–20 cm (6–8 inches) long and bears concentrically grooved pyramids on each of the large plates (scutes). The upper shell is brown, and the neck and legs are reddish.

The wood turtle is semiaquatic and hibernates in late fall in stream banks or other areas adjacent to streams. It mates and often forages in streams during late winter and early spring. As summer approaches, both females and males become largely terrestrial and seek their food—fruits and berries, small invertebrates, eggs, and carrion—in the stream's floodplain and adjacent uplands. Female wood turtles lay between 3 and 18 eggs in a clutch during the middle of spring, and hatchlings emerge about 60 to 70 days later.

CHAPTER 8
AMPHIBIANS

Members of the group of vertebrate animals characterized by their ability to exploit both aquatic and terrestrial habitats are called amphibians. The name *amphibian*, derived from the Greek *amphibios* meaning "living a double life," reflects this dual life strategy—though some species are permanent land dwellers, while other species have a completely aquatic mode of existence.

More than 6,500 species of living amphibians are known. First appearing about 340 million years ago during the Middle Mississippian Epoch, they were one of the earliest groups to diverge from ancestral fish-tetrapod stock during the evolution of animals from strictly aquatic forms to terrestrial types. Today amphibians are represented by frogs and toads (order Anura), newts and salamanders (order Caudata), and caecilians (order Gymnophiona). These three orders of living amphibians are thought to derive from a single radiation of ancient amphibians, and although strikingly different in body form, they are probably the closest relatives to one another.

As a group, the three orders make up subclass Lissamphibia. Neither the lissamphibians nor any of the extinct groups of amphibians were the ancestors of the group of tetrapods that gave rise to reptiles. Though some aspects of the biology and anatomy of the various amphibian groups might demonstrate features possessed by reptilian ancestors, amphibians are not the intermediate step in the evolution of reptiles from fishes.

Salamander (Salamandra terrestris). Jacques Six

Modern amphibians are united by several unique traits. They typically have a moist skin and rely heavily on cutaneous (skin-surface) respiration. They possess a double-channeled hearing system, green rods in their retinas to discriminate hues, and pedicellate (two-part) teeth. Some of these traits may have also existed in extinct groups.

Members of the three extant orders differ markedly in their structural appearance. Frogs and toads are tailless and somewhat squat with long, powerful hind limbs modified for leaping. In contrast, caecilians are limbless, wormlike, and highly adapted for a burrowing existence. Salamanders and newts have tails and two pairs of limbs of roughly the same size; however, they are somewhat less specialized in body form than the other two orders.

Many amphibians are obligate breeders in standing water. Eggs are laid in water, and the developing larvae are

Green frog (Rana clamitans melanota). Norman R. Lightfoot/Photo Researchers

essentially free-living embryos; they must find their own food, escape predators, and perform other life functions while they continue to develop. As the larvae complete their embryonic development, they adopt an adult body plan that allows them to leave aquatic habitats for terrestrial ones. Even though this metamorphosis from aquatic to terrestrial life occurs in members of all three amphibian groups, there are many variants, and some taxa bear their young alive. Indeed, the roughly 6,200 living species of amphibians display more evolutionary experiments in reproductive mode than any other vertebrate group. Some taxa have aquatic eggs and larvae, whereas others embed their eggs in the skin on the back of the female; these eggs hatch as tadpoles or miniature frogs. In other groups, the young develop within the oviduct, with the embryos feeding on the wall of the oviduct. In some species, eggs develop within the female's stomach.

Olympic torrent salamander (Rhyacotriton olympicus). U.S. Fish and Wildlife Service

GENERAL FEATURES OF AMPHIBIANS

The three living orders of amphibians vary greatly in size and structure. The presence of a long tail and two pairs of limbs of about equal size distinguishes newts and salamanders (order Caudata) from other amphibians, although members of the eel-like family Sirenidae have no hind limbs. Newts and salamanders vary greatly in length; members of the Mexican genus *Thorius* measure 25 to 30 mm (1 to 1.2 inches), whereas *Andrias*, a genus of giant aquatic salamanders endemic to China and Japan, reaches a length of more than 1.5 metres (5 feet).

Frogs and toads (order Anura) are easily identified by their long hind limbs and the absence of a tail. They have only five to nine presacral vertebrae. The West

African goliath frog, which can reach 30 cm (12 inches) from snout to vent and weigh up to 3.3 kg (7.3 pounds), is the largest anuran. Some of the smallest anurans include the South American brachycephalids, which have an adult snout-to-vent length of only 9.8 mm (0.4 inch), and some microhylids, which grow to 9 to 12 mm (0.4 to 0.5 inch) as adults. The long, slender, limbless caecilians (order Gymnophiona) are animals that have adapted to fossorial (burrowing) lifestyles by evolving a body segmented by annular grooves and a short, blunt tail. Caecilians can grow to more than 1 metre (3 feet) long. The largest species, *Caecilia thompsoni*, reaches a length of 1.5 metres (5 feet), whereas the smallest species, *Idiocranium russeli*, is only 90 to 114 mm (3.5 to 5 inches) long.

Amphibians occur widely throughout the world, even edging north of the Arctic circle in Eurasia; they are absent only in Antarctica, most remote oceanic islands, and extremely xeric (dry) deserts. Frogs and toads show the greatest diversity in humid tropical environments. Salamanders primarily inhabit the Northern Hemisphere and are most abundant in cool, moist, montane forests; however, members of the family Plethodontidae, the lungless salamanders, are diverse in the humid tropical montane forests of Mexico, Central America, and northwestern South America. Caecilians are found spottily throughout the African, American, and Asian wet tropics.

For many years, habitat destruction has had a severe impact on the distribution and abundance of numerous amphibian species. Since the 1980s, a severe decline in the populations of many frog species has been observed. Although acid rain, global warming, and ozone depletion are contributing factors to these

AMPHIBIAN CHYTRIDIOMYCOSIS

Amphibian chytridiomycosis is a disease affecting amphibians, especially frogs, caused by the fungus *Batrachochytrium dendrobatidis*. *B. dendrobatidis*, known among herpetologists as the amphibian chytrid or simply Bd, has been implicated in the extinction or population decline of many amphibians around the world. The fungus was formally described in 1999 after it was isolated from infected captive poison frogs (such as the South American poison-arrow frog, *Dendrobates auratus*). It was the first chytridiomycete fungus known to infect vertebrates—its closest relatives being saprophytic fungi (that is, fungi that live off of dead matter) and other fungi that infect algae, plants, and invertebrates. At present, the disease is pandemic, and the fungus is regarded as an exotic or invasive species in most areas.

Some evidence suggests that Bd originated in populations of platanna (*Xenopus laevis*), an African clawed-frog species widely used in biological research; however, this evidence remains inconclusive. It is thought that the disease was first transferred to natural amphibian populations through introductions of infected *Xenopus*, but other species and modes of transmission (such as the pet trade, the food trade, and other human activities) also exist.

Although humans likely cause the long-distance movement of Bd, once it has been introduced to an area, it spreads rapidly between amphibians by means of free-swimming infectious reproductive cells called zoospores. Once a zoospore has encountered a potential host, it encysts upon the surface of the skin and penetrates one of the host's epidermal cells. Then the zoospore grows into a mature thallus that ultimately releases 40–100 zoospores over its 4–5-day life cycle. In species where Bd is highly pathogenic, as in those belonging to the genus *Atelopus*, the infection may cover most of the epidermis. As the skin degrades, gas exchange with the environment and electrolyte balance are disrupted. The infected animals eventually succumb to cardiac arrest due to significant reductions in sodium and potassium concentrations in their blood plasma.

Bd has become a global threat to amphibian biodiversity. According to published reports, it has infected members of well over one hundred species. (Most authorities argue that this figure is likely a gross underestimate.) The International Union for Conservation of Nature (IUCN) has declared only 35 amphibian species as formally extinct since 1500 CE; however, some 130 additional species are presumed to have gone extinct in the wild since 1980. Many of these modern extinctions have been attributed to Bd. Since most documented population declines and extinctions have occurred in either temperate or tropical montane regions, Bd is thought to survive and grow best under cool, moist conditions. In addition, it has appeared in habitats ranging from rainforest to desert, and it is present on all continents except Antarctica.

At local scales, Bd can have devastating effects on amphibian communities. For example, in El Cope, Pan.—where Bd has been conclusively shown to infect local amphibian species—the disease occurred in 52 of the 70 described amphibian species in the area and caused a 90 percent reduction in overall amphibian density. Many experts suspect that Bd is at the root of similar damage at many other sites (such as Monteverde, C. Rica, and the rainforests of Queensland, Austl.), though it has not been proved to be the cause.

reductions, a full explanation of the disappearance in diverse environment remains uncertain. A parasitic fungus, the so-called amphibian chytrid (*Batrachochytrium dendrobatidis*), however, appears to be a major cause of substantial frog die-offs in parts of Australia and southern Central America and milder events in North America and Europe.

ECONOMIC IMPORTANCE

Amphibians, especially anurans, are economically useful in reducing the number of insects that destroy crops or transmit diseases. Frogs are exploited as food, both for local consumption and commercially for export, with thousands of tons of frog legs harvested annually. The skin secretions of various tropical anurans are known to have hallucinogenic effects and effects on the central nervous and respiratory systems in humans. Some secretions have been found to contain magainin, a substance that provides a natural antibiotic effect. Other skin secretions, especially toxins, have potential use as anesthetics and painkillers. Biochemists are currently investigating these substances for medicinal use.

CHAPTER 9
FROGS AND TOADS

Frogs and toads make up the order Anura, which is also called Salientia, one of the major extant orders of the class Amphibia. Because of their wide distribution, frogs and toads are known by most people around the world. The name *frog* is commonly applied to those forms with long legs and smooth, mucus-covered skins, *toad* being used for a variety of robust, short-legged anurans, especially those with rough skins. The name *toad* is applied so unevenly that one member of a family may be called a toad and a closely related member a frog. The familiar members of the family Bufonidae may be distinguished as "true toads." There are roughly 5,400 species of living anurans.

Painted reed frogs (Hyperolius viridiflavus). © Digital Vision/ Getty Images

Frogs are used as teaching tools from grade school through college. One of the first biology lessons many children receive is through the rearing of the larvae, known as tadpoles or pollywogs, in science classes. Students become familiar with frog anatomy and embryology in biology courses. People in various parts of the world eat frog legs, and some kinds of toads are used in insect control. Certain South American Indians use the poisonous secretions of some kinds of frogs for poison arrows and darts , and now biochemists are studying the possible medical uses of the constituents of the poison. The biologist interested in evolution finds a vast array of interesting and often perplexing problems in the study of frogs, such as the relatively sudden decline of many frog species since the late 20th century.

SIZE RANGE AND DIVERSITY OF STRUCTURE

Although all frogs are readily recognizable, there are great varieties of sizes and of structural modifications. Many frogs are tiny animals; perhaps the smallest is the Brazilian *Psyllophryne didactyla*, adults of which measure 9.8 mm (0.4 inch) or less in body length (with legs drawn in), whereas the West African goliath frog, *Conraua goliath*, has a body length of nearly 300 mm (12 inches). Many anurans have smooth, moist skins. Toads of the genus *Bufo* are familiar as "warty" amphibians, the skin being highly glandular and covered with tubercles (small, round nodules). Frogs of many other families have rough, tubercular skins, usually an adaptation for life in the less humid environments. The opposite extreme is found in the small arboreal (tree-dwelling) frogs of the tropical American family Centrolenidae, in which the skin on the underside is thin and transparent, and the heart and viscera can be seen through the skin. In most species, cutaneous gas exchange (that is, breathing through the skin) supplements the oxygen taken in by the lungs; however, the lungless *Barbourula kalimantanensis* of Borneo obtains all its oxygen through its skin.

Most frogs move by leaping. The long and powerful hind limbs are straightened rapidly from the crouching position, propelling the frog through the air. Many arboreal frogs—especially members of the families Hylidae, Rhacophoridae, Centrolenidae, and others—have adhesive disks on the ends of the fingers and toes and leap from branch to branch or from leaf to leaf. The families Bufonidae, Rhinophrynidae, and Microhylidae and certain burrowing species in other families have relatively short hind limbs and move forward by series of short hops. Some bufonids actually walk instead of hopping. Highly modified members of the hylid subfamily Phyllomedusinae have opposable digits on the hands and feet and walk slowly along branches, deliberately grasping the branch in the manner of tiny lemurs. Many kinds of frogs have membranous webbing between the fingers and toes; in the aquatic species, the webbing on the feet aids in swimming. The extreme in this specialization is seen in the aquatic family Pipidae. Members of that family normally never leave the water. In regions of the Earth subjected to long dry periods, frogs must seek cover to avoid desiccation; they have behavioral and structural adaptations to conserve water.

Although many frogs are unimpressively coloured, some species are brilliantly marked. The most common colours are brown, gray, green, and yellow. Uniformly coloured frogs are the exception rather than the rule. The markings of a frog may seem bold when observed

out of the natural habitat, but they usually are con-
cealing or visually disruptive when the frog is in its
environment .

DISTRIBUTION AND ABUNDANCE

Because of their morphological and physiological adaptations, frogs are able to inhabit most regions of the world
except the extremely cold landmasses at high latitudes
and some oceanic islands that they have been unable to
colonize because of the barriers provided by salt water.
Frogs live in desert regions below sea level and in montane areas up to elevations above 4,560 metres (15,000
feet). Some members of the genus *Rana* live north of the
Arctic Circle. Although widely distributed on Earth,
frogs are most diverse and abundant in the tropics, and
five or six of the 28 families are restricted to the tropics.
In most temperate areas of the world, the number of species of frogs at any one locality is usually fewer than 10,
but in the tropics, especially in rainforests, the number
of species is much greater. At one locality in the upper
Amazon basin in eastern Ecuador, 83 species are known
to occur, about the same number as is known for all of the
United States.

In a complex environment such as a tropical rainforest, the large number of species of frogs partition
the environmental resources in a variety of ways. In the
humid tropics, frogs can be active throughout the year,
but many species are seasonal in their breeding activity. Various kinds of sites and different seasons are used
for calling and egg laying; such temporal and spatial
separation avoids interspecific competition. Frogs feed
mostly on insects and other invertebrates, and the abundance of food in tropical rainforests probably places no

competitive restrictions on this aspect of environmental resources. Some large species eat vertebrates, including small rodents and other frogs.

BREEDING BEHAVIOUR AND REPRODUCTION

The breeding behaviour is one of the most distinctive attributes of the Anura. Because the eggs can develop only under moist conditions, most frogs place their eggs in bodies of fresh water. Many species congregate in large numbers at temporary pools for short breeding seasons. Others breed along the mountain streams where they live year-round. In the latter species and in those that breed on land, there is no great concentration of breeding individuals at one place.

In all cases, the mating call produced by the male attracts females to the breeding site. It has been observed in the field and in the laboratory that the females can discriminate between mating calls of their own species and those of other species. At a communal breeding site, such as a pond, swamp, or stream, differences in specific calling sites of the males help the frogs to maintain their identities. Differences in mating calls, however, constitute the principal premating isolating mechanism that prevents hybridization of closely related species living in the same area and breeding at the same time and place. Frogs have rather simple vocal cords, in most species a pair of slits in the floor of the mouth opening into a vocal pouch. Air is forced from the lungs over the vocal cords, causing them to vibrate and thus produce sound of a given pitch and pulsation. The air passes into the vocal pouch, which, when inflated, acts as a resonating chamber emphasizing the same frequency or one of its harmonics. In this manner, different kinds of frogs produce different calls.

Most frogs are considered to be placid animals, but recent observations have shown that some species exhibit aggressive behaviours, especially at breeding time. Male bullfrogs (*Lithobates catesbeianus*) and green frogs (*Rana clamitans*) defend calling territories against intrusion by other males by kicking, bumping, and biting. The South American nest-building hylid, *Hyla faber*, has a long, sharp spine on the thumb with which males wound each other when wrestling. The small Central American *Dendrobates pumilio* calls from the leaves of herbaceous plants. Intrusion into a territory of one calling male by another results in a wrestling match that terminates only after one male has been thrown off the leaf. Males of the Central American dendrobatid *Colostethus inguinalis* have calling sites on boulders in streams. The intrusion by another male results in the resident uttering a territorial call, and, if the intruder does not leave, the resident charges him, attempting to butt him off the boulder. Females of the Venezuelan *C. trinitatus* wrestle in defense of territories in streambeds.

Females move toward and locate calling males. Once the male clasps the female in a copulatory embrace called amplexus, she selects the site for depositing the eggs. In the more primitive frogs (the families Ascaphidae, Leiopelmatidae, Bombinatoridae, and Discoglossidae and the mesobatrachians), the male grasps the female from above and around the waist (inguinal amplexus), whereas in the more advanced frogs (neobatrachians) the position is shifted anteriorly to the armpits (axillary amplexus). The latter position brings the cloacae of the amplectic pair into closer proximity and presumably ensures more efficient fertilization.

EGG LAYING AND HATCHING

Most frogs deposit their eggs in quiet water as clumps, surface films, strings, or individual eggs. The eggs may be freely suspended in the water or attached to sticks or submerged vegetation. Some frogs lay their eggs in streams, characteristically firmly attached to the lee sides or undersides of rocks where the eggs are not subject to the current. The large pond-breeding frogs of the genus *Rana* and toads of the genus *Bufo* apparently produce more eggs than any other anurans. More than 10,000 eggs have been estimated in one clutch of the North American bullfrog, *L. catesbeianus*. The habit of spreading the eggs as a film on the surface of the water apparently is an adaptation for oviposition in shallow temporary pools and allows the eggs to develop in the most highly oxygenated part of the pool. This type of egg deposition is characteristic of several

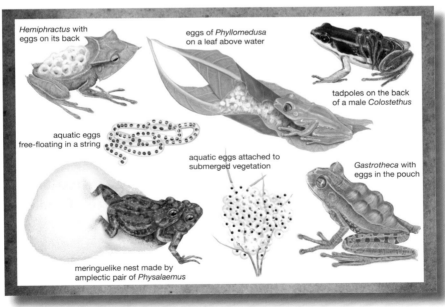

Anuran breeding specializations. Encyclopædia Britannica, Inc.

groups of tree frogs, family Hylidae, in the American tropics—one of which, *Smilisca baudinii*, is known to lay more than three thousand eggs. Frogs breeding in cascading mountain streams lay far fewer eggs, usually no more than two hundred.

The problem of fertilization of eggs in rapidly flowing water has been overcome by various modifications. Some stream-breeding hylids have long cloacal tubes so that the semen can be directed onto the eggs as they emerge. Some other hylids have huge testes, which apparently produce vast quantities of sperm, helping to ensure fertilization. Males of the North American tailed frog, *Ascaphus truei*, have an extension of the cloaca that functions as a copulatory organ (the "tail") to introduce sperm into the female's cloaca.

Males of at least three South American species of *Hyla* build basinlike nests, 25 to 30 cm (10 to 12 inches) wide and 2 to 5 cm (1 to 2 inches) deep, in the mud of riverbanks. Water seeps into the basin, providing a medium for the eggs and young. Calling, mating, and oviposition take place in the nest, and the tadpoles undergo their development in the nest.

Some bufonoid frogs in Leptodactylidae and ranoid frogs in Ranidae and other families build froth nests. The small, toadlike leptodactylids of the genus *Physalaemus* breed in small, shallow pools. Amplexus is axillary, and the pair floats on the water; as the female exudes the eggs, the male emits semen and kicks vigorously with his hind legs. The result is a frothy mixture of water, air, eggs, and semen, which floats on the water. This meringuelike nest is about 7.5 to 10 cm (3 to 4 inches) in diameter and about 5 cm (2 inches) deep. The outer surfaces exposed to the air harden and form a crust covering the moist interior in which the eggs are randomly distributed. Upon hatching, the tadpoles wriggle down through the decaying froth into the water.

VOCAL SAC

The vocal sac is the sound-resonating throat pouch of male frogs and toads (amphibians of the order Anura). Vocal sacs are outpocketings of the floor of the mouth, or buccal cavity. Frogs display three basic types of vocal sacs: a single median throat sac, paired throat sacs, and paired lateral sacs. (Lateral sacs are located just rearward of the angle of the jaw on each side of the head.) All three types, whether single or paired, open into the buccal cavity by paired slits. Each slit is located on either side of the base of the tongue.

A calling frog typically inflates his sac or sacs prior to calling or simultaneously with the production of the first call. The sac is inflated with air from the lungs. If another call is forthcoming and the male frog is not in the process of calling, air is still held in the sac. Sound is produced by a controlled rush of air through the larynx and across its vocal cords. The resulting sound vibrations are amplified by the resonating qualities of the vocal sac or sacs. Unlike vocalization processes of many other vertebrates, frogs broadcast sound without expelling air. Air does not exit the mouth; rather, it cycles back and forth between the buccal cavity and lungs.

FROM TADPOLE TO ADULT

Many frogs have an aquatic, free-swimming larval stage (tadpole). After a period of growth, the tadpole, also called polliwog, undergoes metamorphosis, in which the tail is lost and limbs appear. These are only two of the most obvious changes that take place. Tadpoles have a cartilaginous skeleton, thin nonglandular skin, and a long coiled intestine; they lack jaws, lungs, and eyelids.

Among the first changes that take place is the appearance of hind limb buds, which grow and develop into differentiated hind limbs, complete with toes, webbing, and tubercles (small, round nodules). Much later the forelimbs emerge through the skin of the operculum (gill covering), and the tail begins to shrink, being absorbed by the body. The mouth of the tadpole begins to change. As the horny denticles (toothlike projections) and papillae, if present, disappear, the jaws and true teeth develop. The eyelids develop, and mucous glands form in the skin. The vertebral column and limb bones ossify, and the adult digestive system differentiates as the long coiled intestine shrinks to the short, thick-walled, folded intestine of the adult.

Upon completion of metamorphosis, the tadpole emerges onto land as a young froglet or toadlet. The tadpole stage can be as short as two weeks or as long as three years. For most species the tadpole stage lasts from one to three months.

Just how and where the changes from larva to adult take place are highly varied—a fascinating aspect of the study of frogs. The differences in modes of life history reflect varied environmental conditions. In various evolutionary lines in frogs, there is a strong propensity to breed away from water.

The tadpoles of the pond breeders characteristically have rather large bodies and deep caudal (tail) fins, which in some have a terminal extension, as do the familiar swordtail fishes (*Xiphophorus*). The mouth is relatively small, either at the end of the snout or on the underside, and usually contains rather weak denticles. These tadpoles swim easily in the quiet water and feed on attached and free-floating vegetation, including algae.

In contrast, stream tadpoles have depressed bodies, long muscular tails, and shallow caudal fins. The mouth is relatively large and usually contains many rows of strong denticles. In highly modified stream tadpoles, the mouth is ventral and modified as an oral sucker, with which the tadpole anchors itself to stones in the stream. Such tadpoles move slowly across stones, grazing on the coating of bacteria and algae as they move.

Most tadpoles complete their development in two or three months, but there are notable exceptions. Tadpoles of spadefoot toads, genus *Scaphiopus*, develop in temporary rain pools in arid parts of North America, where it is imperative for the tadpoles to complete their development before the pools dry up. Some *Scaphiopus* tadpoles metamorphose about two weeks after hatching. In the northern part of its range in North America, the tadpoles of the bullfrog *L. catesbeianus* require three years to undergo their development.

Some tree frogs of the family Hylidae deposit their eggs in water that has pooled in parts of trees. Several tropical species of *Hyla* lay their eggs in the water held in the overlapping bases of leaves of epiphytic bromeliads high in trees. Their tadpoles, which are slender with long, muscular tails, develop in small quantities of water high above the ground. The Mexican hylid, *Anotheca spinosa*, lays its eggs in bromeliads or in water-filled cavities in trees. The small tadpoles, like those of *Hyla*, feed on aquatic insect larvae, such as those of mosquitoes, but the larger tadpoles of *Anotheca* apparently feed only on the eggs of frogs.

A modification of the basic pattern of depositing aquatic eggs is the placement of eggs on vegetation above water. This pattern occurs in some arboreal hylids, rhacophorids, ranids, and all species of the family Centrolenidae. *H. ebraccata*, a small Central American tree frog, deposits its eggs in a single layer on the upper surfaces of horizontal leaves, just a few inches above the pond. Upon hatching, the tadpoles wriggle to the edge of the leaf and drop into the water. The Mexican *H. thorectes* suspends 10 to 14 eggs on ferns overhanging cascading mountain streams. The phyllomedusine hylids in the American tropics suspend clutches of eggs from leaves or stems above ponds. Males call from trees. Once a female has been attracted and amplexus takes place, the male placidly hangs onto the back of the female as she descends to the pond and absorbs water. This accomplished, she climbs into a tree, selects an oviposition site, and deposits eggs until her water supply is depleted. She again descends to the pond and repeats the performance at a different site until the entire complement of eggs is deposited. Upon hatching, the tadpoles drop into the pond below.

Most of the tree frogs of the family Centrolenidae are less than 2.5 cm (1 inch) long. Males call from leaves of trees or bushes over cascading mountain streams in the American tropics. Individuals return to the same leaf night after night. Attracted females are clasped on the leaf, and egg deposition takes place there immediately. A highly successful male may have three or four egg clutches on his leaf, each consisting of only about two dozen eggs. Upon hatching, the tadpoles drop into the streambed. If a tadpole lands on a stone, it flips about vigorously until it falls into the water, where it hides in the loose gravel on the bottom of the stream.

EGG LAYING ON LAND

Many kinds of frogs lay their eggs on land and subsequently transport the tadpoles to water. The ranid genus *Sooglossus* of the Seychelles islands and all members of the family Dendrobatidae in the American tropics have terrestrial eggs. Upon hatching, the tadpoles adhere to the backs of adults, usually males. The exact means of attachment is not known. The frogs carry the tadpoles to streams, bromeliads, or pools of water in logs or stumps where the tadpoles complete their development. The most unusual example of tadpole care is exhibited by the mouth-brooding frog, or Darwin's frog, *Rhinoderma darwinii*, in southern South America. An amplectic pair deposits 20 to 30 eggs on moist ground. When the eggs are about ready to hatch, with the embryos moving, the male picks up some eggs with his tongue. The eggs pass through the vocal slits in the floor of his mouth and into the vocal sac. The eggs hatch, and the larvae complete their development in the large vocal sac. Upon metamorphosis the young frogs emerge from the male's mouth.

The European midwife toad, *Alytes obstetricans*, also displays a curious breeding behaviour. Inguinal amplexus takes place on land; at the time of oviposition, the female extends her legs to form a receptacle for the string of 20 to 60 eggs. After fertilizing the eggs, the male moves forward on the back of the female and pushes his legs into the string of eggs until they are wound around his waist and legs. Then the female departs. The male carries the eggs with him on land until they are ready to hatch, at which time he moves to a pond where the eggs hatch and complete their development.

The hylid *Gastrotheca marsupiata*, one of several so-called marsupial frogs, lives in the high Andes of South America. During amplexus, the male exudes a quantity of semen, which flows into the female's pouch. The female extrudes eggs a few at a time; these are pushed into her pouch by the male, who uses the hindfeet to catch and push the eggs. The eggs are fertilized in the pouch, where they hatch and the tadpoles begin their development. Subsequently the female moves to a pond, where the tadpoles emerge from the pouch and complete their development in the water.

In each of the above instances of parental care, there is a trend away from the aquatic environment. Far fewer eggs (fewer than 50) are laid in comparison with those species depositing eggs in the water. The bonds with the aquatic environment have been partially broken, for, although the tadpoles must develop there, the eggs are effectively terrestrial; however, they are not truly so, because they lack the necessary embryonic membranes (allantois and amnion) to maintain physiological balance, and they also have no shell. Consequently, if they are to survive and develop, the eggs must be maintained in moist places, such as damp soil or a part of the parental body. Water and waste products are transported through the membranes by osmosis.

DIRECT DEVELOPMENT FROM EGG TO FROGLET

The next evolutionary step in mode of life history is the elimination of the larval stage, thereby completely severing the ties with the aquatic environment. Direct development of the egg, in which the larvae undergo their development within the egg membranes and emerge as tiny froglets, occurs in many species, in a dozen or more families (such as Leiopelmatidae, Pipidae, Leptodactylidae, Bufonidae, Brachycephalidae, Hylidae, Myobatrachidae, Sooglossidae, Arthroleptidae, Ranidae, and Microhylidae). Typical direct development of terrestrial eggs occurs in the many species of the leptodactylid genus *Eleutherodactylus* of Central and South America and the West Indies. During axillary amplexus, the female deposits a clutch of eggs in a moist place (beneath a log or stone, amid leaf litter, in a rotting stump, in moss, or in a bromeliad). The parents depart, leaving the eggs to develop and subsequently hatch. In some *Eleutherodactylus* species and in the New Zealand leiopelmatid *Leiopelma hochstetteri*, the hatching froglet still has a tail. In *Leiopelma*, at least, vigorous thrusts of the tail are used to rupture the egg membranes. Soon after hatching, the tail is completely absorbed.

Brooding of terrestrial eggs is known in a few species. Females of two species of *Eleutherodactylus* that lay their eggs on leaves of bushes or trees sit on the eggs. Apparently this brooding serves to prevent desiccation of the eggs by dry winds. Females of the Papuan microhylid *Sphenophryne* lay their few eggs beneath stones or logs and sit on top of them until they hatch.

Direct development occurs in several species of hylid marsupial frogs (*Gastrotheca*) living in mountain rainforests in northwestern South America. In these frogs, amplexus is axillary, and the female raises her cloaca so that the eggs, which are extruded one at a time, roll forward on her back and into the pouch. There the eggs develop into froglets. Large, external, gill-like structures envelop the developing embryo. These structures, which are attached to the throat of the embryo by a pair of cords, apparently function in respiration. These frogs live high in trees and complete their life cycle without descending to the ground. Thus, they are rare in collections, and their biology is poorly known.

Some other South American genera of Hylidae also exhibit the phenomenon of direct development of eggs carried on the backs of the females. In *Flectonotus* and *Fritziana* the eggs are contained in one large basinlike depression in the back, whereas in other genera, such as the Surinam toad (*Pipa pipa*) and its relatives, each egg occupies its own individual depression. In *Hemiphractus* gill-like structures and cords similar to those in *Gastrotheca* are present. At hatching, the expanded gill adheres to the modified skin of the maternal depression and is attached to the young by the pair of cords. The female carries the young until they are sufficiently well developed to care for themselves. The manner of detachment of gill from female and young is unknown.

The strictly aquatic *P. pipa* of northern South America has direct development, in this case in the water. Amplexus is inguinal, and the pair rests on the bottom of the pond. The female initiates vertical circular turnovers, at the height of which she extrudes a few eggs. These are fertilized, fall against the belly of the then upside-down male, and are pushed forward onto the female's back, where they adhere and become enclosed in tissue. When developed, the young frogs emerge from the skin of the female's back.

The small African bufonids of the genus *Nectophrynoides* undergo internal uterine development in a fashion that is apparently similar to that of placental mammals. By some unknown means, fertilization is internal, and the young are born alive. It is noteworthy that the evolution of live birth has taken place independently in all three living orders of amphibians, for this phenomenon also occurs in salamanders and caecilians.

FEEDING HABITS

The great majority of frogs feed on insects, other small arthropods, or worms, but some larger species eat vertebrates. The South American leptodactylid *Ceratophrys varius* and the large bufonid *B. marinus* eat other frogs and small rodents. The superficially similar Solomon Island ranid, *Ceratobatrachus guentheri*, and the South American hylids, *Hemiphractus*, eat other frogs. Large North American bullfrogs, *L. catesbeianus*, have been reported to consume other frogs, mice, small snakes, and even small turtles.

FORM AND FUNCTION

Adult anurans are easily recognized, by the layperson and specialist alike, by the short body and elongated hind limbs, the absence of a visible neck, and the absence of a tail. The compact body has been attained by a reduction of the number of trunk vertebrae and the fusion of tail vertebrae into a single rodlike bone, the coccyx, or urostyle (tail support). The lengthening of the hind limbs has been attained in part by the elongation of two bones (astragalus and calcaneum) in the foot. Considering the variety of habitats occupied by anurans, there is remarkably little gross variation in body plan. The female is usually larger than the male. In most frogs the tympanic membrane is visible as a prominent disk on each side of the head. Correlated with a sound-oriented existence, the larynx is also well developed, often accompanied by single or paired inflatable resonating sacs.

SKIN TOXINS

All frogs have poison glands in the skin, well developed in many diverse groups. In the Dendrobatidae the skin

Arrow-poison frog (genus Dendrobates*).* Joseph T. Collins, Museum of Natural History, University of Kansas

secretions are especially toxic. *Dendrobates* and *Phyllobates* are small, diurnal frogs living in Central and South America that are brilliantly coloured solid red, yellow, or orange or patterned with bold stripes or crossbars. These bright patterns are believed to act as warning colours to ward off predators. One nonpoisonous South American leptodactylid, *Lithodytes lineatus*, mimics the dendrobatid *P. femoralis*, thus gaining protection from predators.

The biochemical properties of amphibian skin toxins are highly varied, most being complex nitrogenous compounds. The toxically active ingredients are of various types, from local irritants to convulsants, hallucinogens, neurotoxins (nerve poisons), and vasoconstrictors (acting to narrow blood vessels). The medical importance of these ingredients is now being investigated. Although these skin secretions irritate human skin and mucous membranes, they do not cause warts.

Coloration

The skin toxins of most frogs do not provide security from predators. In fact, frogs are a basic food for many snakes, birds, and mammals. Edible anurans rely on modifications of shape, skin texture, and colour, supplemented by behaviour, to escape detection. These modifications may reach remarkable extremes. Hylids of the South American genus *Hemiphractus* live on the forest floor among leaf litter and have flattened bodies that enable them to blend well with dead leaves. Several tree frogs, rough-skinned and greenish gray, resemble lichens when flattened out on tree trunks. The coloration of many frogs changes from night to day. In most species the colour is darker and the pattern more distinct by day than by night, but the reverse is true for some tree frogs that inhabit semiarid regions. Colour change is brought about through the stimuli of light and moisture, which create a physiological change and result in contraction or expansion of the melanophores (pigment cells) in the skin.

More difficult to comprehend is the striking array of colours on the hidden surfaces of frogs. Many frogs that are rather dull or uniformly coloured when in a resting position have bright colours or patterns on the flanks, groin, posterior surfaces of the thighs, and belly. For example, the South and Central American hylid *Agalychnis calcarifer*, when observed sleeping by day, is nothing more than a green bump on a leaf. The eyes are closed, the hind limbs drawn in close to the body, and the hands folded beneath the chin. Upon moving, the frog creates a striking appearance, previously hidden surfaces showing a deep golden orange interrupted by vertical black bars on the flanks and thighs. These so-called flash colours are common in frogs and are thought to serve in species recognition or in confusing predators. Some colour patterns obviously do confuse predators. The South American leptodactylids of the genus *Eupsophus* have a pair of brightly coloured "eyespots" on the rump. When approached by a potential predator, the frog lowers its head and elevates the rump, thus confronting the predator with a seemingly much larger head.

STRUCTURAL MODIFICATIONS

Structural modifications allow certain specialized frogs to survive dry periods. Some arboreal frogs hide in bromeliad plants, which hold water in the axils of their leaves. Among the Hylidae are genera that have the head modified into a bony casque ("helmet") and the skin co-ossified with the underlying bone. The head is used by some species to plug the constricted base of the bromeliads and by others to plug up holes in trees, the frogs surviving the dry season by using what little moisture is trapped in the cavity.

Most toads of the genus *Bufo* and many genera in the families Rhinophrynidae, Pelobatidae, Myobatrachidae, Leptodactylidae, Hylidae, Ranidae, and Microhylidae burrow in sand, soil, or mud. Many of these species have the tubercles (small, round nodules) on the middle (metatarsal) part of each foot, modified into a spade-shaped digging organ. The animals are highly resistant to desiccation and conserve water in the body by the mucous skin secretions that tend to make the skin impermeable. This modification is carried to the extreme in some desert frogs, which secrete a cocoon formed of numerous layers of hardened molted skin.

CHAPTER 10
TYPES OF ANURANS

Frogs and toads are divided into three groups. The first group contains a sampling of familiar species, whereas the second group is a collection of species that possess unusual physical or behavioral characteristics. The third group highlights species whose toxins are dangerous to humans.

FAMILIAR SPECIES

A number of species of frogs and toads are familiar to people in temperate environments. Many of these species, such as the bullfrog, common frog, and wood frog, are well known because they are distributed across whole continents.

BULLFROGS

Bullfrogs (*Lithobates catesbeianus*) are semi-aquatic frogs in family Ranidae named for their loud call. This largest North American frog, native to the eastern United States and Canada, has been introduced into the western United States and into other countries. The name is also applied to other large frogs, such as *Pyxicephalus adspersus* in Africa, *Rana tigerina* in India, and certain of the Leptodactylidae of South America.

The bullfrog's coloration ranges from green to olive or brown with a white to yellowish belly and dark-barred legs. Body length is to about 20 cm (8 inches); hind legs to 25 cm (10 inches). Large adults weigh 0.5 kg (1 pound) or more. Bullfrogs usually live in or near bodies of still water. They

Bullfrog (Lithobates catesbeianus*)*. Photos.com/Jupiterimages

breed in early summer; the eggs are laid in water and hatch into dark-spotted greenish brown tadpoles. Depending on climate, the tadpole stage lasts one to three years. Many bullfrogs are caught for food.

CHORUS FROGS

Chorus frogs (*Pseudacris*), which are also called swamp tree frogs or swamp cricket frogs, constitute several species of tree frogs belonging to the family Hylidae. Chorus frogs are found in North America from Canada to the southern United States and the northern reaches of Mexico. They are predominantly terrestrial and live in thick herbaceous vegetation and low shrubbery. They are not as adept at climbing as are most other hylids.

Chorus frogs typically have a trilling call and a light streak on the upper lip. Most species are about 2.5 to 3 cm (1 to 1⅕ inches) long, but the little grass frog (*P. ocularis*) reaches a maximum of 1.9 cm (¾ inch), and Strecker's chorus frog (*P. streckeri*) may grow to 4.5 cm (1⅘ inches).

COMMON FROGS

The common frog (species *Rana temporaria*) is a largely terrestrial frog (family Ranidae) native to Europe. It ranges from Great Britain to central Russia. It is known in continental Europe as either grass frog or russet frog. The common frog is smooth-skinned, and adults are 7 to 10 cm (2.8 to 3.9 inches) long. Colour and markings vary from gray to greenish, brown, yellowish, or red with few to many spots of reddish brown or black.

The common frog frequents damp, shaded areas. It breeds in the spring, when water temperature reaches about 14 °C (57 °F). The females lay 1,000 to 4,000 eggs. The eggs hatch quickly, and tadpoles metamorphose in roughly three months.

Common frog (Rana temporaria). Eric Hosking/Bruce Coleman Inc.

CRICKET FROGS

Cricket frogs make up either of two species of small, nonclimbing North American tree frogs of the genus *Acris* (family Hylidae). Their call is a series of rapid clicks, sounding much like the song of crickets. They occur in the eastern and central United States, usually along the open, grassy margin of ponds, streams, and other shallow bodies of water. There are two species: *A. crepitans* and *A. gryllus*. The cricket frog attains a maximum length of about 3.8 cm (1.5 inches). Its skin is slightly warty and brown or green, with a dark triangle on the head and usually a reddish, whitish, or green stripe along the back.

FIRE-BELLIED TOADS

The fire-bellied toad (*Bombina*) is a small amphibian (family Bombinatoridae) characterized by bright orange markings on the undersides of its grayish body and limbs. The common fire-bellied toad (*B. bombina*) is a pond

Fire-bellied toad (Bombina orientalis). Charles Mohr—The National Audubon Society Collection/Photo Researchers

dweller about 5 cm (2 inches) long. When disturbed it raises its forearms and arches its head and hind legs over its back. Resting on the lower part of its tautly curved abdomen, it freezes with the bright colours of its underside on display. This reaction to danger, the "unken reflex," is thought to be a warning signal to indicate to potential predators that the skin of the frog is poisonous.

The genus *Bombina* includes four other species, one European and three Asian. These also have brightly marked undersides. All breed in water. Tadpoles develop rapidly and often undergo metamorphosis in less than 45 days.

Green Frogs

The green frog (subspecies *Rana clamitans melanota*) is a common aquatic frog (family Ranidae) found in ponds, streams, and other bodies of fresh water in the northeastern United States. The green frog is 5 to 10 cm (2 to 4 inches) long and green to brownish in colour. The back and legs are characteristically spotted or blotched.

Another race of this species, the bronze frog (*R. c. clamitans*), is found in such places as swamps and streamsides of the southeastern United States. It is brown above and grows to about 8.5 cm (3.3 inches). Its call, like that of the green frog, is a sharp, twanging note. The European marsh, pool, and edible frogs are also known as green frogs.

Marsh Frogs

The marsh frog (*Rana ridibunda*), which is also called lake frog, is a large aquatic frog of the "true frog" family Ranidae, occurring naturally from France to the Urals and by introduction in southern England. This species seldom occurs more than 1 to 2 metres (3 to 6.5 feet) from the edge of permanent water. It is the largest of the European ranids; females grow to 13 cm (5 inches) long, whereas males grow to 9 cm (3.5 inches) long.

The pool frog (*R. lessonae*) is the other species of European aquatic frogs. They may interbreed with marsh frogs to produce a hybrid form called the European edible frog (*R. esculenta*). Male and female edible frogs may breed with males and females of either *R. ridibunda* or *R. lessonae* to produce viable offspring. However, breeding between male and female edible frogs results in infertile eggs or offspring incapable of surviving.

WOOD FROGS

The wood frog (*Rana sylvatica*) is a terrestrial frog (family Ranidae) of forests and woodlands. It is a cool-climate species that occurs from the northeastern quarter of the United States and throughout most of Canada to central and southern Alaska.

The wood frog is tan to brown with a distinctly dark facial mask. Its maximum length is approximately 8.25 cm (3.25 inches), and its maximum weight is approximately 8 grams (0.3 ounce). It is an early spring breeder, using the vernal pools created by meltwater and late winter rains. Breeding occurs between early March and early May, during which females lay a globular mass of several hundred to a few thousand eggs. Development is moderately fast and temperature-dependent. Metamorphosis takes place over the subsequent two to three months. The male's voice is a ducklike quack.

It has been shown that wood frog tadpoles may be conditioned to perceive predators, such as salamanders, as threats by the odours they give off, provided that the predator's chemical cues were paired with those of injured tadpoles. Later, when the conditioned tadpoles encountered a predator's odour, they stopped swimming and

Wood frogs (Rana sylvatica). Karl H. Maslowski

became still. In contrast, wood frog embryos exposed to a predator's odours alone were at a higher risk to perceive such odours as nonthreatening upon reaching the tadpole stage.

UNUSUAL SPECIES

Some groups of frogs and toads are notable because of a particular physical feature or behaviour. Physically, the glass frogs are some of the most striking species. One of the more peculiar egg-laying strategies is that employed by the Tungara frog, a species that creates foamy nests of fertilized eggs that float upon the water. Tadpoles of Surinam toads hatch from eggs embedded into the back of their female parent.

GLASS FROGS

Glass frogs (family Centrolenidae) constitute a group of tree frogs found in the New World tropics, some species of which have transparent bellies and chests. In glass frogs the viscera are visible, and an observer can see the heart pumping blood into the arteries and food moving through the gut. There is no satisfactory explanation for this transparency, and not all species have a "glass" underside. Viewed from above, most glass frogs appear light green. Their patterning ranges from uniform green to green with white to yellow spots that mimic glass frog eggs. Glass frogs have expanded digit tips that aid in climbing, and this trait allows most to live in trees or shrubs along forest streams.

Glass frogs include more than 120 species in three genera (*Centrolene*, *Cochranella*, and *Hyalinobatrachium*). They occur from tropical lowland forests to mid-elevation mountain forests. Most species are small, with adults ranging from 20 to 30 mm (0.8 to 1.2 inches) in total length. In a few species adults are larger, attaining a maximum length of nearly 80 mm (3 inches).

For mating to occur, males must first call to females. Calling males sit on leaves—either the top or underside depending upon the species—over streams or lake edges. When a female comes, she does not descend to the water with the amplexing male. Instead, they mate on the calling leaf where she deposits her eggs. After she departs, the male often remains to protect the eggs from predators and call additional females. Some males will attract other females and thus have several egg clutches in various developmental stages to guard. When the tadpoles hatch, they fall into the water below. Tadpoles usually live and feed amidst the leaf litter and stream-side detritus until they metamorphose into froglets. One of the major egg predators are "frog flies," which lay their eggs on the egg masses. The flies' eggs hatch quickly, and the maggots feed on the frog embryos.

LEOPARD FROGS

Leopard frogs, a group of North American anurans (family Ranidae), occur throughout North America (except in the coastal band from California to British Columbia) from northern Canada southward into Mexico. At one time the leopard frog was considered a single species, *Rana pipiens*, but during its wide use as a laboratory frog from the 1940s to the 1960s, developmental and physiological differences were noted in frogs from different geographic areas. These differences and the distinct morphologies indicated that several species were characterized by a similar colour pattern. At present, leopard frogs are contained within the *Pantherana* clade, which is known informally as the *Rana pipiens* complex. In the United States and Canada, nine species are recognized: *R. berlandieri*, the Rio Grande leopard frog; *R. blairi*, the Plains leopard frog; *R. chiricahuensis*, the Chiricahua leopard frog; *R. fisheri*, the Vegas Valley leopard frog (now extinct); *R. onca*, the relict leopard frog; *R. pipiens*, the northern leopard frog; *R. sphenocephala*, the southern leopard frog; *R. subaquavocalis*, the Ramsey Canyon leopard frog; and *R. yavapaiensis*, the lowland leopard frog.

All leopard frogs are relatively slender-bodied and long-legged, with pointed snouts. They range from about 6 to 10 cm (2 to 4 inches) in head-body length. All have a pattern of ellipsoidal to circular dark spots on their backs, the size, shape, and colour

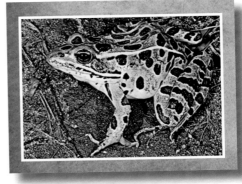

Leopard frog (Rana pipiens). John Kohout/ Root Resources

of which differ among species. All are semiaquatic frogs and generally associated with marshy habitats.

In the 1960s several populations of *R. pipiens* from Vermont to Minnesota experienced major population crashes. The reason for these declines is not completely known; however, pollution, habitat loss, increases in ultraviolet radiation resulting from the thinning of the ozone layer, disease, and overharvesting by laboratories and collectors are often cited. Although not recognized at the time, this event is thought to portend the worldwide amphibian decline that began about 1970 and continues to the present day. While many leopard frog populations have survived and returned to near normal levels, the leopard frogs of the upper Midwest have a high incidence of developmental malformations.

MIDWIFE TOADS

The midwife toad is a slow-moving, terrestrial amphibian represented by four species of the genus *Alytes* (family Discoglossidae). The best-known species is *A. obstetricans.* These western European toads live in forests and often near ponds and streams in open areas. Midwife toads are about 5 cm (2 inches) long and plump, with warty, dull-gray skin.

Midwife toads are nocturnal and thoroughly terrestrial. Toward evening, the males reveal their presence by a clear whistling note. Mating takes place on land and occurs throughout the spring and summer. The eggs are large and yellow, and they are produced in two rosarylike strands of gelatinous capsules. While the eggs are being extruded, the male discharges milt (sperm-containing fluid) over them to effect fertilization. Once he has fertilized the eggs, the male twists the egg strings around his legs and waist and returns to his usual moist retreat. If the weather is exceptionally dry, the male makes periodic trips to moisten the eggs and prevent their dehydration. When the time for hatching arrives, after about three weeks, the male enters the water; the larvae, measuring slightly more than 1.3 cm (0.5 inch), emerge from their egg envelope, which is not abandoned by the male until all the young are liberated.

SPADEFOOT TOADS

The spadefoot toad is a relatively smooth-skinned amphibian of either the Old World genus *Pelobates* or of the genera *Scaphiopus* and *Spea* of North America. All spadefoot toads are classified in the family Pelobatidae. Spadefoot toads have a broad, horny "spade" projecting from the inside of each hind foot that is used by the animals in burrowing.

The European spadefoot (*Pelobates fuscus*) is found in Europe and Central Asia, usually in sandy regions. Some related species have more restricted ranges. It is about 6 to 7.5 cm (2 to 3 inches) long and spends the day underground.

At least seven species of spadefoots are found in regions of Canada, the United States, and Mexico, where soils are sandy. These animals are about 4 to 9 cm (1.5 to 3.5 inches) long and are also nocturnal burrow dwellers. In warm weather after a heavy rain, they emerge to breed in temporary ponds. The young of the western, arid-country forms normally hatch quickly and transform into adults before the ponds dry up; those of the eastern spadefoot develop more slowly.

SPRING PEEPERS

Spring peepers (*Pseudacris crucifer*) are small tree frogs (family Hylidae) found in woodland areas in the eastern United States and Canada. Outside of the breeding season, when it may be found in ephemeral woodland ponds, it is seldom seen.

Spring peeper (Pseudacris crucifer). U.S. Geological Survey

The spring peeper, with its high, whistling call, is one of the first frogs to vocalize and breed in spring. Larvae metamorphose into tiny froglets in two to three months. It is grayish, tan, or olive brown with an X-shaped, often irregular, brown mark on its back, and it grows to a length of about 2 to 3.5 cm (0.75 to 1.3 inches).

SURINAM TOADS

Surinam toads (*Pipa pipa*) are aquatic South American toads (family Pipidae) in which the eggs are incubated on the back of the female. The Surinam toad is about 10 to 17 cm (4 to 7 inches) long. It has a flat, squarish body, small eyes, and a flat head with loose flaps of skin on the snout and jaws. The digits end in small, star-shaped appendages that aid food finding. It eats a variety of small vertebrates and invertebrates.

The Surinam toad mates in water. As each egg is released, it is fertilized and pressed by the male to the back of the female. In the next several hours, the skin grows around the eggs to enclose them in a cyst with a horny lid. After about 80 days' development, the young emerge as miniatures of the adult. The Surinam toad is one of seven species of *Pipa*. In five of the other species, the young emerge as tadpoles.

Surinam toads (Pipa pipa), *showing* (top) *the dorsal and* (bottom) *the ventral surfaces.* © Jane Burton/Bruce Coleman Ltd.

TAILED FROGS

Tailed frogs (*Ascaphus truei*) belong to the frog family Ascaphidae (order Anura). The species is restricted to cold, clear forest streams of the Pacific Northwest region of the United States and Canada. It is one of many species that disappears when old-growth forests are cut.

The "tail" found on the male is actually an extension of the cloaca, an internal chamber that receives waste materials and reproductive products. This extension serves to transfer sperm directly into the cloaca of the female in the swift current of mountain streams. Breeding occurs in the fall, and the female stores the sperm until the following summer, when the eggs are laid. Because eggs are deposited in cold streams, they require nearly two months to hatch. The tadpole stage may last up to three years, and adults reach sexual maturity at seven or eight years.

Tailed frog (Ascaphus truei). George Porter—The National Audubon Society Collection/Photo Researchers

TUNGARA FROGS

Tungara frogs (*Physalaemus pustulosus*), which are also called Central American mud-puddle frogs, are terrestrial, toad-like frogs common in moist, lowland sites from Mexico to northern South America.

The frog is cryptically coloured, its rough brown skin matching the leaf litter in which it lives. Although a mere 25–35 mm (1–1.4 inches) in length, this small amphibian consumes a wide range of insects; unlike many frogs of its size, it does not specifically feed on ants.

The breeding behaviour and calls of the tungara frog have been well studied. At the onset of the wet-season rains, males seek out small, shallow pools. From the pools, they begin calling at dusk, producing a series of clucks, glugs, mews, and whines. This attracts other male and female tungaras to the site, but it also attracts predators such as snakes, opossums, bats, and other frogs. Calling males can be seen floating on the water, their vocal sacs inflated on both sides of the body. Some males initiate the chorus and call persistently; others only answer, and some remain silent.

After mating is initiated, the female carries the male to a nesting spot, generally somewhat removed from the calling site. There they spend up to an hour and a half constructing a nest: the female lays a combination of eggs and jelly, which the male collects with his hind feet, fertilizes, and whips into a foam mass the size of a fist. These foam nests float on the water and may have 100–200 eggs within them. The eggs hatch before the end of two days, and the brown, nocturnal tadpoles descend from the foam into the water, where they will eat detritus. If the pool has dried, the tadpoles will aggregate beneath the foam, where they can survive for up to five days. Tungara frogs may reproduce two to three months after metamorphosis. Tungara frogs belong to the family Leptodactylidae.

POISONOUS SPECIES

Although all amphibians produce toxins, several frogs and toads produce chemicals that can be dangerous to human beings and other animals. Toxin production is a defensive measure. Toxins produced by some frogs and toads, such as certain types of narrow-mouthed toads, merely irritate the skin of human beings. Poisons produced by the genera *Dendrobates* and *Phyllobates* are so strong that they can be lethal to humans if they come into contact with the victim's mucous membranes.

NARROW-MOUTHED TOADS

Narrow-mouthed toads constitute the amphibian family Microhylidae, which includes 10 subfamilies and more than 60 genera and more than 300 species. Narrow-mouthed toads are found in North and South America, Africa, Asia, and Australia. Many are small, stocky, and smooth skinned with short legs, small heads, pointed snouts, and narrow mouths. They live on land, underground, or in trees and are generally secretive in nature. Most species are less than 8 cm (3 inches) long.

The eastern narrow-mouthed toad, *Gastrophryne carolinensis,* is a small, terrestrial microhylid of the United States. It is gray, reddish, or brown with darker stripes, spots, or blotches. The Mexican narrow-mouthed toad, or sheep frog (*Hypopachus cuneus*), is similar but is larger and has a yellow stripe on its back. It hides in burrows, pack rat nests, or, as does the eastern narrow-mouth, under objects lying on the ground.

A variety of microhylids are found in Asia and Africa. The genus *Breviceps* (rain frogs) includes a number of plump, short-faced, African species. These live and breed

Eastern narrow-mouthed toad (Gastrophryne carolinensis). George Porter—The National Audubon Society Collection/Photo Researchers

on land. *B. gibbosus* is a burrowing South African form that is traditionally thought to control the coming of rain.

Among the Asian microhylids are *Glyphoglossus molossus*, a pug-nosed native of southeastern Asia, and *Kaloula pulchra*, a frequent visitor to gardens in Indochina. The African genus *Phrynomerus* (sometimes separated as the family Phrynomeridae) includes about five species of arboreal frogs; *P. bifasciatus* is a black and red, striped form whose skin secretions are strong enough to irritate human skin.

PANAMANIAN GOLDEN TOADS

Panamanian golden toads (*Atelopus zeteki*)—which are also called Panamanian golden frogs—are small, bright yellow toads, often with a few black spots or blotches; they are found at moderate elevations in the central part of Panama. Considered to be one of the most beautiful frogs in Panama, where it is endangered and legally protected, the golden toad has attracted so much attention that it has become a national symbol.

The Panamanian golden toad's skin contains a potent water-soluble toxin called zetekitoxin, which affects nerve cells and protects the toad from most predators. However, if minor precautions are taken, these toads can be safely handled.

Aspects of its natural history are not fully investigated. Females are larger than males, measuring about 53 mm (2 inches) to the males' 45 mm (1.8 inches). The toad is terrestrial and diurnal (active during the day). Males maintain small territories along forest streams. When males encounter one another, they sometimes engage in waving of their forefeet as a signal of aggression or defense. Males also communicate acoustically, emitting a very soft and trilled mating call. Eggs are presumably laid in strings attached to rocks at the bottom of fast-flowing streams, where the tadpoles develop and grow. The tadpoles have a ventral sucker that may be used for remaining attached to rocks or other substrata in the streams. Panamanian golden toads and other species of the genus *Atelopus* are members of the family Bufonidae, as are most toads. Some authorities, however, classify the genera *Atelopus* and *Bradycephalus* as a separate family called the stub-footed toads (Atelopodidae).

PICKEREL FROGS

Pickerel frogs (*Rana palustris*) are dark-spotted amphibians (family Ranidae) that typically inhabit meadows, cool streams, and sphagnum bogs in eastern North America. The pickerel frog is about 5 to 7.5 cm (2 to 3 inches) long and has lengthwise rows of squarish spots on its golden or brownish skin.

When the pickerel frog leaps it reveals the orange or yellow on the inner surfaces of its hind legs. The skin secretions, which protect this frog from snakes, are reported also to be toxic to other frogs.

Poison Frogs

Poison frogs (family Dendrobatidae)—which are also called poison dart frogs, dart-poison frogs, or poison arrow frogs—constitute approximately 180 species of New World frogs characterized by the ability to produce extremely poisonous skin secretions. Poison frogs inhabit the forests of the New World tropics from Nicaragua to Peru and Brazil, and a few species are used by South American tribes to coat the tips of darts and arrows. Poison frogs, or dendrobatids, are small and range from 12 to 19 mm (0.5 to 0.75 inch) from snout to vent in the minute poison frogs (*Minyobates*) to about 65 mm (2.6 inches) in the skunk frog (*Aromobates nocturnus*).

All frogs (order Anura) produce poisonous skin secretions; however, humans do not notice the toxicity or suffer skin irritation when handling most species. Nonetheless, handling one of the brightly coloured dendrobatids, such as *Dendrobates* and *Phyllobates*, requires caution because their alkaloid skin secretions are potentially lethal if absorbed through human mucous membranes or passed into the body through a cut on the skin. In fact, the skin secretion of the true poison dart frog, or golden poison frog (*Phyllobates terribilis*), is so toxic that the tip of a dart rubbed across its back picks up sufficient poison to kill a large bird or a monkey. The origin and production of the toxic skin secretions remains uncertain, but at least in some dendrobatids it appears to be derived from their

Kokoa frog or South American poison arrow frog (Dendrobates auratus).
George Porter—The National Audubon Society Collection/Photo
Researchers

consumption of beetles, their primary prey. When kept in
captivity and fed a diet devoid of beetles, the skin secretions of poison frogs lack the highly toxic alkaloids.

Aposematic (conspicuous) or warning coloration is
common among distasteful and poisonous species of
many plants and animals. The coloration of poison frogs
commonly include reds, oranges, yellows, and even bright
blues and greens on a black or dark background. Not all
dendrobatids are so poisonous or brightly coloured; many
are patterned with shades of brown and well camouflaged
(as in *Colostethus*), and their skin secretions are generally
nontoxic and nonirritating.

Parental care of the young, which is often performed
by the male, occurs in all poison frog species. The male
attracts a female to his residence beneath a leaf or log,
and she lays the eggs and often departs. The male remains

to guard the clutch; however, in some species the female remains. When the tadpoles hatch, the parent allows the tadpoles to swim or crawl up onto his or her back. They are subsequently carried to a nearby body of water (such as a stream, a pond, or a tree-hole). There, the tadpoles slide off the back of the parent and into the water to complete their development.

Superficially, the mantelline frogs of Madagascar (family Mantellidae) appear nearly identical to the dendrobatids; however, they are not closely related. The similarities between the two groups are attributed to convergent evolution. Also, both are comparable in terms of physical size, as mantellines range from 15 to 120 mm (0.6 inch to nearly 5 inches) from snout to vent, although most species are less than 60 mm (about 2.5 inches) long. While the skin secretions of the mantellines have not been thoroughly studied, the secretions of *Mantella* are toxic and capable of killing vertebrate predators.

Mantellines include more than 100 species in three genera of terrestrial to arboreal (tree-dwelling) forms that live in semiarid scrubland to rainforest habitats. Some species lay eggs on leaves that overhang bodies of water, and hatching larvae then drop into the water. Other species lay terrestrial eggs that develop either directly into froglets or into a nonaquatic, nonfeeding tadpole stage. In addition, parental care occurs in some mantelline species with terrestrial eggs.

CHAPTER 11

NEWTS, SALAMANDERS, AND CAECILIANS

Salamanders (order Caudata) and caecilians (order Gymnophiona) make up the other two major groups of amphibians. Salamanders are relatively well known in temperate regions of North America, Europe, Japan, and China. In contrast, caecilians are less well known since most species live underground in tropical regions. Not to be overlooked, newts are partially terrestrial salamanders of the family Salamadridae, a caudatan family that also contains so-called true salamanders. The distinction made between newts and true salamanders is an informal one, however.

CAUDATA

Caudata, which is also called Urodela, is one of the major extant orders of the class Amphibia. It includes salamanders and newts. The relatively small and inconspicuous salamanders are important members of north temperate and some tropical ecosystems, in which they are locally abundant and play important roles. They are important as subjects of experimental studies in embryology, developmental biology, physiology, anatomy, biochemistry, genetics, and behaviour. Convenient size, low food requirements, low metabolic rate, and hardiness make them useful laboratory animals.

NEWTS

*Warty newt (*Triturus cristatus*). Toni Angermayer*

Newt is a generic name used to describe several partially terrestrial salamanders within family Salamandridae. The family is divided informally into newts and "true salamanders" (that is, all nonnewt species within Salamandridae regardless of genus). There is little distinction between the two groups.

Salamandridae is second in diversity to the lungless salamanders (family Plethodontidae); the family is made up of 15 genera of true salamanders and over 50 species of newts. Salamandridae has a spotty geographic distribution throughout the Northern Hemisphere and occurs from western Europe to the Urals, from southern China to Japan, on the west coast of North America, and east of the Rocky Mountains in the eastern United States. Salamandrids range from moderately slender to robust-bodied forms. All have well-developed limbs and tails. They are usually less than 20 cm (8 inches) in total length, and many are less than 10 cm (4 inches). Newts have rough skin, and the skin of many salamanders is rugose (wrinkled).

Adults of most species lay eggs in water, and individuals pass through an aquatic larval stage before metamorphosing into adult-like body forms. Three life histories occur among salamandrids with aquatic larvae. In some genera, such as the Asian *Cynops* and the European *Pleurodeles*, the larvae metamorphose in the water, and juveniles and adults remain aquatic. In the European newts (*Triturus*) and western North American newts (*Taricha*), the larvae metamorphose into terrestrial juveniles that remain terrestrial as adults; adults return to water only for courtship and egg deposition. In the eastern North American newts (*Notophthalmus*), the larvae metamorphose into a terrestrial juvenile, referred to as the eft stage; efts spend two to four years on land. As they begin to mature sexually, they return to water and become aquatic as adults.

Live-bearing salamandrids, such as the alpine salamander (*Salamandra atra*) and Luschan's salamander (*Lyciasalamandra luschani*), also exist; they retain their eggs in the oviduct and give birth to miniature adultlike offspring. A few other species lay eggs on land.

All members of Salamandridae are toxic and have either poisonous skin or glands that secrete poison when threatened. In general, the terrestrial species, such as *Taricha*, and the efts of some aquatic species have the most-toxic skin secretions. One species, the Spanish ribbed newt (*Pleurodeles waltl*), combines its poisonous skin secretions with sharp barbs running along the sides of its body; the barbs are ribs that can be forced through the animal's skin when threatened. Commonly, these poisonous salamanders are brightly coloured to advertise their toxicity to potential predators.

SIZE RANGE AND DIVERSITY OF STRUCTURE

The most typical salamanders are short-bodied, four-legged, moist-skinned vertebrates about 100 to 150 mm (about 4 to 6 inches) long. The tail is usually about as long as the body. There is much variation in size, and terrestrial salamanders range from 40 to nearly 350 mm (1.5 to nearly 14 inches), with a few exceeding 1 metre (39 inches) in length. Members of most species live in moist places on land but must return to water to breed. Others are completely terrestrial. Wholly aquatic salamanders attain larger sizes than do terrestrial ones, the former reaching a maximum of 180 cm (about 6 feet). Salamanders may retain gills throughout life, lose the gills but retain a spiracle or gill slit, completely metamorphose and lose both gills and gill slits, or entirely bypass the aquatic larval stage and develop directly, hatching as miniature adults. Many aquatic species resemble their terrestrial relatives in body

AMPHIUMAS

Amphiumas (*Amphiuma*), which are also called Congo eels or Congo snakes, are North American salamanders that belong to the family Amphiumidae (order Caudata). There are three known species. Because they are long and slender and have inconspicuous legs, amphiumas are often mistaken for eels or snakes. The body is gray or brown and paler on the lower side. The usual habitat is swamps and drainage ditches.

Although there are both three-toed and one-toed species, the most widely distributed (Virginia to Louisiana) is *Amphiuma means,* which usually grows to 46–116 cm (18–46 inches) in length and has two toes on each foot. Amphiumas have strong jaws and sharp teeth and, unlike most salamanders, can bite viciously. Their diet consists chiefly of crayfish, clams, snails, and other small animals. Fertilization is internal, and the female lays from 40 to 350 eggs in a single clutch.

form, but the aquatic genera *Siren* and *Pseudobranchus* lack hindlimbs, and *Amphiuma* has an extremely elongated body, short tail, and diminutive legs; several cave-dwelling forms (*Proteus*, *Haideotriton*, *Typhlomolge*) are blind and almost without pigment.

DISTRIBUTION AND ABUNDANCE

Salamanders, with the exception of one subfamily, are classic examples of animals with a distribution restricted to the north temperate regions of both the Eastern and Western hemispheres; 9 of the 10 families are found almost entirely in northern regions that lie outside the tropics. Typically, salamanders occur in moist, forested habitats, where they are often common in aquatic and terrestrial communities. Members of the family Salamandridae extend south to extreme northern Africa, the southern foothills of the Himalayas, northern Vietnam, and the islands of Hainan, Taiwan, and Okinawa. Some ambystomatids reach the southern margins of the Mexican Plateau, but only the lungless salamanders (plethodontids) have truly entered the tropics. One group of plethodontids, the bolitoglossines, occupies a wide variety of tropical habitats in the New World—from northern Mexico to southern Brazil and central Bolivia—and contains nearly half of all recognized species of salamanders, which is an indication that the plethodontids have been extremely successful in the tropical environment. Other areas in which salamanders are both speciose and abundant include temperate North America (Appalachian and Ozark uplands; Pacific coastal areas with a moist habitat), western Europe, Japan, and China.

NATURAL HISTORY OF CAUDATANS

Most caudatans require at least periodic visits to aquatic environments throughout their lives. In many species, fertilization and egg laying must occur in aquatic environments. Most terrestrial species prefer damp, shaded places, and some salamanders even inhabit caves. Salamanders overwhelmingly prey on insects, which are usually captured with the tongue and quickly drawn into the mouth.

LIFE CYCLE AND REPRODUCTION

Most salamanders are terrestrial or semiterrestrial as adults, but many return to aquatic habitats to breed. Courtship, which is relatively simple in hynobiids and cryptobranchids, is increasingly elaborate and prolonged in the more highly evolved families. In primitive species constituting the suborder Cryptobranchoidea, the egg is fertilized externally. The females deposit sacs or strings of eggs that may be grasped by the male, who then sheds milt (which contains the sperm) over them. Nothing is known of courtship in sirens, but they, too, may have external fertilization, for the males lack the cloacal glands that produce the spermatophore, or sperm case, in species with internal fertilization, and the females lack spermathecae—chambers inside the cloaca used for sperm storage. However, sirens also lay single eggs, a behaviour that would not be facilitated by external fertilization.

All other species of salamanders have internal fertilization and more complex courtship behaviour, which often differs in details between species. The male deposits from one to many spermatophores on the ground or other surface. These consist of a gelatinous base, which is produced by cloacal glands, and a so-called sperm cap at the tip. The female moves by herself or is led by the male onto the spermatophore, and she takes the sperm mass into her cloaca. Breeding often occurs in ponds, but some salamandrids and most plethodontids breed on land. Egg deposition may take place shortly after mating but in many plethodontids may be delayed for several months, the eggs being fertilized by stored sperm. Eggs are laid in masses in streams or ponds, often in the shallows near shore. Many salamandrids lay eggs singly, while plethodontids typically lay eggs in clusters in terrestrial sites—e.g., under surface objects, in rotting logs, or underground. Some species deposit eggs in tree cavities, and tropical species may deposit them in bromeliad plants (various genera of the family Bromeliaceae), the leaves of which are arranged so that they often hold water and thus provide a moist habitat. Frequently, the female stays with the eggs until they hatch, a period of several weeks to many months. The number of eggs varies greatly and is correlated with adult size. Aquatic forms deposit as many as 400 eggs, terrestrial forms as few as five or six.

Members of most families pass through an aquatic larval stage that lasts for a period ranging from a few days to several years. A short period of metamorphosis usually occurs before the terrestrial phase of the life cycle begins. The newly metamorphosed salamander is usually very small, and up to several years may elapse before it is sexually mature.

Some salamander species never metamorphose and thus retain most of their larval characteristics. In other species, individuals or populations may occasionally fail to metamorphose. Still other species undergo partial metamorphosis, a state in which the adult retains larval or juvenile features (paedomorphosis). This condition characterizes all salamanders to a degree but is particularly evident in species such as *Necturus maculosus* (mud puppy) and *Ambystoma mexicanum* (axolotl), which retain gills and other larval structures throughout life. These animals breed in what is essentially a larval state. This extreme condition, which characterizes the Proteidae and Sirenidae, is also found in the Dicamptodontidae, Plethodontidae, and Ambystomatidae. In most species the permanent larval state is determined by heredity, but in some it is induced by environmental factors, such as unfavourable terrestrial conditions resulting from drought or cold. The most complete metamorphosis is found in the families Hynobiidae, Salamandridae, Ambystomatidae, Dicamptodontidae, and Plethodontidae.

Most species of the family Plethodontidae differ from members of all other families in that their eggs develop entirely on land, with no aquatic larval stage. The hatchling has either rudimentary gills that soon disappear or none at all and, in virtually all respects, is a miniature of the adult.

Females of the genera *Salamandra* and *Mertensiella* (Salamandridae) may retain the fertilized eggs in the reproductive tract for a variable amount of time. The fire salamander (*Salamandra salamandra*) deposits relatively advanced larvae in the water. In the alpine salamander (*Salamandra atra*) and *Mertensiella*, fully metamorphosed individuals are born. One individual develops from the first egg in each oviduct, the tube leading from the ovary to the outside. Initially, the young salamander lives on its own yolk supply; later it eats the yolk of the other eggs. It develops enlarged gills that form an intimate association with the walls of the oviduct to convey nutrients to itself. The gills are lost shortly before birth. Such salamanders are the only members of the order that bear live young.

Larval salamanders are exclusively aquatic. They may occur in a variety of habitats, from temporary ponds to permanent swamps, rivers, slow-moving streams, mountain brooks, springs, and subterranean waters. In all habitats they are exclusively carnivorous, feeding primarily on aquatic invertebrates. In most salamander larvae, feeding is accomplished by a "gape-and-suck" method, in which the throat is expanded, or gaped, to produce a suction that draws water and prey into the opened mouth. Skin flaps around the mouth direct the water movement. The larvae are well equipped with teeth, which aid in holding and shredding prey. Pond larvae have a high fin on the upper side of the tail that extends far anteriorly and large gills. Limbs are rather slow to develop. By contrast, stream larvae have a low, short tail fin, small gills, and limbs that develop early.

Metamorphosis, although a period of major reorganization, is not so dramatic as that in frogs. In the final stages, metamorphosis is usually a rapid process; it is mediated by several hormones produced by the thyroid and pituitary glands. The following events typically occur during metamorphosis: loss of the gills, closure of the gill slits, appearance of a tongue pad and reorganization of the gill skeleton and musculature to produce the mechanical system necessary for projecting and retracting the tongue, enlargement of the mouth and eyes, development of eyelids, and major changes in the structure of the skull and skin.

AXOLOTLS

The axolotl (*Ambystoma*, formerly *Rhyacosiredon* or *Siredon, mexicanum*) is a salamander of the family Ambystomatidae (order Caudata), notable for its permanent retention of larval features, such as external gills. It is found in lakes near Mexico City, where it is considered edible. The name axolotl is also applied to any full-grown larva of *Ambystoma tigrinum* (tiger salamander) that has not yet lost its external gills. *A. mexicanum* grows to about 25 cm (10 inches) long and is dark brown with black speckling. Both albino and white mutants, as well as other colour mutants, are common. The legs and feet are rather small, but the tail is long. A fin extends from the back of the head to the tip of the tail. A lower fin extends from between the hind legs to the tip of the tail.

LOCOMOTION

Locomotion is by means of limbs and by sinuous body movements. Elongated species of the genera *Phaeognathus*, *Batrachoseps*, *Oedipina*, and *Lineatriton* have reduced limbs and rely mainly on body movements for rapid locomotion. Species of the genus *Aneides* have arboreal (tree-dwelling) tendencies, and their long legs and digits, expanded toe tips, and prehensile (grasping) tails make them effective climbers. Some salamanders of the genera *Ixalotriton*, *Nyctanolis*, *Dendrotriton*, *Pseudoeurycea*, and *Chiropterotriton*, found in the New World tropics, are similarly adapted. Others, members of the genus *Bolitoglossa*, have extensively webbed forefeet and hindfeet with indistinct digits, allowing them to move across moist leaves and other smooth surfaces.

BEHAVIOUR AND ECOLOGY

Adult salamanders are nearly all nocturnal (i.e., active mainly at night) animals. They may be highly seasonal, remaining hidden underground until the breeding season, or they may emerge from hiding places on any evening when moisture and temperature are at the proper levels. Fallen logs, rocks, crevices in soil, and surface litter commonly provide daytime refuge. Home ranges of salamanders are small, often less than 3 or 4 square metres (about 30 to 40 square feet), and in favourable areas some of the smaller species can be very abundant, occasionally numbering thousands per acre.

Most terrestrial species live near the surface of the ground, often in thick leaf litter and rock piles. Some enter subterranean retreats, sometimes by way of burrows made by mammals and invertebrates. Caves are often occupied during cold or dry periods. Climbing species live on rock faces and in crevices, in trees, on broad-leaved herbs and shrubs, and in bromeliads. Many species are semiaquatic, frequenting streamside and spring habitats throughout their lives. The terrestrial species that have direct development have been able to free themselves entirely from reliance on standing or flowing water. Among the bolitoglossine plethodontids, species are found in habitats ranging from true deserts and frigid alpine areas to tropical rain forests and from sea level to elevations of more than 4,000 metres (13,000 feet).

FOOD AND FEEDING

Insects are by far the most important food of salamanders. All terrestrial salamanders initially contact the prey with the tongue, which retracts quickly to deliver the quarry into the mouth. Some members of the Salamandridae and Plethodontidae, however, have evolved highly specialized tongue-protrusion mechanisms. These are especially well developed in the tropical plethodontids, many of which are arboreal. The tongue can be extended from the mouth for a considerable distance and retracted almost instantaneously, with the prey attached to the sticky tongue pad.

The gill skeleton found in larvae has evolved into a bio-mechanically efficient tongue-projection mechanism in adults, and most of the tongue skeleton is shot from the mouth with the tongue pad on the end; in contrast, in frogs only the soft parts of the tongue leave the mouth. When the tongue is maximally projected, the retractor muscles are stretched; because contraction of these muscles takes place at the same time as the protractor muscles are contracted, the tongue is rapidly returned to the mouth.

FORM AND FUNCTION

Salamanders possess a unique collection of physical features. The skin plays several roles, but the most important is the one that it plays in respiration. In addition, cartilage is an important supporting structure in salamanders. Salamanders also rely on a relatively simple nervous system and well-developed olfactory and vomeronasal organs.

SKIN AND EXTERNAL FEATURES

The most distinctive and important feature of amphibians in general and salamanders in particular is their smooth, moist skin. This organ consists of an epidermis, or surface tissue, that is several layers thick and a rather thick dermis containing mucous and poison glands as well as pigment cells. The integument, or skin, is highly vascular and serves a major respiratory function. The poison glands of some species produce some of the most virulent toxins known. The fleshy tongue pad contains many mucus-secreting glands.

Most species are drab gray or brown, but some, especially the more poisonous ones, are spectacularly coloured, with bright spots, blotches, or streaks. The few integumentary specializations include keratinized skins of the terrestrial stages of many salamandrids, keratinized claws in stream-dwelling hynobiids, and glands that to some degree stimulate sexual activity by making the female more receptive. Cryptobranchids have large, lateral folds of skin that serve respiratory functions.

LUNGLESS SALAMANDERS

Lungless salamanders (family Plethodontidae) account for more than 370 species of lungless amphibians dependent largely on cutaneous respiration (gas exchange through moistened skin). Plethodontidae is the largest group of salamanders, and its members occur predominantly in the Americas from southern Canada to the Amazon basin in Brazil. A few species also occur spottily in Sardinia, northern Italy, and the Korean peninsula. Adult plethodontids range in size from approximately 25 mm (1 inch) in head and body length in the Mexican pygmy salamander (*Thorius*) to 36 cm (14 inches) in Bell's false brook salamander (*Pseudoeurycea bellii*). The length of the animal's tail usually equals or slightly exceeds its head and body length. Most plethodontid species are between 40 and 120 mm (1.6 and 4.7 inches) in head and body length. Since they lack lungs, all plethodontids breathe through their skin and the mucous membrane in the mouth and throat; these surfaces must remain moist at all times in order to absorb oxygen.

All lungless salamanders possess a pair of nasolabial grooves, and each groove extends from the upper lip to a nostril. The salamander touches its snout to a surface (nose tapping), and capillary action moves odour particles up the groove into the sensory cells in the vomeronasal organ of the nose. Plethodontids rely on odours for chemical alarm cues, directions to food sources, and cues for courtship and other social behaviour. Smaller species eat a wide variety of small invertebrates that range from worms to insects and mites. Larger plethodontids also consume invertebrates, and some of them even prey on other salamanders.

Plethodontid lifestyles vary widely and range from fully aquatic to entirely terrestrial. Some terrestrial forms are semiburrowing, whereas others are arboreal (tree dwelling). About 35 species—spanning the genera *Eurycea*, *Gyrinophilus*, *Pseudotriton*, and *Stereochilus*—lay aquatic eggs that hatch into free-swimming larvae, which eventually metamorphose into adultlike juveniles. Other species are characterized by embryos that complete their development within the egg capsule and hatch directly as adultlike juveniles.

Family Plethodontidae is divided phylogenetically into the subfamilies Desmognathinae and Plethodontinae. The desmognathines are made up of two genera (*Desmognathus* and *Phaeognathus*) and 18 species strictly limited to eastern North America. Desmognathine salamanders range from fully terrestrial forms, such as the Red Hills salamander (*P. hubrichti*), to aquatic forms, such as the black-bellied salamander (*D. quadramaculatus*). All desmognathine species lay eggs, and females guard the eggs regardless of whether the eggs hatch into larvae or into adultlike juveniles.

The plethodontines are made up of more than 25 genera and 250 species that occur throughout the range of the family. All are egg layers, and the majority of species in this group have eggs that develop directly into adultlike forms; however, some aquatic species have free-living larvae. Most other plethodontines are forest species, and over four dozen of these belong to *Plethodon*, the most diverse North American genus. The majority of species in this genus live on the floors of forests and woodlands that have been fragmented by human activity. *Bolitoglossa* and *Pseudoeurycea*, two genera found in mountainous areas in the New World tropics, possess their greatest diversity in middle-elevation cloud forests; some of these species are arboreal and live in epiphytes. Web-toed salamanders, plethodontines of the genus *Hydromantes*, prefer nonforested areas; they mainly inhabit rock crevices in desertlike environments in Europe, California, and Baja California. The embryos of all terrestrial and arboreal plethodontines undergo direct development and hatch into adultlike forms. Females of most species guard their eggs.

BONES AND CARTILAGE

The rather weak skull of adults is composed of various paired and unpaired bones. These bones may fuse or be lost in different groups, and their presence and arrangement are important in classification. Much of the fusion and loss of skull bones is associated with a trend toward tongue feeding. Small, double-cusped teeth line the margins of the jaw and spread over parts of the palate. They are important in holding but not chewing the prey.

Cartilage plays an important role in the salamander head, especially in supportive structures in the throat region. These are ossified (bony) to different degrees, with more cartilage in the more highly evolved groups. Species such as the bolitoglossine plethodontids that display tongue protrusion often have flexible, cartilaginous tongue skeletons. In larvae and permanently gilled species the tongue is not developed.

The vertebrae constituting the spinal column are generalized with centrums (i.e., ventral, or lower, sections connecting with the adjacent vertebrae) that are rather poorly developed. The notochord (i.e., a resilient, flexible cord of specialized cells passing through the vertebral column) is usually persistent in adults. An intervertebral cartilage forms the articulation between vertebrae. If it remains cartilaginous, the vertebrae are said to be amphicoelous (biconcave, or depressed on both the anterior and posterior sides), but, if it mineralizes or ossifies, the vertebrae are termed opisthocoelous (bulged on the anterior side and depressed on the posterior side). There is one cervical vertebra with a characteristic projection called the odontoid process and two large facets for articulation with the skull. There may be from 11 (*Ambystoma talpoideum*) to 60 (*Amphiuma*) dorsal, or trunk, vertebrae, all but the last one or two usually bearing ribs. Most salamanders have from 14 to 20 trunk vertebrae. One sacral vertebra, two to four caudosacral vertebrae, and from about 20 to more than 100 (*Oedipina*) caudal, or tail, vertebrae complete the column. Many plethodontids are capable of autotomizing, or dropping off, the tail, a valuable defense mechanism in the event that the tail is grasped or bitten by a predator. These salamanders have various specialized features associated with the last caudosacral and the first caudal vertebrae, between which the break usually occurs.

The limbs and girdles are similar to those of generalized vertebrates. The pectoral, or chest, girdle, supporting the forelimbs, is relatively reduced, and the fused elements remain largely in a cartilaginous condition. An ypsiloid cartilage, attached to the front of the pelvic girdle, is used in exhalation in several groups, especially ambystomatids, dicamptodontids, hynobiids, and salamandrids. Digits and digital bones have been lost in many different groups. There are never more than four fingers, but nearly all species have five toes.

NERVOUS SYSTEM AND SENSE ORGANS

The nervous system is almost diagrammatically simple in anatomy, although this apparent simplicity is not primitive but mainly a secondary evolutionary derivation. The generalized brain is rather small. The relatively large cerebrum (collectively, the two large anterior lobes of the brain) is associated with the large and important olfactory and vomeronasal organs, both of which are used for smelling. The surprisingly complex social organization of these organisms is largely based on olfaction. The eyes, usually large and well developed, are reduced and nearly lost in some cave-dwelling species. Vision is especially important in terrestrial foraging, because the projection of the tongue is guided visually. Certain parts of the inner ear are large and well developed. Hearing mechanisms of the salamander are not fully understood. There is no middle ear cavity and no external ear. One middle ear bone rests in the structure known as the vestibular fenestra. The other bone of the middle ear rests in the posterior part of the fenestra and is joined by muscles to the pectoral girdle. In most species these bones

OLMS

Olm (Proteus anguinus)*, darkened by exposure to light.* Jacques Six

Olms (*Proteus anguinus*) are blind salamanders belonging to the family Proteidae (order Caudata). It lives in the subterranean streams in karst areas of the Adriatic coast from northeastern Italy southward into Montenegro. As an aquatic cave dweller, the olm has lost its skin pigmentation, and its vestigial but light-sensitive eyes are covered with skin. It retains numerous larval traits, such as well-developed gills, a lateral line system, and tiny limbs. The olm grows to about 30 cm (12 inches) long and has a normally white (unpigmented) body, red gill plumes, a narrow head, and a blunt snout.

Olms reproduce by either laying eggs or giving birth to live young. Temperature appears to be the factor that determines which reproductive strategy is used, with colder water triggering the bearing of live young. Adults commonly produce two live larvae using the live-bearing strategy, whereas they may produce up to 70 eggs using the egg-laying strategy.

are variously fused or lost, so that only one survives. The spinal cord and the peripheral nervous system—i.e., the paired cranial and spinal nerves—are generalized in their structure, and there are distinct brachial and sacral plexuses, both of which are important nerve networks that supply the limbs.

MUSCLES AND ORGAN SYSTEMS

The generalized musculature of the trunk exhibits little differentiation. The abdominal muscles show increasing degrees of differentiation in the fully metamorphosed, more derived taxa. The hyobranchial and branchiomeric muscles and some abdominal muscles (rectus abdominis) are highly specialized in those species that use the tongue to capture prey.

The simple digestive system includes a short, nearly straight gut. The lungs are relatively simple, saclike organs in primitive groups. In stream-dwelling members of several families, the lungs are greatly reduced; they are entirely absent in all plethodontids.

The circulatory system is characterized by a highly developed vascularization of the body surface. The heart is simple, with one ventricle (i.e., a chamber that pumps blood out of the heart) and two atria (chambers that receive blood from the rest of the body); separation between the two atria is not distinct in lungless forms.

The urogenital system consists of an elongated kidney with a distinct sexual segment and a posterior concentration of large renal units, which filter urine from the blood. Testes, the male sex glands, are small and compact, increasing in size with age. Ovaries of females are thin sacs. The cloaca is relatively complex in more derived groups, with a spermatheca in females and several sets of cloacal glands in both sexes.

CELL STRUCTURE AND BIOCHEMISTRY

Salamanders have enormous genomes that contain more nucleic acid and larger chromosomes in each cell than any tetrapods. The genomes vary greatly in size among species, even within a family. Large genomes impose large cell size, which means that small salamanders have relatively few cells. The apparent anatomic simplicity of salamanders may be a direct and phylogenetically secondary outcome.

EVOLUTION

Salamanders are very ancient survivors of a Mesozoic (251 to 66.5 million years ago) radiation. The cryptobranchids, sirenids, proteids, and amphiumids are all unusual, considering that they are tetrapods, in that they are fully to mainly aquatic and have retained larval traits (paedomorphosis) to a great degree. The other families have adults that are generalized terrestrial tetrapods, but several of these families have few species and limited distributional ranges. The hynobiids, plethodontids, and salamandrids are the most diverse in structure and ecology. These groups have evolved along parallel lines, and features such as highly projectile tongues, loss of lungs, and loss of fifth toes have evolved repeatedly, even within the same family. The combination of parallel evolution and paedomorphic evolution has made phylogenetic analysis difficult. Several genera—such as *Ambystoma*, *Bolitoglossa*, *Hynobius*, and *Plethodon*—are very speciose, and within the Plethodontidae there has been much cryptic speciation that has been revealed by application of biochemical techniques.

Fossils have contributed little as yet to the understanding of salamander evolution. The earliest definitive salamander from the Middle to Late Jurassic Period (187 to 144 million years ago) may be the sister taxon (Karauridae) of all other salamanders. Several other families (Prosirenidae, Scapherpetonidae, Batrachosauroididae) are known only from fossils. The relationships of salamanders to other living and fossil amphibians are unclear, but recent workers consider the three living groups to form the subclass Lissamphibia.

GYMNOPHIONANS

Gymnophiona, which is also called Apoda, is one of the three major extant orders of the class Amphibia. Its members are known as caecilians, a name derived from the Latin word *caecus*, meaning "sightless" or "blind." The majority of this group of wormlike amphibians live underground in humid tropical regions throughout the world. Because of their relatively hidden existence, caecilians are unfamiliar to the layperson and are not usually considered in discussions about amphibians. They are nevertheless a fascinating group of highly specialized amphibians about which there is still much to be learned.

SIZE AND RANGE

Several species of caecilians in the South American genus *Caecilia* exceed 1 metre (about 3.3 feet) in total length; the largest known caecilian is *C. thompsoni*, at 152 cm (about 60 inches). The smallest caecilians are *Idiocranium russeli* in West Africa and *Grandisonia brevis* in the Seychelles; these species attain lengths of only 98–104 mm (3.9–4.1 inches) and 112 mm (4.4 inches), respectively.

DISTRIBUTION AND ABUNDANCE

Caecilians are found in tropical areas throughout the world. Of the three families that inhabit southern Asia, one occurs in geographically separated pockets in India, Southeast Asia, Borneo, and the Philippines. Three families are widespread in the American tropics, but only two are endemic; two families occur in Africa, and one is endemic. On the Seychelles there are three genera native to the islands, although caecilians are not found on any other islands in the Indian Ocean. None have been found on Madagascar or New Guinea. Approximately 170 caecilian species are known to exist, and up to five species have been found to inhabit the same area in the Amazon rainforest.

Natural History of Caecilians

Information about annual reproductive patterns among caecilians is limited. The breeding period of some Asiatic ichthyophiids seems to be aseasonal or at least without seasonal constraints. At least one species, *Ichthyophis glutinossus* in Sri Lanka, mates only during the rainy season. Females of viviparous species have a biennial reproductive cycle; the viviparous *Dermophis mexicanus* in Guatemala mates in the early part of the rainy season, and gestation takes one year.

All caecilians are believed to have internal fertilization. This is achieved by means of the phallodeum, a copulatory organ in males that is modified from the cloacal wall. Eggs of all members of the families Ichthyophiidae and Rhinatrematidae are deposited in burrows in mud that is close to water. The females watch over these clutches, which may hold up to 54 eggs. Upon hatching, the larvae leave the burrows to make their homes in ponds and streams. Some caecilians deposit eggs on land, and in different species these hatch as larvae or small adults. Three families have viviparous species to which usually no more than four young are born at one time. Aquatic typhlonectids are viviparous and produce larvae. The caecilian fetus emerges from the egg membrane as soon as its meagre yolk supply is exhausted; it uses its deciduous teeth, adapted for scraping, to obtain secretions and epithelial tissues from the oviduct lining.

The diet of terrestrial caecilians is mainly earthworms and other soft-bodied prey. Feeding either aboveground or in subterranean burrows, terrestrial caecilians are believed to locate their quarry by means of a chemosensory tentacle on each side of the head. They capture their prey with their powerful recurved teeth, masticate, and swallow. Aquatic caecilians, the typhlonectids, prey on fishes, eels, and aquatic invertebrates.

FORM AND FUNCTION

Caecilians have long, limbless, cylindrical bodies that abruptly end behind the cloaca or short tail. Annuli (primary grooves) in the skin encircle the body and form segments. In some taxonomic groups, secondary and tertiary grooves partially circumscribe the body. Within the tissue of the annuli, bony scales of dermal origin usually occur. The heads of caecilians are blunt, and their skulls are bony and compact. Centres of ossification have fused, which has reduced the number of independent cranial bones in caecilians in comparison with anurans and salamanders. For example, a single bone, the os basale, forms both the floor of the braincase and the posterior part of the skull. Teeth are found on all jaw bones, and a palatal series of teeth appears in addition, medial to the maxillary series. A U-shaped facet, which articulates with the quadrate and also has a long retroarticular process that

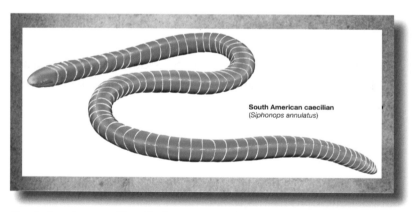

South American caecilian
(Siphonops annulatus)

South American caecilian (Siphonops annulatus). Drawing by S. Jones serves as an attachment site for three major jaw muscles, is located on the lower jaw.

The vertebral column is made up of an atlas (the first vertebra of the neck) and 95 to 285 trunk vertebrae; no differentiated sacral vertebrae are present. Double-headed ribs are found on all vertebrae except the atlas and the terminal three to six vertebrae. Of the three amphibian orders, only caecilians have an axial musculature in which all the hypaxial components, excluding the subvertebral musculature, form an outer muscular sheath. This sheath, which is anchored to the skin by fibrous connective tissue, is all but disconnected from the vertebral musculature and thereby allows the skin and superficial muscles to move as a single unit. The degenerate eyes are covered with bone or skin. These adaptations make it possible for the caecilian to feed, reproduce, and avoid enemies within their subterranean realm. The features of aquatic caecilians of the family Typhlonectidae are representative of secondary adaptations.

CONCLUSION

Both reptiles and amphibians face unique environmental challenges. Some of these challenges result from the ways in which each group relates to its physical environment, whereas others result from human activities. The temperature of the surroundings strongly affects reptile metabolism. As a result, they consider the temperature of the air, water, and surfaces they crawl upon when going about their daily activities. On the other hand, since amphibians rely on their skin as an organ of respiration, most species remain close to watery or damp environments.

Through unique anatomical characteristics and complex behaviours, reptiles are resilient creatures that live in all but the coldest environments. Many reptiles, however, suffer the consequences of human activity. Some reptiles (such as lizards and turtles) are hunted for the meat they provide, whereas snakes are hunted for their skins. In some areas, snakes are killed because they threaten livestock or are considered dangerous to humans.

Each year, many sea turtles and other marine turtles are unintentionally captured in crab and lobster traps or the nets of fishing fleets. Oil washed ashore during nesting season on Gulf of Mexico beaches, a result of the 2010 Deepwater Horizon drilling rig disaster, threatened to obliterate an entire generation of sea turtles, particularly the endangered loggerheads. As for the tuataras, since the time of Maori arrival in New Zealand, they have become the unwilling victims of cat and rat introductions to their habitats.

Because they inhabit both aquatic and terrestrial environments, and thus they are subjected to the environmental pressures of each one, amphibians are thought to serve as early indicator organisms of environmental degradation. Amphibians are especially sensitive to pollution, because harmful chemicals can be easily absorbed by the skin, and to habitat loss, since many species have specialized habitat requirements. In recent years, a number of amphibian populations have declined as a result of the global outbreak of *Batrachochytrium dendrobatidis*, a fungus that covers and degrades the skin.

No one can say with any certainty what will happen to any particular reptile or amphibian species in the future. Yet based on their long record of survival thus far--fossilized evidence suggests these creatures have been around since prehistoric time--reptiles and amphibians should be a prescence on planet Earth for years to come.

GLOSSARY

allotriploid Used to define an organism that has at least two sets of chromosomes passed down from each parent.

arboreal Used to describe a creature that lives in or frequents trees.

ecothermic Used to describe an organism requiring an external heat source to elevate its body temperature.

extirpation Localized extinction.

carapace The bony or chitinous case covering the back or part of the back of an animal; a turtle's shell.

carrion The rotting flesh of a dead animal, on which certain animals that took no part in the kill feed.

chemoreception The process by which organisms respond to external chemical stimuli by using the senses of taste and smell.

cloaca In vertebrates, the common chamber and outlet into which the intestinal, urinary, and genital tracts open.

clutch A nest of eggs or young hatchlings.

cutaneous respiration Breathing through the skin.

dewlap A pocket or fan of loose skin that hangs under the neck of an animal.

herbivore An animal that lives on plant life, not the meat of prey.

molt The process by which an animal sheds its skin or feathers.

neurotoxins A poisonous protein complex that acts on the central nervous system; venom.

occipital condyle A protuberance on reptile physiognomy, where the skull attaches to the first vertebra.

parthenogenesis The process by which a species is able to reproduce independent of sex and without fertilization.

prehension The ability to grab or take hold of an object.

scutes The bony plates that make up a turtle's shell.

seta A slender, usually rigid or bristly and springy organ or part of an animal or plant.

thermoregulation The process by which an organism maintains an optimum temperature.

vivaparity The process by which a fertilized egg grows inside the mother's body until the young animal is capable of living outside the womb.

vomeronasal Used to describe an organ on each side of an animal's nose that enables the creature to detect and communicate through chemicals such as pheromones.

zygodactylous Having toes that are arranged so that there are two in front and two behind.

BIBLIOGRAPHY

REPTILES

General surveys of reptiles and their life histories, with many photographs, are found in H.M. Cogger and R.G. Zweifel, *Encyclopedia of Reptiles and Amphibians*, 2nd ed. (2003); and Tim Halliday and Kraig Adler (eds.), *The New Encyclopedia of Reptiles and Amphibians* (2002). College-level texts that provide an excellent overview of reptiles and general herpetology include George R. Zug, Laurie J. Vitt, and Jan P. Caldwell, *Herpetology: An Introductory Biology of Amphibians and Reptiles*, 2nd ed. (2001); and F. Harvey Pough et al., *Herpetology*, 3rd ed. (2004).

Well-organized field guides and taxonomic summaries with excellent maps and photographs include Mark O'Shea and Tim Halliday, *Reptiles and Amphibians*, ed. by David A. Dickey (2002); Tim Halliday and Kraig Alder (eds.), *Firefly Encyclopedia of Reptiles and Amphibians* (2002); Roger Conant and Joseph T. Collins, *A Field Guide to Reptiles and Amphibians: Eastern and Central North America*, 3rd ed. (1998); John Coborn, *The Mini-Atlas of Snakes of the World* (1994); Roy W. McDiarmid, Jonathan A. Campbell, and T'Shaka A. Touré, *Snake Species of the World: A Taxonomic and Geographic Reference*, 3 vol. (1999–); and John B. Iverson, *A Revised Checklist with Distribution Maps of the Turtles of the World* (1997). In addition, B. Gill and T. Whitaker, *New Zealand Frogs and Reptiles* (1996), provides a general overview of tuataras.

Carl Gans et al. (eds.), *Biology of the Reptilia*, 19 vol. (1968–98), is a highly technical series of detailed reviews on various aspects of reptilian anatomy, physiology, behaviour, ecology, and embryology. Ludwig Trutnau and Ralf Sommerlad, *Crocodilians: Their Natural History and Captive Husbandry* (2006), is an invaluable resource that covers crocodilian evolution and classification, ecology, conservation and management, physiology, and behaviour. Other technical treatments that consider various aspects of the anatomy, natural history, and ecology of living reptiles include Richard A. Seigel, Joseph T. Collins, and Susan S. Novak, *Snakes: Ecology and Evolutionary Biology* (2001); Jonathan A. Campbell and William W. Lamar, *The Venomous Reptiles of the Western Hemisphere*, 2 vol. (2004); G.C. Grigg, F. Seebacher, and C. Franklin (eds.), *Crocodilian Biology and Evolution* (2001); and L.J. Vitt and E.R. Pianka (eds.), *Lizard Ecology: Historical and Experimental Perspectives* (1994).

The evolution of reptiles within the context of other vertebrates is carefully considered in Robert L. Carroll, *Patterns and Processes of Vertebrate Evolution* (1998); and Michael J. Benton *Vertebrate Paleontology*, 3rd ed. (2005). A succinct overview of the various evolutionary adaptations possessed by lizards is presented in Eric R. Pianka, *Lizards: Windows to the Evolution of Diversity* (2006). Ronald Orenstein, *Turtles, Tortoises, and Terrapins: Survivors in Armor* (2001), is a popular and well-illustrated account that addresses turtle conservation and evolution as well as natural history. A highly accessible treatment of the evolution of flight in pterosaurs and other reptiles is found in Phillip J. Currie, *The Flying Dinosaurs: The Illustrated Guide to the Evolution of Flight* (2002). A semi-technical review of dinosaur evolution, biology, and research is found in James O. Farlow, *The Complete Dinosaur*, ed. by M.K. Brett-Surman (1999). Anthony J. Martin, *Introduction to the Study of Dinosaurs*, 2nd ed. (2006), provides a general treatment of dinosaur evolution that highlights the process of paleontological research.

LIZARDS

A succinct overview of the various evolutionary adaptations possessed by lizards is presented in Eric R. Pianka, *Lizards: Windows to the Evolution of Diversity* (2006).

General surveys of lizards and their life histories, with many photographs, are found in Harold G. Cogger and Richard G. Zweifel (eds.), *Encyclopedia of Reptiles & Amphibians*, 2nd ed. (1998). General herpetology textbooks include George R. Zug, Laurie J. Vitt, and Janalee P. Caldwell, *Herpetology: An Introductory Biology of Amphibians and Reptiles*, 2nd ed. (2001); and F. Harvey Pough et al., *Herpetology*, 3rd ed. (2004). Summaries of modern trends in research as they relate to lizard ecology, physiological ecology, and behaviour include Laurie J. Vitt and Eric R. Pianka (eds.), *Lizard Ecology: Historical and Experimental Perspectives* (1994); John W. Wright and Laurie J. Vitt (eds.), *Biology of Whiptail Lizards: Genus Cnemidophorus* (1993); and Stanley F. Fox, J. Kelly McCoy, and Troy A. Baird (eds.), *Lizard Social Behavior* (2003).

Worthy regional accounts of lizards and other herpetofauna include Christopher J. Glasby, Graham J.B. Ross, and Pamela L. Beesley (eds.), *Amphibia & Reptilia* (1993), a packed but highly readable technical manual with summary accounts of the biology and anatomy of all families of Australian amphibians and reptiles; Roger Conant and Joseph T. Collins, *A Field Guide to Reptiles & Amphibians: Eastern and Central North America*, 3rd ed., expanded (1998), an excellent guide to the herpetofauna of eastern North America; and Brian I. Crother (ed.), *Scientific and Standard English Names of Amphibians and Reptiles of North America North of Mexico, with Comments Regarding*

Confidence in Our Understanding, 6th ed. (2008), an annotated list of all amphibians and reptiles in North America
with comments on the validity of each species.

Important taxonomic works, not easily read by the
layperson but fundamental to the understanding of lizard
classification, include Steven C. Anderson, *The Lizards
of Iran* (1999); T.C.S. Avila-Pires, *Lizards of Brazilian
Amazonia (Reptilia: Squamata)* (1995); Brian I. Crother
(ed.), *Caribbean Amphibians and Reptiles* (1999); and Albert
Schwartz and Robert W. Henderson, *Amphibians and
Reptiles of the West Indies: Descriptions, Distributions, and
Natural History* (1991).

SNAKES

Harry W. Greene, *Snakes: The Evolution of Mystery in
Nature* (1997), surveys snake diversity and biology and is
complemented by stunning photography. John Coborn,
The Atlas of Snakes of the World (1991), discusses the
care of snakes and snakebites in addition to describ-
ing each family and genus. Carl H. Ernst and George
R. Zug, *Snakes in Question: The Smithsonian Answer Book*
(1996), provides answers to many of the questions most
frequently asked about snakes. Tony Phelps, *Poisonous
Snakes*, rev. ed (1989), covers the rear-fanged colubrids,
the elapids, and the vipers. *The Ultimate Guide: Snakes*
(1997), a video produced for the Discovery Channel
by Partridge Films, portrays snakes in the wild and
also includes computer graphics and interviews with
researchers.

Roy W. McDiarmid, Jonathan A. Campbell, and
T'Shaka A. Touré, *Snake Species of the World: A Taxonomic
and Geographic Reference*, vol. 1 (1999–), constitutes the
first of a comprehensive series. F. Harvey Pough (ed.),
Herpetology, 2nd ed. (2001), is a college-level textbook.

TURTLES AND TUATARAS

Carl H. Ernst and Roger W. Barbour, *Turtles of the World* (1989), also available in a CD-ROM version (2000), briefly describes every family, genus, and species of turtle. John B. Iverson, *A Revised Checklist with Distribution Maps of the Turtles of the World* (1992), is a taxonomic summary of the world's turtles with an individual distribution map for each species. Michael W. Klemens (ed.), *Turtle Conservation* (2000), is a semitechnical examination of the biological and environmental issues of turtle conservation.

Ronald Orenstein, *Turtles, Tortoises, and Terrapins: Survivors in Armor* (2001), is a popular and well-illustrated account that addresses conservation and evolution as well as natural history. Peter L. Lutz, John A. Musick, and Jeanette Wyneken (eds.), *The Biology of Sea Turtles*, 2 vol. (1996–2003), collects reviews by several authors of major aspects of sea turtle biology, including reproduction, navigation, physiology, and ecology.

C. Kenneth Dodd, Jr., *North American Box Turtles: A Natural History* (2001), is a technical summary of the life cycle of the familiar box turtle. Carl H. Ernst, Roger W. Barbour, and Jeffrey E. Lovich, *Turtles of the United States and Canada* (1994), thoroughly reviews the biology of each species of turtle found in those countries. Two field and natural history guides to regional terrestrial and freshwater turtles are Richard C. Boycott and Ortwin Borquin, *The Southern African Tortoise Book*, rev. ed. (2000), covering the southern third of Africa; and Indraneil Das, *Colour Guide to the Turtles and Tortoises of the of Indian Subcontinent* (1991). John Cann, *Australian Freshwater Turtles* (1998), reviews all species of Australian turtles and includes superb colour photographs of all species.

A general overview of tuataras can be found in B. Gill and T. Whitaker, *New Zealand Frogs and Reptiles* (1996); and G.R. Zug, L.J. Vitt, and J.P. Caldwell, *Herpetology: An Introductory Biology of Amphibians and Reptiles* (2000). The latter is a college-level textbook that contains reviews of fossil history, anatomy, systematics, and natural history. A treatment of the tuatara's characteristics and habits, its interaction with the Maori people, and its conservation is found in Richard L. Lutz, *Tuatara: A Living Fossil* (2005).

AMPHIBIANS

An accurate introduction to amphibians and reptiles, complete with excellent illustrations and photographs, is provided in Harold G. Cogger and Richard G. Zweifel (eds.), *Encyclopedia of Reptiles & Amphibians*, 2nd ed. (1998). A popular and engaging review of amphibian biology is given in Robert C. Stebbins and Nathan W. Cohen, *A Natural History of Amphibians* (1995). A college-level textbook covering all aspects of herpetology from fossil history to the conservation of amphibians and reptiles is George R. Zug, Laurie J. Vitt, and Janalee P. Caldwell, *Herpetology: An Introductory Biology of Amphibians and Reptiles*, 2nd ed. (2001).

More-comprehensive treatments of herpetology include William E. Duellman and Linda Trueb, *Biology of Amphibians* (1986, reissued 1994); and F. Harvey Pough et al., *Herpetology*, 3rd ed. (2004). In addition, Martin E. Feder and Warren W. Burggren (eds.), *Environmental Physiology of the Amphibians* (1992), is a thorough compendium of amphibian physiology.

Michael J. Benton, *Vertebrate Paleontology*, 2nd ed. (1997), is a textbook treatment with comprehensive and technical reviews of vertebrate paleontology. Hans-Peter Schultze and Linda Trueb (eds.), *Origins of the Higher*

Groups of Tetrapods (1991), reviews tetrapod evolution and classification.

A number of worthy regional accounts of herpetofauna are also available. Christopher J. Glasby, Graham J.B. Ross, and Pamela L. Beesley (eds.), *Amphibia & Reptilia* (1993), is a packed but highly readable technical manual with summary accounts of the biology and anatomy of all families of Australian amphibians and reptiles. Roger Conant and Joseph T. Collins, *A Field Guide to Reptiles & Amphibians: Eastern and Central North America*, 3rd ed., expanded (1998), is an excellent guide to the herpetofauna of eastern North America; and Brian I. Crother (ed.), *Scientific and Standard English Names of Amphibians and Reptiles of North America North of Mexico, with Comments Regarding Confidence in Our Understanding*, 6th ed. (2008), is an annotated list of all amphibians and reptiles in North America with comments on the validity of each species.

G. Kingsley Noble, *The Biology of the Amphibia* (1931, reprinted 1954), is the classic English-language work on amphibians.

ANURANS

General herpetology texts that investigate various aspects of order Anura include Christopher J. Glasby, Graham J.B. Ross, and Pamela L. Beesley (eds.), *Amphibia & Reptilia* (1993); and George R. Zug, Laurie J. Vitt, and Janalee P. Caldwell, *Herpetology: An Introductory Biology of Amphibians and Reptiles*, 2nd ed. (2001). Albert Hazen Wright and Anna Allen Wright, *Handbook of Frogs and Toads of the United States and Canada*, 3rd ed. (1995), is a well-documented account of North American frogs and toads with many black-and-white photographs. William E. Duellman and David M. Dennis, *The Hylid Frogs of*

Middle America, expanded ed., 2 vol. (2001), is a detailed study of the taxonomy, distribution, life history, and ecology of the tree frogs of Mexico and Central America. An excellent identification manual for frogs in the western United States is Robert C. Stebbins, *A Field Guide to Western Reptiles and Amphibians,* 3rd ed. (2003). A modern taxonomy of anuran families is provided in Linda S. Ford and David C. Cannatella, "The Major Clades of Frogs," *Herpetological Monographs,* 7:94–117 (1993).

Classic works on anurans include Ronald Maxwell Savage, *The Ecology and Life History of the Common Frog (Rana temporaria temporaria)* (1961), a well-documented study of the biology of this species in England; and H.W. Parker, *A Monograph of the Frogs of the Family Microhylidae* (1934, reprinted 1966), a thorough account of one of the most interesting families of frogs.

CAUDATANS

Relationships of salamanders to other amphibians are analyzed in A.R. Milner, "The Paleozoic Relatives of Lissamphibians," *Herpetological Monographs* 7:8–27 (1993); and G.J. McCowan and S.E. Evans, "Albanerpetonid amphibians from the Cretaceous of Spain," *Nature,* 373:143–145 (Jan. 12, 1995). An overview of both the fossil record and living salamanders is provided in G.R. Zug, L.D. Vitt, and J.D. Caldwell, *Herpetology,* 2nd ed. (2001). A review of the biology and natural history of North American salamanders is provided in James W. Petranka, *Salamanders of the United States and Canada* (1998).

Phylogenetic relationships of the families of salamanders are the subject of several recent investigations, and a consensus is gradually growing. A general review of this controversial topic is found in A. Larson and W.W. Dimmick, "Phylogenetic Relationships of the

Salamander Families: An Analysis of Congruence Among Morphological and Molecular Characters," *Herpetological Monographs*, 6:77–93 (1993). Treatments of specific taxa based mainly on morphological traits include the following: on Ambystomatidae, H.B. Shaffer, "Phylogenetics of Model Organisms: The Laboratory Axolotl, *Ambystoma mexicanum*," *Systematic Biology*, 42(4):508–522 (1993); on Plethodontidae, "Symposium on the Biology of Plethodontid Salamanders," *Herpetologica*, 49(2):153–237 (1993); on Rhyacotritonidae, David A. Good and David B. Wake, *Geographic Variation and Speciation in the Torrent Salamanders of the Genus Rhyacotriton (Caudata: Rhyacotritonidae)* (1992); and on Salamandridae, Richard A. Griffiths, *Newts and Salamanders of Europe* (1996).

GYMNOPHIONANS

William E. Duellman and Linda Trueb, *Biology of Amphibians* (1986, reissued 1994), offers the first general review of caecilians' biology and anatomy. A more recent and less detailed review of caecilians is available in George R. Zug, Laurie J. Vitt, and Janalee P. Caldwell, *Herpetology: An Introductory Biology of Amphibians and Reptiles*, 2nd ed. (2001). The most comprehensive review of caecilians is Werner Himstedt, *Die Blindwühlen* (1996).

INDEX